Married to Genius

Books by Jeffrey Meyers

BIOGRAPHY
A Fever at the Core: The Idealist
  in Politics
Katherine Mansfield
The Enemy: A Biography of
  Wyndham Lewis
Hemingway
Manic Power: Robert Lowell
  and His Circle
D.H. Lawrence
Joseph Conrad
Edgar Allan Poe: His Life and
  Legacy
Scott Fitzgerald
Edmund Wilson
Robert Frost
Bogart: A Life in Hollywood
Gary Cooper: American Hero
Privileged Moments: Encounters
  with Writers
Wintry Conscience: A Biography
  of George Orwell
Inherited Risk: Errol and Sean
  Flynn in Hollywood and
  Vietnam
Somerset Maugham: A Life
Impressionist Quartet: The
  Intimate Genius of Manet and
  Morisot, Degas and Cassatt
Modigliani: A Life

CRITICISM
Fiction and the Colonial
  Experience
The Wounded Spirit: T.E.
  Lawrence's *Seven Pillars of
  Wisdom*
A Reader's Guide to George
  Orwell

Painting and the Novel
Homosexuality and Literature
D.H. Lawrence and the
  Experience of Italy
Disease and the Novel
The Spirit of Biography
Hemingway: Life into Art

BIBLIOGRAPHY
T.E. Lawrence: A Bibliography
Catalogue of the Library of the
  Late Siegfried Sassoon
George Orwell: An Annotated
  Bibliography of Criticism

EDITED COLLECTIONS
George Orwell: The Critical
  Heritage
Hemingway: The Critical
  Heritage
Robert Lowell: Interviews and
  Memoirs
The Sir Arthur Conan Doyle
  Reader
The W. Somerset Maugham
  Reader

EDITED ORIGINAL ESSAYS
Wyndham Lewis: A Revaluation
Wyndham Lewis *by Roy
  Campbell*
D.H. Lawrence and Tradition
The Legacy of D.H. Lawrence
The Craft of Literary Biography
The Biographer's Art
T.E. Lawrence: Soldier, Writer,
  Legend
Graham Greene: A Revaluation

Married to Genius

Jeffrey Meyers

southbank
publishing

This edition published in May 2005 by Southbank Publishing
P. O. Box 394, Harpenden, Herts, AL5 1XJ

www. southbankpublishing. com

Distributed in the USA by Trafalgar Square Publishing,
P. O. Box 257, Howe Hill Road, North Pomfret, Vermont 05053

A CIP catalogue record for this book is available from the British
Library.

ISBN 1 904915 09 4

2 4 6 8 10 9 7 5 3 1

Typeset by Avocet, Typeset, Chilton, Aylesbury, Bucks
Printed and bound in Great Britain by CPD, Ebbw Vale, Wales

For Rube

Tolstoy
Shaw
Conrad
Joyce
Woolf
Mansfield
Lawrence
Hemingway
Fitzgerald

Photo Credits

Table of Contents

Introduction

I

Married to Genius is a biographical work that considers the relation between emotional and artistic commitment in the marriages of nine modern writers: Tolstoy, Shaw, Conrad, Joyce, Virginia Woolf, Katherine Mansfield, D. H. Lawrence, Hemingway and Fitzgerald. These authors made a serious commitment to the claims of ordinary life and believed that marriage provided their most profound personal relationship. They found in marriage a confirmation and extension of the self, a stronghold of affection that encouraged and tested their capacity for love, a union that left them free for individual development, an antidote to the modern fear of alienation, and a strengthening bond that was deeply valuable to an artist engaged in psychic survival and in creating order out of chaos. Women like Jessie Conrad and Nora Joyce, who had modest egos and docile natures, comforted their high-strung husbands and provided the stable family life that enabled them to write their books. But other wives, creative and egoistic themselves, provoked and challenged their husbands to conflict and creativity.

The lives of these authors reveal the pressures and strains of modern marriage, and their creative impulse was directly inspired by their emotional and intellectual conflicts. Tolstoy's *Anna Karenina*, Shaw's *Getting Married*, Conrad's *The Secret Agent*, Joyce's *Ulysses*, Woolf's *Night and Day*, Mansfield's *Je ne parle pas français*, Lawrence's *Women in Love*, Hemingway's *A Farewell to Arms* and Fitzgerald's *Tender is the Night* are all autobiographical. A discussion of these works in the context of both the author's marriage and the spouse's portrait of the artist in memoirs, diaries, letters, essays and fiction, reveals new insights about the imaginative process, and about the way these major writers attempt to integrate life and art and to resolve the crucial conflict between domestic and creative fulfilment.

Lawrence, who was both complemented and completed by his union with Frieda, defined 'the long course of marriage as a long event of perpetual change, in which a man and a woman mutually build up their souls and make themselves whole.' In his major novels Lawrence tried to unite the desire for individual freedom – what he called star-like isolation, self-determination and integrity with the need for the security of permanent marriage. Though he did not always see the struggle as two-sided, as an equal surrender of the self for both man and woman, his concepts of sexual freedom, bisexuality and homosexuality were far ahead of his time and have had a powerful influence on our own era. Novelists like Lawrence and Fitzgerald, who inherited a nineteenth-century idea of the wife's role but helped to formulate the twentieth-century concept of woman, both exemplified and portrayed the archetypes of modern marriage that had a profound effect on contemporary consciousness and conduct. Lawrence represents the struggle for sexual domination and the problems of a rootless and isolated marriage, and Fitzgerald the fatality of success and the anguish of alcoholism and madness.

In both of these marriages the wives struggled to make their husbands aware of their needs and desires. For Frieda Lawrence and Zelda Fitzgerald, who were gifted and beautiful women with powerful egos, rejected their traditional role. Though Frieda left a bourgeois husband and family for a penniless, wandering writer, and Zelda married a glamorous and apparently unconventional novelist, they both discovered they were expected to take a subservient place in the artistic lives of their husbands. The emotional tension that developed from this conflict led to personal unhappiness, but also stimulated the husband's creative powers. For Lawrence and Fitzgerald felt that passion, with all its dangers, was the source of creative endeavour. The imaginative faculty of these artists gave them extraordinary insight but made them extremely difficult to live with, for the intense egoism that was so necessary to creativity was frequently fatal to marriage. As Lawrence asserted: 'You have to have something vicious in you to be a creative writer. It is the something vicious, old-adamish, incompatible to the "ordinary" world, inside a man, which gives an edge to his awareness.'

II

In contrast to the authors considered in *Married to Genius*, there were many modern writers who believed that marriage and art were mutually exclusive. As Yeats observes in 'The Choice':

> The intellect of man is forced to choose,
> Perfection of the life or of the work.

In 'The Lesson of the Master' (1888), the sociable but inveterate bachelor Henry James expresses the conflict between family life and the higher pursuit of art. The great writer Henry St George (speaking for the author whose name he shares) explains to the young aspirant Paul Overt that marriage interferes with the sacrificial quest for artistic perfection and that a man endangers his work if he devotes himself to personal rather than to intellectual passion:

> 'One's children interfere with perfection. One's wife interferes. Marriage interferes.'

'You think then the artist shouldn't marry?'

'He does so at his peril – he does so at his cost.'

'Not even when his wife's in sympathy with his work?'

'She never is – she can't be! Women haven't a
conception of such things. . . .'

'You can't do it without sacrifices. . . . I've made none.
I've had everything. In other words I've missed
everything. . . .'

'Are there no women who really understand – who can
take part in a sacrifice?'

'How can they take part? They themselves are the
sacrifice.'

The lonely philosopher Friedrich Nietzsche, who had asked in *Zarathustra*: 'who can wholly comprehend *how* strange man and woman are to each other?' agreed that the artist must sacrifice his family life but accepted this deprivation with far less equanimity than James. As Nietzsche wrote to his friend Overbeck in 1886: 'I feel that all the things which I *need* as a *philosophus radicalis* – freedom from profession, wife, child, fatherland, creed, etc. etc. – are just so many *deprivations*, insofar as I fortunately am a living being and not merely an analysing machine.' And Thomas Mann, who was strongly influenced by Nietzsche, also believed that art evolved from suffering and isolation, and that happiness was forbidden to the artist. Mann once planned a story about a writer whose marital happiness extinguished his imaginative life – until the wife's infidelity spurred him to creation. The reconciliation of marriage and art, which Mann had portrayed in *Royal Highness* (1909), became absolutely impossible in his greatest work, *Doctor Faustus* (1947), when the hero, Adrian Leverkühn, makes a diabolic pact and renounces earthly love for seven years of creative genius.

Franz Kafka, a wretched and recalcitrant lover who was twice engaged but could never commit himself to matri-

mony, fortified himself in 1913 by summarising, in a characteristically extreme form, all the arguments against marriage.
Though Kafka could not endure life alone, he could only
create in solitude. He hated everything that did not relate to
art, and thought he would never be able to give up his
tedious job if he married. He was torn between self-love and
self-surrender, and feared the connection with and absorption by a woman. And he felt that even if his wife transformed him into a fearless and powerful man, it might
undermine the foundation of his work, which was based on
anguish and on torment. The very qualities that made Kafka
a great artist – his pathological sensitivity, his morbid introspection, his self-hatred and self-torture, his fanatical
commitment to the 'disease' of literature – all precluded
marriage. As Kafka explained to his loyal fiancée, Felice
Bauer, who absolutely refused to take him seriously or to
believe that anyone could *really* be like that: 'Of the four men
I consider to be my true blood-relations (without comparing
myself to them either in power or in range), Grillparzer,
Dostoyevsky, Kleist, and Flaubert, Dostoyevsky was the only
one to get married, and perhaps Kleist, when compelled by
outer and inner necessity to shoot himself on the Wannsee,
was the only one to find the right solution.' Unlike Yeats and
Mann, who followed Flaubert's advice: 'Be orderly and
regular in your life, like a bourgeois, so that you may be wild
and original in your work,' writers like James, Nietzsche and
Kafka believed that marriage was hostile and even fatal to art.

In the modern period the homosexual writer, who
subverted the very concept of marriage, symbolised the
opposition to ordinary life and the devotion to art. For
homosexual writers ignored or attacked heterosexual love,
and were forced to portray it in a false and distorted fashion.
At the end of *A Passage to India* (1924) the hero Fielding,
speaking for the homosexual Forster, cynically calls marriage
a muddled and risky absurdity:

Marriage is too absurd in any case. It begins and continues
for such very slight reasons. The social business props it up
on one side, and the theological business on the other, but
neither of them are marriage, are they? I've friends who
can't remember why they married, no more can their
wives. I suspect that it mostly happens haphazard, though
afterwards various noble reasons are invented. About
marriage I am cynical.

And Forster admits: a 'cause of my sterility [is] weariness of
the only subject that I both can and may treat – the love of
men for women & vice versa. . . . I shall never write another
novel after it [*A Passage to India*] – my patience with *ordinary*
people has given out.'

Carl Jung believes that the artist's conflict can never be
completely resolved because his personal life is tragically
compromised by his creative gift. As he writes of the artist in
'Psychology and Literature' (1930):

His life cannot be otherwise than full of conflicts, for two
forces are at war within him: on the one hand the justified
longing of the ordinary man for happiness, satisfaction, and
security, and on the other a ruthless passion for creation
which may go so far as to override every personal desire.
If the lives of artists are as a rule so exceedingly unsatisfactory, not to say tragic, it is not because of some sinister
dispensation of fate, but because of some inferiority in
their personality or an inability to adapt. A person must
pay dearly for the divine gift of creative fire.

According to this influential theory, which originates in
Plato's *Ion* and is reinforced by Romantic and Decadent
concepts of art, the artist is essentially diseased and can only
create if he is divorced from the comforts and advantages of
life. In a review of *Death in Venice*, Lawrence wrote of Thomas

Mann: 'He has never given himself to anything but his art. This is all well and good, if his art absorbs and satisfies him, as it has done some great men, like Corot. But then there are the other artists, the more human, like Shakespeare and Goethe, who must give themselves to life as well as to art.' The creative artist defined by James and Jung substitutes art for life and sacrifices ordinary pleasure for what he believes to be a superior joy. But the artist defined by Lawrence creates art *from* life, and often 'sacrifices' the spouse by transmuting flesh and blood into art. These writers used their personal experience in marriage for the themes and characters of their fiction. They drew on living people and frequently exploited the feelings of those closest to them, and their works both reflected and affected their married life. Though Jung's statement applies to Nietzsche, Kafka and the writers discussed in my book, *Homosexuality and Literature*, the lives of the artists in *Married to Genius* refute this negative theory. Though they provoked and endured many quarrels and crises, they were nevertheless sustained by the love and inspired by the conflict of marriage.

Leo and Sofya Tolstoy
THE BONDAGE OF LOVE

'Everyone carries in himself an image of woman
derived from the mother; by this he is determined to
revere women generally, or to hold them in low
esteem, or to be generally indifferent to them.'
NIETZSCHE, *Human, All-Too-Human*

The half-century of conflict between the paradoxical genius,
Leo Tolstoy, and his neurotic but strong-willed wife, Sofya
Behrs, ended melodramatically with his flight and her
attempted suicide. Their quarrel, which concerned sex, love,
property, art, fame and religion, began in the early days of
their marriage and ended in a struggle literally to the death,
with neither one ever fully understanding nor tolerating the
other. Their final battle was fully documented in their private

diaries, memorialised by members of the Tolstoy circle, recounted in books by their children, and presented to a fascinated public by newspapermen and photographers.

Tolstoy and Sofya were both, in different ways, opposed to the social and sexual norms they had inherited from their aristocratic and feudal society, which was torn by contradictions and close to collapse. Men of this class were permitted to satisfy their gross sexual appetites on peasant women and *demimondaines*. But their wives, brought up to find sex repugnant, were expected to be pure, idealised virgins: lovely, innocent and uneducated before marriage, and continuously bearing children after it. Sofya, who was egoistic and hypersensitive, rebelled inwardly against her sexual and maternal stereotype, but found an outlet for her unhappiness only in hysteria and recrimination.

Tolstoy, a nobleman and great landowner, who was lord of his family and the serfs in his care, married Sofya when he was about to enter the most creative phase of his life. But when his romantic love for Sofya soon faded, he experienced social and sexual revulsion, saw himself as Sofya's victim, and denounced love and marriage as a fraudulent illusion. In the early 1880s, after twenty years of marriage, Tolstoy began to reject the life and values of his class and made radical changes in his personal habits. Sofya became the symbol of the conventional norms that he hated, and he came into sexual and social conflict with her.

Tolstoy had a dual and contradictory character. His powerful eroticism, psychological sensitivity and commitment to social reform, which were vital to his creative life, involved an understanding and acceptance of the world. But this side of his character clashed with his asceticism, mysticism and search for a spiritual existence which rejected this world. The conventional Sofya, who was inevitably confused and distressed by these unresolved contradictions, believed his behaviour was both cruel and irrational. The great psychic drama of Tolstoy's life was the painful repudiation of his early idealism, and the bitter recognition that he could never completely control his sexual passions.

I

Count Leo Tolstoy, an old friend of the Behrs family, was thirty-four when he fell madly in love with the eighteen-year-old Sofya in 1862. Sofya, the second daughter of a successful doctor, was an attractive and unsophisticated girl who had grown up in the society of the Russian Imperial court and absorbed its aristocratic values. Tolstoy, after attending a university and serving as an officer in the army, had travelled in Europe and then taught at a school he had founded for peasant children on his country estate, Yasnaya Polyana. He was already well-known as the author of *Childhood-Boyhood-Youth* (a great favourite of Sofya's) and of *Sebastopol*, a first-hand account of the campaign in the Crimean War. Like many men of his class, Tolstoy was a debauched egoist who drank, gambled and whored his way through university and the army. But he was also an enlightened idealist who worshipped family life, administered his estate in a progressive fashion and believed in his own artistic destiny. Tolstoy's mother and father had both died before he was ten; and he saw marriage as a way to achieve his ideal of family happiness as well as to control his shameful sexual indulgence.

At the end of August 1862 Tolstoy recorded his confused feelings and fears about Sofya in his diary: 'Spent the evening with the Behrses. A mere child! A beautiful thing! How complicated everything is! If I could only find a clear and honest path. . . . I am afraid of myself. What if this is only the search for love, and not real love! I try to see only her bad traits. A mere child. A lovely thing! . . . I am thirty-four. A repulsive face. Should not think of marriage! I have another calling in life, and that is why so much has been given me.'

These entries reveal Tolstoy's doubts about the difference in their age, appearance, background and ideas; his desire to be objective and fear of being blinded by passion; and the conflicting claims of art and marriage. The situation was also complicated because Tolstoy, according to the conventions of the time, was supposed to court the oldest sister, Elizabeth; and because Sofya, the second of three sisters, already had a serious suitor.

The following month Tolstoy overcame his doubts, expressed his feelings, braced himself for a devastating rejection and warned Sofya about the intensity of his love:

> Tell me honestly if you want to be my wife? But only if you can say it with conviction and from the bottom of your heart. If you have even a shadow of doubt, say no. For God's sake, examine your heart carefully. A 'no' from you will be terrible, but I am prepared for it and I will find strength to accept it. . . . But when I am your husband, it will be horrible if I shall never be loved as I love you.

When Sofya immediately agreed to marry him, he defied all custom and insisted that the wedding, which would calm his passions and eliminate his doubts, take place within a week.

Though the Behrs were the model for the Rostov household in *War and Peace* (1869), Tolstoy's courtship and early married life are faithfully recorded in *Anna Karenina* (1877). Like Tolstoy, 'Levin was in love with the whole family – especially the feminine half of it. . . . In the Shcherbatskys' house he encountered for the first time the home life of a cultured, honourable family of the old aristocracy, of which he had been deprived by the death of his own father and mother. All the members of the family . . . appeared to him as though wrapped in some mysterious, poetic veil.' Levin, like Tolstoy, discovered Kitty's feelings when she deciphered the meaning of some complicated and intimate sentences from the first letter of each word; and he also had a rushed wedding week, and delayed the ceremony for an hour and a half while he searched for a missing dress shirt.

More significantly, Levin made the disastrous mistake of showing Kitty his early diary, which contained 'horrible revelations' of his sexual debauchery. Tolstoy also did this just before his marriage, and though Sofya forgave him, she was shocked, felt polluted and became permanently jealous of his early loves. But Tolstoy may have had other, less conscious and confessional motives for showing his diary, for it was also a boast of his youthful adventures, a warning about his strong passions and a challenge to his young bride to tame and domesticate his animal lusts. He also believed, like St Paul, that one function of marriage was to resolve the struggle between passion and chastity by sublimating lust into love. The young Tolstoy adored his lovely bride, and planned to be the perfect husband and father to a fruitful wife and devoted children. But thirty-five years later in 1898, he had lost all faith in idealistic love, felt it was ridiculously inappropriate to people familiar with the grim realities of marriage, and rather bitterly wrote:

Falling in love is to lighten the struggle between sex, desire and chastity. Falling in love ought to be for a young man who cannot keep to full chastity before marriage, and to release the young men in the most critical years, from 16 to 20 or more, from the torturing struggle. Here is the place for falling in love. But when it breaks out in the life of people after marriage, it is out of place and disgusting.

Sofya, like Tolstoy, was intensely idealistic about marriage; and her daughter Tatiana revealed that on 'the morning after her marriage Sofya was so ashamed that she did not want to leave the bedroom, but hid her face in the pillows and cried.' Sofya's sexual shame was increased by her realisation that

Tolstoy had performed the same act of love with whores and peasant sluts. Though Tolstoy remained faithful to Sofya after their wedding, she could never forget his youthful sexual dissipation. Many years later, in 1891, she wrote in her diary that only her purity and innocence had upheld the marriage ideal; and felt that life would be disastrous if women had the same sexual freedom as men.

> I simply cannot reconcile the ideas of woman's *marriage* and man's debauchery. Marriage cannot be happy after the husband's debauchery. It is a constant wonder to me that we have kept it up so long. What saved our marriage was my childlike innocence and my instinct of self-preserva-tion. I instinctively closed my eyes on his past, and delib-erately refrained from reading these [current] diaries and from questioning him about his past. Otherwise it would have been the end for us both. He doesn't realise that my purity alone saved us from perdition.

The portrayal of Kitty and Levin's marriage in *Anna Karenina* provides a constant contrast and counterpoint to the marriage of Dolly and Stiva, and to Anna's unhappy marriage with Karenin and tragic adultery with Vronsky. In the beginning of the novel Vronsky wins Kitty from Levin and then rejects her for Anna. And Anna must die at the end of the novel, rejected by Vronsky, not because Tolstoy is defending sexual morality, but because she has been a disobe-dient wife and negligent mother.

But the Levins have to struggle to achieve their happiness, and the first three weeks of their marriage are 'the bitterest and most humiliating period of their lives.' Like Sofya, Kitty rejects the idea of a honeymoon trip abroad and chooses to live on her husband's country estate. But her frivolous and shallow upbringing, which leaves her with no real interests, makes her lonely, bored and desperate for some occupation.

Though Levin, like Tolstoy, spends a great deal of time trying to amuse her and realises that he is wasting his life and 'doing next to nothing,' he cannot reconcile his desire to free himself from his wife with his extreme jealousy of any visitors who might interest and attract her.

A few months after their marriage, in January 1863, Tolstoy recorded his jealous torments in his diary and related it to the kind of trivial, wasteful and conventional life he had been forced to lead since his courtship of Sofya:

Today the obvious pleasure she derived from talking to Erlenwein and attracting his attention brought me back to the old height of truth and strength. I can read this over and say: Yes, I know, this is jealousy! This will calm me and do something else to throw me back into the conventional life that I have hated since my youth. I have been leading it for nine months. It is terrible! I am a gambler and a drunkard. I am on a spree of farming and I have wasted nine months, which could have been the best and which I have made almost the worst in my life. All I need to live happily is to be loved by her and by myself and instead, all this time, I have been hating myself. . . . I understand why she enjoys the company of another person no matter how insignificant and no matter how unbearable she makes me feel. I realise that during the last nine months I have been the most insignificant, the weakest, the most senseless, and the most conventional person.

Though Sofya tried to understand Tolstoy's jealousy and recognised that it was an expression of his love, she could not control her own envy of her younger sister, jealousy of his former mistress and anger at his devotion to the peasants. When Tolstoy took Tatiana Behrs to a ball in the nearby town because his wife was ill, the childish Sofya recorded: 'When Lev, in full dress, left with Tatiana for Tula to attend the ball, I began to cry bitterly and cried all evening long. We led a monotonous, secluded, dull life, and when the opportunity arose, I – I was then only nineteen – I could not take advantage of it.' Less than three months after their marriage, Aksinya, a fat and simple peasant wench who was pregnant by Tolstoy, was ordered to wash the floors of the manor house. The sight of her disgusted Sofya, drove her into a frenzy and made her want to 'burn his diary and all his past.' And in November 1862 the aristocratic Sofya, who felt neglected and lonely when Tolstoy was involved with his estate and his school, recorded: 'He disgusts me with his People. I feel he ought to choose between me, i. e. the representative of the family, and his beloved People.' The problems that plagued the Tolstoys during the next fifty years were manifest in the early months of their marriage and reflected in the portrayal of Levin and Kitty in *Anna Karenina*. They were sexually incompatible; jealous of each other's interests, friends and feelings; and in conflict about Tolstoy's desire to live the simple life of the peasants.

II

Sofya soon became absorbed in Tolstoy's work and in her own children. He began to write *War and Peace* in 1863, shortly after his marriage. His extremely subtle portrayal of female characters in that novel and in *Anna Karenina* provides a strong contrast to the superficial portraits of women in his early books, and reflects his intimacy with his wife and her criticism of the novel. Sofya's brother Stephen claimed that she copied the nearly illegible manuscript of the massive novel seven times; and though she resented Tolstoy's absorption in his work, she had an almost penitential commitment to it: 'I try to persuade myself that there is a joy in doing one's *duty*, and I make myself copy manuscripts and do all kinds of things which are supposed to be my *duty*, but sometimes my will protests against it, and I want some *personal* joy.' As she stoically asserted: 'My fate has been to serve my husband, the author. Perhaps I ought not to complain; for I have served a man who was worthy of the sacrifice.' Though Sofya derived satisfaction from participating in Tolstoy's work, she also wanted him to love her and recognise the value of *her* work.

Sofya recognised Tolstoy's genius, but regretted that he did not apply his profound artistic insight to his life: 'If he had only a fragment of that deep psychological understanding which is shown in his books he must surely have understood . . . the depth of my pain and despair.' But in *War and Peace*, which was finally published in 1869, Prince Andrey condemns the bondage of marriage and gives his friend Pierre the following advice:

Never, never marry, my dear fellow! That's my advice: never marry till you can say to yourself that you have done all you are capable of, and until you have ceased to love the woman of your choice and have seen her plainly as she is, or else you will make a cruel and irrevocable mistake. Marry when you are old and good for nothing – or all that is good and noble in you will be lost. It will be wasted on trifles. Yes! Yes! Yes! Don't look at me with such surprise. If you marry expecting anything from yourself in the future you will feel at every step that for you all is ended, all is closed except the drawing-room, where you will be ranged side by side with a court lackey and an idiot!

Though Tolstoy had written this work of consummate genius during the first six years of his marriage, he felt that domestic bondage was based on deception, precluded achievement and transformed a man of promise into a 'lackey and an idiot.' Tolstoy was totally absorbed in himself and his work, believed he was the only one who had sacrificed himself in marriage, and was completely unaware that Sofya resented her servile role and was also desperately unhappy.

In the twenty-five years between 1863 and 1888 Sofya had thirteen children. Three of them died in infancy and two in childhood, and the rest survived to take sides in their parents' quarrel, edit the Tolstoys' diaries and write their own memoirs. Tolstoy expressed his ambivalent feelings about the birth of his first child, Sergei, through Levin, who felt nothing but fear and aversion and 'was oppressed by a new sense of apprehension – the consciousness of another vulnerable region. And this consciousness was so painful at first, the apprehension lest that helpless being should suffer was so acute, that it drowned the strange thrill of unreasoning joy and even pride which he had felt when the infant sneezed.' Tolstoy was furious when his wife was unable to feed their son and had to hire a peasant wet nurse.

After the birth of their fifth child Marya in 1871, Sofya suffered an almost fatal attack of puerperal fever. But when she expressed fears about another pregnancy Tolstoy was deeply offended, and she continued to bear an infant every other year. When she became pregnant with her twelfth child Alexandra in 1884, she felt physically and emotionally exhausted by the endless births, nursing and illnesses, and unsuccessfully tried to abort the child. At the end of this pregnancy she quarrelled with Tolstoy about the trivial matter of selling horses, and he decided to leave the 'house inhabited and managed by insane people' – his family. The excitement seemed to induce labour and as she prayed for death, Tolstoy repented and returned home to find 'the bearded ruffians' – his elder sons - playing whist. Their daughter was born the next morning.

Another characteristic family scene – a sudden flare up, with extreme accusations and threats to leave – took place during the following year, 1885. According to Sofya:

Lev worked himself into a state of fury and depression. . . .
We had been getting along beautifully; not a single
disagreeable word, not a single argument. 'I have come to
tell you that I want a divorce; I cannot live like this.' . . .
Dumbfounded, I asked: 'What has happened?' 'Nothing,
but if you keep adding to a load, a horse stops and cannot
go any farther.' I had no notion of what he meant. Then he
began to scream, to hurl accusations and harsh words at me,
and the scene became more disgusting every minute. I tried
to keep my temper but when he finally said that 'the very
air around me was infected' I gave orders to bring my trunk
and began to pack. . . . He begged me to stay. I gave in, and
then suddenly hysterical tears began. It was horrible! . . . Just
imagine, Lev shaking all over and convulsed with sobs. I felt
so sorry for him. Four of the children – Tatyana, Ilya, Helen
and Mary – were screaming at the top of their voices. I was
stunned.

Sofya's self-pity and self-justification prevented her from
understanding either the situation ('We had been getting
along beautifully') or her husband ('I was stunned'). Though
Tolstoy's request reflected his profound unhappiness, Sofya
claimed she 'had no notion of what he meant' and suggested
that his 'disgusting' accusations were completely irrational.
Though Tolstoy asked for the divorce, Sofya (in her
extremely subjective version of this incident) reversed their
traditional roles and threatened to leave, while Tolstoy
assumed her part and burst into hysterical tears of grief and
frustration before the audience of four startled children. They
could only communicate by the expression of extreme
emotions; and in 1887, Tolstoy summarised their twenty-five
years of married life with the terse understatement: 'Things
could have been better.'

III

Anna Karenina opens with the famous sentence, 'All happy families are alike but an unhappy family is unhappy after its own fashion,' which reflects the Tolstoys' idiosyncratic unhappiness. In 1882 Tolstoy investigated the lives of the poor in Moscow while conducting a population census, was appalled by the filth and disease, decided it was 'impossible to live like this,' and proposed a programme of radical reform in his book, *What Are We to Do?* The great turning point in Tolstoy's marriage – and the first of three great crises with Sofya – took place in 1883 when Tolstoy came to the conclusion that property was evil and suddenly decided to give up the management of his house, his land and his literary copyrights. Tolstoy gave his inexperienced wife the power of attorney, and she had to learn the business of managing the estate, publishing and selling subscriptions of his books, and dealing with government censors. Sofya believed he had acted in an absurd and terrible way, and wrote, with considerable justification: he 'has thrown the weight of everything on my shoulders – children, house, land, all the business affairs, books, everything – and continues to despise me and to torture me with his selfish indifference.'

In 1883 Tolstoy also made a radical change in his personal habits. He wore peasant clothes, gave up his servants, cleaned his own room, lit the stoves, cut the wood, carried the water, learned shoemaking and persuaded his daughters to wear his hand-made footwear. He also attempted to simplify his life by systematically abandoning his favourite pleasures. He gave up hunting in 1884, meat and alcohol in 1887, and tobacco in 1888. It was impossible for Sofya – with her 'frivolous and shallow upbringing,' her aristocratic beliefs and title of Countess, her twenty years of married life supported by an army of servants and retainers, and her desperate need for money and security to compensate for the lack of love – to understand or tolerate Tolstoy's bizarre behaviour. For he not only defied all the conventions of class and society, but also threatened the financial well-being of herself and her numerous children.

Sofya, who refused to wear Tolstoy's shoes, quite rightly thought he was better as an artist than an artisan, and recognised his aesthetic and moral dichotomy. 'There were two men in Lev,' she wrote, 'a novelist of genius and a poor moralist who simply amazed people by the paradoxical contradiction of his ideas. . . . One hadn't time to change one's life to suit one's husband's spiritual whims, and to follow him in his ideas.' Her children, in the mid-1880s, shared her feelings; and Tolstoy, who could not sympathise with their 'meaningless' existence nor convince them of his beliefs, forfeited his parental and moral authority. He felt isolated and even scorned within his own family, and was forced into the ungrateful role of a discontented old man. As he sadly wrote in his diary of 1884:

I find it very difficult to be with the family. I find it difficult because I cannot share their feelings. All their joys, examinations, social successes, music, clothes, shopping – all this I consider misfortune and an evil, but I cannot explain this to them. I try to talk to them, but they seem unable to grasp my words. They refuse to think about the meaning of my words, and instead feel that I am inconsiderate to mention the subject. In my weaker moments – and this is one of them – their heartlessness amazes me. How can they fail to see that during the last three years I have not only suffered, but that I have been deprived of my life? I have been assigned the role of a grumbling old man, and I am nothing else in their eyes. If I should share their lives, I should be disloyal to the truth, and they would be the very first to point out any inconsistency to me. If I continue sadly to watch their insane behaviour, I am a grumbling old man like all other old men.

The well-publicised photographs of the patriarchal and white-bearded Tolstoy in his peasant blouse and high boots attracted legions of disciples and humble followers who gravitated to Yasnaya Polyana to sit at the Master's feet and enjoy his *largesse*. Sofya's resentment of Tolstoy's infatuation with the peasants, which dated from the early days of her marriage, intensified considerably in the late 1880s with the arrival of the professional 'Tolstoyans' in their greasy sheepskin coats and muddy felt boots. Sofya disdainfully referred to them as the 'dark ones,' and her comical diary entry of 1890 did not fail to note the disparity between Tolstoy's lofty ideas and his base followers: 'The "dark" ones have arrived: Popov, that inane and stupid Asiatic, and that fat fool of a Khokhlov, of shopkeeper origin. And those are the followers of a great man! Miserable abortions of human society, aimless babblers, uneducated loafers.'

Tolstoy's daughter Alexandra, who became sympathetic to her father's ideas but shared her mother's fastidiousness and snobbery, agreed with Sofya about the parasitic disciples: 'They never gave any tips [to the servants], they brought in a lot of dirt, they made spots on the parquet floors, they reeked of tar and they always managed to insinuate themselves right into the Count's study' and to interfere with his work. Alexandra found a bovine Swedish writer, who appeared in 1892, particularly objectionable: 'He lies on the grass like a cow, digs in the earth, rinses himself in the Don River, eats a lot, lies in the kitchen – and that's all. . . . It proved impossible to dislodge the Swede.' Even the proletarian writer, Maxim Gorky, confirmed in vivid detail their mean motives and religious hypocrisy, and thought the 'dark ones' infected Tolstoy's house 'with a spirit of hypocrisy, cowardice, mercenary and self-seeking pettiness and legacy-

hunting. . . . Nearly all of them like to moan and kiss one
another; they all have boneless perspiring hands and lying
eyes.'

IV

Though Tolstoy's story, 'The Kreutzer Sonata,' concerns the
bizarre confessions of Pozdnyshev who was acquitted of
murdering his wife in a *crime passionnel*, it is also an extremely
autobiographical work which summarises the Tolstoys'
marital conflicts of the 1880s. The story mentions his wife's
horror when he shows her the diary of pre-marital love
affairs, his own lust and jealousy, their quarrel about nursing
the first child, his wife's suicide attempts and his unsuccessful
efforts to run away from home. This extremely misogynistic
story is also an attack on the hypocrisy of marriage. 'What is
vilest about it,' states the embittered husband, 'is that in
theory love is something ideal and exalted, but in practice it
is something abominable and swinish.'

Though Sofya gave birth to their thirteenth child, Ivan,
when Tolstoy was writing 'The Kreutzer Sonata' in 1888, he
strongly advocated chastity in the 'Afterword' to the story.
Sofya was naturally disturbed by this unpleasant paradox and
wrote in her diary: 'He is killing me very systematically. . . .
It would be terrible to become pregnant again; for all would
learn of his shame and would repeat with malicious joy a
joke just now invented in Moscow society: "There's the real
'Afterword' of 'The Kreutzer Sonata.'"'

When the story was finally published in 1891 (after having
been delayed for three years by government censorship), the
public inevitably related it to Tolstoy's own marriage. Sofya
recorded that 'He couldn't have hurt anyone more than he
had hurt me with his last book. . . . It has wounded me and
has disgraced me in the eyes of the whole world, and has
destroyed the last remnant of love between us.'

Sofya condemned as false the description of female passion in the story, contrasted Tolstoy's lust with her own purity, and complained 'His sensuality is contagious, and yet my whole moral being *protests* against it, for I never wanted it. All my life I have dreamed sentimentally of an ideal and spiritual relationship – but not *that*.' But after twenty-seven years of married life, Tolstoy's suggestion that they sleep in separate rooms seemed to destroy the meaning of her life. As she noted in 1891, the wife 'at times becomes passionate towards her husband and expects to be satisfied. Woe to her if he has ceased to love her.' Sofya also emphasised the strong contrast between Tolstoy's theory and practice of chastity: 'If only the people who read 'The Kreutzer Sonata' with such a feeling of veneration could look for a moment at the erotic life he lives – and which alone makes him happy and cheerful – they would cast this little god from the pedestal on which they have placed him.' Sofya wanted a spiritual relationship but expected to be sexually satisfied, complained that Tolstoy did not sleep with her but claimed that she gave him erotic cheer. Tolstoy was equally inconsistent, for the sybarite and saint were always at war within him. He was a reformed rake who preached chastity but continued to have sexual relations into extreme old age.

V

In 1891 Tolstoy again astounded his wife and family by deciding to give away the rights of all his literary works published after 1881, the beginning of his moralistic and didactic phase, and the year he published *What Men Live By*. During the violent arguments about this renunciation, Tolstoy's last resort was always a threat to leave home and Sofya's a vow to kill herself. After a quarrel about literary rights in 1891 Sofya rushed out of the house, ran toward the railroad tracks and (like Anna Karenina) planned to throw herself under a train. But she ran into her brother-in-law who restrained her without much difficulty and escorted her home.

This quarrel was still raging in 1895, when Sofya's hysteria became much worse after the death, at the age of seven, of her adored youngest son, Ivan. Sofya claimed the rights of Tolstoy's recent stories for her very profitable edition of his complete works, the family's main source of income. When Tolstoy opposed her wishes Sofya was again inspired by one of his suicidal characters, and said that she 'wanted to go off and freeze to death, somewhere in the Sparrow Hills, in the woods. I liked the idea, so I recall, that in the story ['Master and Man,' 1895] Vasili Andreyevich froze to death and that I too would freeze to death because of that story.' Sofya, who ran into the snow in her bare feet, remembered weeping and screaming: '"Let them take me to the police station, or take me to the lunatic asylum!" Lev dragged me back and I kept tumbling on the snow.'

The mutual threats and recriminations, which continued throughout the final decades of Tolstoy's marriage, reached a second crisis in 1897 when Sofya once again acted out the life of a fictional character. Like Pozdnyshev's wife in 'The Kreutzer Sonata,' she became infatuated with a young composer and pianist, S. I. Taneyev, who became the passive recipient of her passionate though platonic feelings. The narrator says of the musician: 'He was a worthless man in my opinion and according to my estimate. And not because of the significance he acquired in my life but because he really was so.' And Tolstoy repeated this accusation against the actual Taneyev in his diary of 1896:

It is dreadfully painful and humiliatingly embarrassing that a complete stranger, a person of no use, of no kind of interest, should be directing our lives, poisoning the last years or year of our life; it is humiliating and agonizing, that we must be governed by when he goes where, by what rehearsals, by when he plays. It is horribly, horribly disgusting and shameful.

Though Taneyev was a superfluous luxury, he was extremely interesting to Sofya, displaced her love for her husband and dominated the life of the family.

Tolstoy finally became so jealous and exasperated by Sofya's love affair with Taneyev that in 1897 he again decided to leave home. He wrote a letter to Sofya (which was not opened until after his death in 1910) that explained his spiritual quest and foreshadowed his final flight in the last year of his life. Tolstoy thanked his wife for their thirty-five years of married life, and asked her to 'let me go of your own free will; do not seek for me, do not find fault with me, do not condemn me.' He could not longer 'continue to live as I have been living these sixteen years, at one time struggling and harassing you, at another yielding to those influences and temptations to which I was accustomed.' But the main reason was that, having reached his seventieth year, he wanted to retire into the forest in order to 'dedicate the last years of his life to God and not to jokes, puns, gossip and lawn tennis.'

Tolstoy did not escape in 1897 any more than he did in 1884, when Alexandra was born. But he continued to record his intense anger with Sofya in his diary entries of 1897–99, which expressed in a more extreme form the misogynistic ideas of *The Kreutzer Sonata* as well as his perennial conflict of lust and love. Though Sofya had once inspired his most attractive fictional heroines, she now provoked his most violent denunciations of women:

Woman is generally stupid. . . . She cannot understand the simplest thing; she cannot see farther than the present moment and there is no self-control and no patience (except child-birth and the care of children). . . . For 70 years I have been lowering and lowering my opinion of women and still it has to be lowered more and more. The woman question! How can there not be a woman question? Only not in this, how women should begin to direct life, but in this, how they should stop ruining it.

The aged and thoroughly embittered Tolstoy condemned the confusion of sexual desire with spiritual love; and felt that reason should control and repress passion rather than 'adorn it with peacock feathers of spirituality' – as he himself had done when he first met Sofya. He also wanted to destroy all the illusions about marriage: he insisted on the dissociation of marriage and happiness, repeated the idea of domestic bondage that he had expressed in *War and Peace*, stated that men were tortured and contaminated by the moral defects of their wives, and in a fit of almost Swiftian revulsion, emphasised the disgusting imperfections of the female body:

The chief cause of unhappiness in married life is that people have been taught to think that marriage means happiness. The incentive for marriage is sex attraction, which takes the form of promises and hopes of happiness – a view supported by public opinion and by literature. But marriage cannot cause happiness. Instead, it always means torture, with which man has to pay for satisfying his sex urge. These tortures are lack of freedom, servility, satiety, revulsion, all sorts of moral and physical defects in one's mate, which one is forced to endure, such as temper, stupidity, dishonesty, vanity, drunkenness, laziness, greed, cupidity and immorality – all defects that it is much more difficult to endure in others than in oneself and which make one suffer as if they were one's own – and such physical imperfections as ugliness, slovenliness, odours, diseases, insanity, and many others that are even more unbearable.

VI

The third crisis of Tolstoy's marriage took place in 1910, the last year of his long life, and concerned the same moral issues and sexual conflicts that he had failed to resolve in the earlier quarrels. In 1910 Sofya became locked in a deadly struggle with V. G. Chertkov, an ex-Guards officer who, like Tolstoy, was interested in the welfare of the peasants and the relation of social questions to the teaching of the Gospels. Tolstoy had met Chertkov in 1883, considered him his closest friend and main apostle of his ideas, and had chosen him – and not Sofya – as the posthumous editor of his works. As Sofya struggled with Chertkov for control of Tolstoy's private diaries, which she claimed defamed her 'as a tormentor whom it is necessary to *resist*,' she was actually defaming *Tolstoy's* character in her own diaries. Three of her sons, fearful of losing their inheritance, actively supported Sofya, while two daughters, Tatiana and Alexandra, sided with Tolstoy. Sofya was madly jealous of Chertkov (as Tolstoy had been of Taneyev), accused Tolstoy of having homosexual relations with him, and reversed their original roles (the voluptuary and virgin) by insisting that her eighty-two-year-old husband resume sexual relations with her. As she pitifully wrote in June 1910: 'I am insanely jealous of Leo Nikolaevich's intimacy with Chertkov. I feel that he has taken from me all that I have lived by for forty-eight years. I was so accustomed to love him, take care of him, and look after his works! And now I am completely thrown aside. He finds me a burden.'

During this final struggle, Sofya's diary and behaviour revealed the very worst side of her character. She was both prudish and flirtatious, selfish and stubborn, nagging and domineering, wallowed in her sense of personal grievance, ostentatiously assumed the role of martyr, constantly imagined fatal attacks of illness, and often threatened to kill herself. She never understood Tolstoy's commitment to social reform, his impressive though unsuccessful attempts to transcend his human limitations, and his quest for a spiritual existence. She justified her violent opposition to his ideas by unjustly stating he was vain, ambitious, selfish and hypocritical; suggested that his abandonment of property and effort to live a simple life were merely poses adopted to attract publicity and increase his popularity; and believed his saintly demeanour disguised a secret corruption. Sofya countered Tolstoy's criticism of her ignorance and materialism by condemning his humiliating exposure of their marriage in 'The Kreutzer Sonata' as well as his premarital passions with whores and peasant women: 'I told him he was ambitious and vainglorious, and he said I was always out for money, and that he had never seen such a greedy and stupid woman. I said that he had made it his business to humiliate me, all my life, because he had never had anything to do with decent women.'

On 22 June 1910, when Sofya was sixty-five and Tolstoy nearly eighty-two, she suffered a severe nervous breakdown. She rolled on the floor in hysterics, tried to shoot herself, carried a bottle of opium, constantly threatened to take her own life – and was diagnosed as paranoid. Tolstoy was summoned home from Chertkov's house, where he had tried to escape from Sofya, and as his oldest son Sergei (who was sympathetic to his mother) admits: 'He had to encounter my mother's hysterical attacks, in which the same things were repeated again and again: reproaches, complaints of what she considered to be her unhappy fate, hostile thrusts at Chertkov, insane suspicions, demands that her husband should hand his diaries to her and disclose the contents of his will, threats of suicide.'

In June Tolstoy explained to his friend Goldenweiser that

Sofya 'is unquestionably mentally deranged. She has an *idée fixe* – vanity. She is afraid that people will say that she spoilt my life, and with all her might she wants to prove the opposite – that she alone is good, and that all the rest are scoundrels and liars.' The egoistic belief of both Sofya *and* Tolstoy that 'I alone am good' expressed their fundamental and irrevocable opposition. Though Tolstoy recognised Sofya's condition, he found it difficult to tolerate, and in July told his daughter Alexandra: 'She is finishing me off.'

Sofya's attempt to redeem herself in the eyes of the world merely increased her mania. She felt compelled to spy on Tolstoy in order to discover the location of the private diary he had promised to Chertkov and the secret will of July 1910 which renounced the rights to all his works, including *War and Peace* and *Anna Karenina*, written *before* 1881. On the night of 10 July Tolstoy heard Sofya moving about his room, complained that she was disturbing his sleep and told her to go away. Sofya reports that she literally obeyed his order, 'went away into the garden, and lay for two hours in a thin dress on the wet grass. I was very cold, but I greatly desired to die and still desire to.'

Four days later the desperate and weary Tolstoy wrote a letter to Sofya explaining the three principal causes of their difficulties: his withdrawal from wordly life, her imperious and violent character, and their fundamental disagreement about the meaning of life:

> First, my ever-increasing alienation from the interests of worldly life and the repulsion I felt for it; whereas you did not wish to and could not part with them, not having in your soul the principles that led me to my convictions. That was quite natural and I cannot reproach you for it . . . . Secondly, then, these last years your character has become more and more irritable, despotic and unrestrained. . . . And the third, chief, and most fatal thing, for

which neither you nor I are to blame, is our completely opposite conception of the meaning and purpose of life.

Though he did not blame Sofya for her worldliness and her philosophy of life, he made it clear that her despotic temperament was sufficient to make his existence intolerable.

But Sofya could not respond to Tolstoy's rational explanation and personal criticism, and their domestic difficulties grew worse. In August Tolstoy condemned her perversion of love, which was no longer redeemed by the unselfish care of her children, and had degenerated into a destructive and devouring egotism: 'There is no love, but demands for love, which are near to hatred and are changing into hatred. Yes, egotism is madness. The children used to save her – an animal love, but still selfless. But when that ended, only a terrible egotism remained, and egotism is the most abnormal state. It is madness.' Tolstoy also records that in August Sofya again became hysterical in front of the entire household: 'Toward evening she began making scenes – running out into the garden, sobs and screams. It went to the point that when I followed her into the garden she screamed, "He is a beast, a murderer, I cannot look at him."'

In October Sofya rearranged the photographs in his study, burnt the portrait of Chertkov and blamed Tolstoy for her behaviour. Like Tolstoy, his daughter Tatiana recognised the comic, operatic and masochistic elements in Sofya's hysterical performances, but could not find a way to control her: 'Mama had a very bad hysterical attack at Yasnaya ... we have the impression that she could easily put a stop to all the tragi-comedy she is producing. . . . Hysterical persons do enjoy their sufferings and the troubles to which they put others.' At the end of the month Tolstoy, who was watched and controlled by Sofya throughout the day and night, reached the breaking point. He compared his life to the

damned in hell and told a friend he had finally decided to
leave home:

> I am stewing in this house as I would in hell. Yes, yes!
> believe me, I am sincere with you! I will not die in this
> house. I have decided to leave for some unknown place
> where no one knows me. Perhaps I shall come to your
> house to die. . . . I have not left, I could not leave before
> for selfish reasons, but now I see that my departure will be
> for the good of the family. There will be fewer arguments,
> and they will sin less.

In the early morning of 28 October Tolstoy was again
awakened by the noise of Sofya searching his desk, and was
overcome by indignation and revulsion. At daybreak, with
only his friend Dr Makovitsky to accompany him, Tolstoy
quietly left Yasnaya Polyana, his ancestral home and birth-
place, forever. As he had done under similar circumstances in
1897, Tolstoy carefully explained his reasons in a letter to his
wife. He told Sofya that he was unable to bear her humiliating scrutiny and their luxurious milieu, and was leaving in
search of final tranquillity:

> My departure will be bitter news for you and I am sorry,
> but please understand and believe me when I say that I
> could not have done anything else. My position in this
> house has become unbearable. In addition to everything
> else, I can no longer live in the luxurious surroundings in
> which I have been living, and I am doing what old men of
> my age should do: I am leaving mundane affairs so I can
> spend the remaining days of my life in peace and solitude.

Sofya, shocked by her husband's departure, raced out to the
laundry float, slipped, fell, sank into the shallow pond and
was rescued. That same day she wrote:

Leo Nikolaevich has *unexpectedly* gone away. O horror! A letter from him telling me not to seek him. He is going away for ever to live the peaceful life of an old man. Having read part of it I immediately in despair threw myself into the middle pond and began to choke in the water. Sasha and Bulgakov pulled me out, and Vanya Shuraev helped them. Utter despair. Why did they save me?

The next day, terrified by the scandalous flight of her husband, who was the most famous man in Russia, she wrote Tolstoy a confused and pathetic letter, filled with endearments. She begged him to come back, threatened suicide, made impossible promises to reform her habits and character, and appealed to his conscience, to the Gospels and to his sense of loyalty as a husband:

Levochka, my dear one, my darling, return home! Save me from a second suicide, Levochka, my life-long friend. I will do everything, everything that you wish! I will cast aside all luxury, your friends shall be mine, I will undergo a cure, and will be mild, tender, and kind. Do come back to me. You must *save* me. You know it is said in the Gospels that a man must never *for any reason* abandon his wife. My dear, my darling, friend of my soul, save me! Return if only to say farewell to me before our inevitable separation.

When Sofya finally tracked down Tolstoy at the Astapovo railroad station, a week later, he refused to see her and quite rightly said, in a telegram to his sons: 'heart so weak that meeting Mama would be fatal for me.' He died in the stationmaster's house, with Chertkov and three of his children at his bedside, on 7 November 1910. The marriage of Tolstoy and Sofya, who both had enormous egos and powerful passions, ended in mutual destruction. Though

Sofya justly wrote in 1897: 'My husband's *strength* broke my life, my personality,' she also martyred Tolstoy and later admitted to Alexandra: 'I knew I was the cause of your father's death.'

The young Tolstoy had extremely conservative ideas about marriage and expected to remake Sofya in his own image. Though she reluctantly agreed to continuous childbearing, she defended her wifely status and the inheritance of her children, and violently opposed Tolstoy's decision to abandon his property and literary rights. She was far too conventional and practical to follow Tolstoy's radical changes and spiritual quests in the early 1880s, immediately saw through and exposed his paradoxical contradictions, and successfully undertook the management of all his affairs when he forced her to do so.

Worn out by childbearing and constant quarrels with her husband, the death of her youngest son and a serious disease, Sofya, who had a strong tendency toward hysteria and self-pity, felt compelled to imitate Tolstoy's passionate and morbid fictional characters, and began to break down after 1906. In the last years of Tolstoy's life she repeated her earlier mistakes, displayed the worst aspects of her character, tortured her husband, and lost the sympathy and support of her family and friends. Her futile efforts to redeem her reputation merely ruined it forever.

Though Tolstoy threatened to leave home in 1883 and again in 1897, he did not do so. He was bound to Sofya by lust, love and loyalty; and remained locked in combat with her for nearly fifty years. His last flight was a desperate but hopeless attempt to free himself from Sofya's intolerable interference in his most intimate affairs, which tormented his life and hastened his death. A famous photograph of their last confrontation provides a powerful contrast to the idealized image of a lovely young girl who was courted by a distinguished author. It shows Sofya as a pathetic old

woman, shut out of Tolstoy's room and peering through a
window at his deathbed. After Tolstoy died she honestly
admitted that she had not understood him: 'Yes, I lived with
Lev for forty-eight years but I never really learned what
kind of a man he was.'

Bernard and Charlotte Shaw
SEXLESS MARRIAGE

'The fickleness of the women I love is only equalled by
the infernal constancy of the women who love me.'

SHAW, *The Philanderer*

'Money guarantees comfort and what you call culture.
Love guarantees nothing.'

SHAW, *Buoyant Billions*

I

George Bernard Shaw and Charlotte Payne-Townshend,
who were married in their early forties, were peculiarly well-
suited to each other. Their marriage made few emotional
demands and tended to reinforce their personal limitations.
Shaw had been a sexual philanderer who maintained a coldly

intellectual and emotionally sterile attitude toward women, and used his conquests to satisfy his egoism and vanity. Charlotte, who was frightened of sex and motherhood, repressed her physical desires and remained essentially unfulfilled. Shaw's basically passionless temperament allowed Charlotte to remain neurotically as well as virginally intact, while she gave him luxury and social status, and protected him from serious involvement with other women. Shaw's biographer, St John Ervine, writes of 'the embarrassing skittishness which he was apt to display when sex relations were involved. He had long been terrified of his own emotions and sought to allay them by laughing them off; but the laugh was always forced. The last twenty years of his life were full of fear of women, and this fear, after Charlotte's death, degenerated into something like mortal terror.' Though Shaw's marriage did not deepen his feelings and extend his understanding of women, it allowed him to stabilise his emotional behaviour and to discipline his intellectual energy.

Shaw was the son of a drunken, impoverished father and a cold, disillusioned mother, with neither taste nor talent for domesticity, who despised her husband and ignored her son. Shaw later admitted that his unhappy childhood made him unusually independent but emotionally retarded, eager to exploit the emotions of others but afraid to show his own feelings: 'Though I was not ill-treated – my parents being quite incapable of any sort of inhumanity – the fact that nobody cared for me particularly gave me a frightful self-sufficiency, or rather a power of starving on imaginary feasts, that may have delayed my development a good deal, and leaves me to this hour a treacherous brute in matters of pure affection.'

The autobiographical hero of Shaw's early novel, *Love Among the Artists* (1886), states that his mother 'did not know how much her indifference tortured me, because she had no idea of any keener sensitiveness than her own. . . . She taught me to do without her consideration; and I learned my lesson.' Shaw's lack of maternal affection turned him into a rather bitter and selfish young man who learned to attract the compensatory love of women – which proved his personal worth and satisfied his ego, without reciprocating their love – which would have involved responsibility and risked rejection. As his Fabian colleague Beatrice Webb wrote: 'The most characteristic paradox of his nature is the union of the fanatic and the manipulator.'

When Shaw was a child of ten Vandaleur Lee, an iconoclastic, possessive and dictatorial 'man of mesmeric vitality and force,' became his mother's singing teacher and shared a house with the family. Though there was no *menage à trois*, Lee undermined the authority of the father, and established for Shaw the model of an ever-present but vicarious participant in the man–woman relationship. Shaw's vanity and theatrical sense nearly always demanded a vicarious participant in his own love affairs, a person who could at once provide an audience for the amorous spectacle, intensify the dramatic interest and admire his masterful control of the situation. His former mistress, Jenny Patterson, became the jealous observer of his liaison with Florence Farr. His friend Beatrice Webb encouraged and recorded Shaw's courtship of Charlotte Payne-Townshend. Charlotte detached him from his emotional entanglement with Bertha Newcombe. And the actress Ellen Terry received a detailed epistolary account of his affair with Charlotte. After their marriage, Charlotte assumed the unwelcome role of vicarious participant in his rather operatic affairs with Erica Cotterill and Mrs Patrick Campbell; and her intense jealousy added an element of excitement that sustained these affairs and prolonged her own torment.

II

Shaw was born in Dublin in 1856 and spent the twenty years between 1872 and 1892 in a desperate struggle against poverty, frustration and neglect. In 1872 Shaw's mother left his hopeless father, went to London, and supported herself and her daughter Lucy by giving singing lessons; and Shaw began to work as a clerk and cashier in a Dublin land agent's office. Four years later Shaw abandoned this tedious work, followed his mother to London and joined her squalid household. He wrote five unsuccessful novels between 1879 and 1883; became a Socialist in 1882 and joined the Fabians two years later; and did increasingly successful music, art and then drama criticism for the *Saturday Review* between 1885 and 1898. He wrote *Widowers' Houses, The Philanderer* and *Mrs Warren's Profession* in the early 1890s, and finally established his reputation as a playwright with *Candida* and *Arms and the Man* in 1894.

Poverty, passivity and shyness kept Shaw 'perfectly continent' until the age of twenty-nine. But when he became acquainted with his mother's pupils and with the female Fabians, he realised that women found him attractive and his sexual activity soon kept pace with his literary life. Ervine reports that in 1888 Shaw 'had six affairs on his hands, three of them languishing, two of them beginning, and one seeming to go passionately on and on,' and he remarks that all the women who loved Shaw were either beautiful or exceptionally intelligent. When Shaw fell deeply in love the following year with the 'clever, good-natured and very good-looking' actress Florence Farr, he severed his languishing platonic connections with the conventional nurse Alice Lockett, the fiery atheist Annie Besant, and the tiresome wife of a polygamous Tory M. P. , Mrs Hubert Bland; and ended his innocent flirtations with two young women in the Fabian circle, Grace Gilchrist and Geraldine Spooner. But the rich, passionate and quick-tempered widow,

Jenny Patterson, who was fifteen years older than Shaw and had seduced him in 1885, was much more difficult to dismiss. She was violently jealous of Shaw's love for Florence, and late one night she burst in on them, used atrocious language, created a shocking scene and had to be forcibly restrained from attacking her rival.

Though Shaw loved Florence for a time, he could never build a permanent relationship based on sexual attraction, for as Ervine writes: 'Her passion was too precise to last, and his too importunate to keep her in thrall.' After a brief courtship of May Morris, the daughter of the Socialist poet William Morris, Shaw had an affair with the talented portrait painter, Bertha Newcombe, the most interesting of his early loves. Beatrice Webb, who had a stormy interview with Bertha after Shaw had lost interest in her and was courting Charlotte, learned 'the story of her relationship to Bernard Shaw, her five years of devoted love, his cold philandering, her hopes aroused by my repeated advice to him ... to marry her – and then her feeling of dismay and resentment against me when she discovered I was encouraging him "to marry Miss Townshend."' Bertha's painful involvement with Shaw had taught her to understand his personality and behaviour, and she gave Beatrice an extremely perceptive analysis of his personal defects, his emotional limitations and his sexual fears. Shaw was:

> a passionless man. He had passed through experiences, and he seemed to have no wish for and even to fear passion though he admitted its power and pleasure. The sight of a woman deeply in love with him annoyed him. He was not in love with me, in the usual sense, or at any rate as he said only for a very short time. . . . Frequent talking, talking, talking of the pros and cons of marriage ... his dislike of the sexual relation and so on, would create an atmosphere of love-making without any need for caresses or endearments.

Both H. G. Wells and Beatrice Webb testified that Shaw was dominated and driven by a fantastic vanity. The former stated, 'He was ruled by a naked, unqualified, ego-centred, devouring vanity such as one rarely meets in life'; and the latter agreed, 'In his relations with women he is vulgar – if not worse – it is a vulgarity which includes cruelty and springs from vanity.' Beatrice Webb, a careful observer of Shaw's behaviour, also discussed the influence of his sexual escapades on the quality of his work:

> He is mistaken if he thinks that it does not affect his artistic work. His incompleteness as a thinker, his shallow and vulgar view of many human relationships . . . these defects come largely from the flippant and worthless self-compla-cency brought about by the worship of rather second-rate women. . . .
>
> Adored by many women, he is a born philanderer; a 'soul' so to speak; disliking to be hampered either by passion or convention and, therefore, always tying himself up into knots which he has to cut before he is free for another adventure.

When she met Charlotte, Beatrice (who disagreed with Ervine about the quality of Shaw's women) believed she had finally found the cure for Shaw's 'philandering follies' in a 'first-rate' lady who would make few emotional demands, and could satisfy his ego, secure his social standing, and provide stability, devotion and material comfort.

III

Charlotte, the daughter of an extremely rich Irish landowner and shareholder, was born in Derry in 1857, and spent her idle and pampered youth attending operas and balls, visiting country houses and travelling extensively on the Continent, in Egypt and in India. Despite all the advantages of wealth, leisure and society, her early life was unhappy. As she told her intimate friend and surrogate son, T. E. Lawrence, in a letter of 1927, her selfish, overbearing and demanding mother had dominated and destroyed her weak but gentle father, tormented the entire family – and inspired her own revulsion against marriage, sex and children:

> My mother was a terribly strong character – managing and domineering. She could not bear opposition: if it was offered she either became violent, or she cried. She felt (genuinely felt) she had sacrificed her life for us & my father . . . & she never ceased telling us so. She felt (quite genuinely) that we none of us loved her enough. . . . My father was gentle & affectionate, well-educated & well-read, very, *very* good, honourable & straight. He was a marvel of patience with my mother, which was terribly bad for her. I think, now, she ought to have been *beaten*: it would have been better for us all, especially for herself. As it was my father led a most unhappy life, & died comparatively young of sheer tiredness. It was a terrible home.

Though Charlotte, a classic Electra, hated her mother and loved her father, she shared her mother's 'managing and domineering' traits, her neurotic tendency toward self-pity and tears, and her feeling that she was insufficiently loved. Her father, who was too weak to deal with his aggressive wife, was defeated by his own pathetic and ineffectual goodness. And Charlotte, who could neither identify with women nor submit to men, developed a pathological fear of sex.

Charlotte's sexual fears were intensified in Rome in 1894 when, at the age of twenty-seven, she met and fell in love with the handsome and successful Swedish doctor, Axel Munthe (who later wrote *The Story of San Michele*). Charlotte's platonic relationship with Munthe (who specialised in the nervous diseases of women) lasted for more than a year before she realised that he could not accept her militant chastity and did not intend to propose marriage. Though Shaw rather frivolously discounted the significance of Charlotte's affair and believed she could be brought to her senses by a tonic rebuke, he recognised that he had won her on the rebound: 'Just before we married she had a serious love affair with Axel Munthe in Italy, and she told me her heart was broken. I answered, "Rubbish! your heart is certainly not broken." And from then on she seemed to attach herself to me.'

The Webbs met Charlotte at the end of 1895, immediately enlisted her in the Fabian cause, urged her to donate £1000 to the Library of the newly formed London School of Economics, and in January 1896 introduced her to Shaw. Charlotte described herself at that time as without family ties, financially independent, unconventional by nature and 'free from the ordinary individual hopes, fears and despairs which are so apt to become chains. Under these circumstances there is nothing to prevent my doing exactly as I choose.' Her great problem, however, was choosing exactly what she wanted to do, and putting herself in touch with ordinary human emotions.

In *Our Partnership* Beatrice Webb gives an insightful and thorough description of Charlotte's unimpressive appearance, romantic and rebellious temperament, ambivalent attitude toward marriage, and generous though tempestuous and unstable spirit:

A large graceful woman with masses of chocolate-brown hair, pleasant grey eyes, *matte* complexion which sometimes looks muddy, at other times forms a picturesquely pale background to her brilliant hair and bright eyes. . . . At moments she is plain. By temperament she is an anarchist. . . . She is romantic but thinks herself cynical. . . . She is by nature a rebel. She has no snobbishness and no convention. . . . She is fond of men and impatient of most women; bitterly resents her enforced celibacy but thinks she could not tolerate the matter-of-fact side of marriage. Sweet-tempered, sympathetic and genuinely anxious to increase the world's enjoyment and to decrease the world's pain. . . . An 'original', with considerable personal charm and certain volcanic tendencies.

Charlotte spent the spring of 1896 in Italy but was invited to join the Webbs and Shaw on their summer holiday in a Suffolk rectory. Charlotte had an infinite capacity for hero-worship and soon became Shaw's constant companion: they bicycled around the countryside in the afternoons and talked late into the night. By the end of the summer Beatrice Webb noted, 'To all seeming, she is in love with the brilliant Philanderer, and he is taken in his cold sort of way with her.'

She continued to see a great deal of Charlotte throughout the winter and the spring of 1897. Beatrice then felt Shaw was losing interest and echoed the doubts of Charlotte's cousin, the Irish novelist Edith Somerville, who thought Shaw 'is too clever to be really in love with Lottie, who is nearly clever, but not quite.' For Beatrice also believed that Charlotte's attachment was much stronger than Shaw's, that he was merely flattered and amused by her devotion, and that he might soon become bored with his study of her idle and rather meaningless existence:

It is obvious that she is deeply attached to him. But I see no sign on his side of the growth of any genuine and steadfast affection. He finds it pleasant to be with her in her luxurious surroundings, he has been studying her and all her little ways and amusing himself by dissecting the rich woman brought up without training and drifting about at the beck of any impulse. I think he has now exhausted the study – observed all that there is to observe. He has been flattered by her devotion and her absorption in him; he is kindly and has a cat-like preference for those persons to whom he is accustomed. But there are ominous signs that he is tired of watching the effect of little words of gallantry and personal interest with which he plied her in the first months of the friendship. And he is annoyed at her lack of purpose and utter incapacity for work.

While courting Charlotte, Shaw was also carrying on a playful but intimate correspondence with the actress Ellen Terry, which provides another picture of his relationship with his 'Irish lady with the light green eyes and the million of money.' Shaw told Ellen Terry that he raised the possibility of marriage only to dismiss it, warned Charlotte not to fall in love with him, and 'lacerated her conscience' at political lectures with denunciations of the parasitic rich while he pondered the solid benefits of '£4000 a year, independent and unencumbered.' In his most interesting letter, written in November 1896, Shaw shrewdly analyses Charlotte's emotional and physical repression, family background, desire for personal freedom, fear of spinsterhood, and conflict between her intellectual theories and her sentimental feelings about marriage in general and himself in particular:

> She doesn't really *love* me. The truth is, she is a clever woman, with plenty of romantic imagination. She knows that what she lacks is physical experience, and that without it she will be in ten years time an old maid. She knows the value of her unencumbered independence, having suffered a good deal from family bonds & conventionality before the death of her mother & the marriage of her sister left her free [in 1891]. The idea of tying herself up again by a marriage before she knows anything – before she has

exploited her freedom & money power to the utmost –
seems to her intellect to be unbearably foolish. Her theory
is that she won't do it. She picked up a broken heart somewhere a few years ago, and made the most of it (she is very
sentimental). . . . She got fond of me and did not coquet
or pretend that she wasn't. I got fond of her because she
was a comfort to me.

Charlotte's money and Shaw's cold intellectuality drew them
together but paradoxically prevented them from overcoming
their emotional disabilities. For Charlotte's great wealth
compensated for her sexual frigidity and allowed her to
marry Shaw on her own terms; and Shaw's facile wit created
the cynical and defensive rationalisation for his own eccentric submission to her wishes.

The turning point of their indecisive relationship (so
different from Tolstoy's impulsive marriage) came a year and
a half later in April 1898 when Charlotte left on a world tour
with the Webbs, but was recalled to London by a wire from
a friend stating Shaw was seriously ill. Shaw had hurt his foot
which developed necrosis of the bone, swelled to the size of
'a large cat,' required two operations and kept him on
crutches for eighteen months. Charlotte removed him from
his incredibly squalid room in Fitzroy Square, rented a house
in the country for his convalescence and began to nurse him
back to health. When they discussed the awkward question
of cohabitation, Shaw discovered that Charlotte's maternal
nursing was indispensable and finally proposed marriage. On
2 June 1898 Shaw placed a comical defence of his marriage
in a London newspaper and publicly denied he had been
prompted by passion: 'As a lady and gentleman were out
driving in Henrietta Street Covent Garden yesterday, a heavy
shower drove them to take shelter in the office of the Super-
intendent Registrar there, and in the confusion of the
moment he married them. The lady was an Irish lady named

Miss Payne-Townshend, and the gentleman was George Bernard Shaw.' After the marriage Charlotte gave Shaw's mother a life annuity, and merged her immense resources with the more modest earnings of her husband.

IV

Though Charlotte overcame most of her doubts about marriage, she could never suppress her horror of sexual relations, her abhorrence of motherhood and her fixed determination never to consummate her marriage. Charlotte failed to relate these unusual feelings to any abnormality in herself and blamed them on her unhappy childhood. Her attempt to explain her feelings to T. E. Lawrence in a letter of May 1927 was less an honest self-analysis than the rationalisation of a selfish, pampered and frightened neurotic who once exclaimed: 'Babies! Who could like them? Disgusting little things.'

> I don't believe, as far as I can remember, that I was born with a dislike of children . . . but, anyway, my own home life made me firmly resolve never to be the mother of a child who might suffer as I have suffered. . . . As I grew older I saw many, & better, reasons for sticking to my resolution. . . . The idea was physically repulsive to me in the highest degree, and my reason did not consent to any of the arguments brought to bear upon me.

Some of these 'arguments' affirming sex and motherhood were expressed by Shaw in his plays. In the Preface to *Getting Married* he condemns the Christian revulsion against sex and states, 'By far the most dangerous of these [doctrinal excesses and extravagances], because it is a blasphemy against life . . . is the notion that sex, with all its operations, is in itself absolutely an obscene thing.' And in his anti-romantic last play, *Buoyant Billions* (1948), about the marriage of an artist and an heiress, the Solicitor (speaking for Shaw) stresses the 'life force,' alludes to Dante and tells Miss Buoyant: 'Celibacy for a woman is *il gran rifiuto*, the great refusal of her destiny, of the purpose in her life which comes before all personal considerations: the replacing of the dead by the living.' But the force of these arguments is undermined by the mechanical connotation of 'operation' and the emphasis on social duty rather than on personal feelings.

Charlotte's managerial capacity and militant chastity also influenced Shaw's portrayal of Saint Joan (1923) – a subject suggested and researched by his wife. 'The evident truth is,' Shaw says of Joan in the Preface to the play, 'that like most women of her hardy managing type she seemed neutral in the conflict of sex because men were too afraid of her to fall in love with her. She herself was not sexless: in spite of the virginity she had vowed.' Unlike many other men, Shaw was not repelled by Charlotte's chastity, and recognised that her residual, matronly sex could inspire affection if not passion.

Shaw agreed to Charlotte's chaste conditions for a number of complicated reasons. Since he found her thoroughly unexciting and unattractive, it was not too difficult for him to renounce his conjugal rights. He unenthusiastically described Charlotte to the beautiful Ellen Terry as 'a ladylike person at whom nobody would ever look twice. . . . Age certainly not less than 37, & looks 40. Perfectly placid and proper and pleasant.' Shaw once recalled that when he was married 'a friend said that my wife had a face like a muffin, and you know that is really what she was like' – both physically and emotionally.

A second reason was that Shaw, as Bertha Newcombe told Beatrice Webb, was a cold, 'passionless' person who *disliked* sexual relations and preferred to 'create an atmosphere of love-making without any need for caresses.' Shaw used sex to capture the affections of women, and it was more a means to power than to pleasure. Finally, Shaw was, at the age of forty-two, weary of the complicated and fundamentally boring emotional entanglements that gave him more irritation than satisfaction once the initial excitement subsided, drained his creative energy and distracted him from his work. As he wrote in *Sixteen Self-Sketches* (1949): 'During the 14 years before my marriage there was always some lady in the case; and I tried all the experiments and learned what there was to be learnt from them. . . . I was never *duped* by sex as a basis for permanent relations nor dreamt of marriage in connection with it.' Sex was an experiment which provided a lesson that could be learned in a brief period of time, without the tedious necessity of marriage. It was far more rational to renounce sex, abandon his bohemian life, solidify his social position and marry a well-born heiress with £4000 a year.

Though Shaw admitted that wealthy, childless people who marry at forty know nothing about marriage 'except as lookers-on,' he also justified his own marriage by affirming in 1949, 'As man and wife we found a new relation in which sex had no part. It ended the old gallantries, flirtations and philanderings for both of us. Even of these it was the ones that were *never consummated* that left the longest and kindliest memories.' Though this statement explains Shaw's preference for sexless flirtations, it erroneously suggests that Charlotte had sexual relations *before* marriage and that he remained entirely faithful to her *after* marriage. In old age Shaw regretted he did not have children and felt he should have insisted on 'physical experience' with Charlotte; but he also admitted there would have been serious problems: 'If we had had children, Charlotte would certainly have quarrelled with me over them, and would have been jealous. Besides, she would never allow anything like that.'

V

Though Shaw realised that Charlotte had rescued him from 'those philandering follies which make me so ridiculous, so troublesome, so vulgar with women,' he too had ambivalent feelings (suggested by the wedding notice), and after Charlotte's death rather regretfully stated: 'I don't think I ought ever to have been married: I am not the marrying kind.' Though he enjoyed the domestic convenience, he resented the emotional limitations of monogamy. He also discussed the marriage question in two plays written in the decade after his union with Charlotte: *Man and Superman* (1903) and *Getting Married* (1908). Shaw stated in *Sixteen Self-Sketches* that John Tanner's hopeless struggle against marriage to Ann Whitehead in the last act of the first play 'is a poignantly sincere utterance which must have come from personal experience.' In his rhetorical peroration Tanner echoes the condemnation of matrimonial bondage expressed by Prince Andrey in *War and Peace* and hyperbolically repeats the conventional cliché that marriage means defeat and decay, the end of freedom and romance, and the extinction of all possibility of achievement:

Marriage is to me apostasy, profanation of the sanctuary of my soul, violation of my manhood, sale of my birthright, shameful surrender, ignominious capitulation, acceptance of defeat. I shall decay like a thing that has served its purpose and is done with; I shall change from a man with a future to a man with a past; I shall see in the greasy eyes of all the husbands their relief at the arrival of a new prisoner to share their ignominy. The young men will scorn me as one who has sold out: to the women I, who have always been an enigma and a possibility, shall be merely somebody else's property – and damaged goods at that: a secondhand man at best.

In both the Preface to *Getting Married* and the play itself, which clearly reflect Shaw's relationship with Charlotte, he criticises the institution of marriage and justifies his own sexual and psychological attitudes. In his prefatory discussion of 'The Impersonality of Sex,' Shaw argues that the choice of a marriage partner should be based on calm, rational judgment and not, as is commonly the case, on insane, delusive and transient passions: 'the wildly extravagant illusions of inexperienced people.' The most disastrous marriages, Shaw believes, are founded almost exclusively on the ephemeral 'appetite' of love, while the most successful unions (like his own) are those 'in which the decisive considerations have had nothing to do with sex, such as liking, money, congeniality of tastes, similarity of habits and suitability of class.'

Shaw's Preface also states the dominant theme of the rather verbose and oratorical play, which is more a disquisition than a drama. *Getting Married* shows that 'men who are bolder freethinkers than Shelley himself can no more bring themselves to commit adultery than to commit any common theft, whilst women who loathe sex slavery more fiercely than Mary Wollstonecraft are unable to face the insecurity and discredit of the vagabondage which is the masterless woman's only alternative to celibacy.' Shaw paradoxically suggests that sceptical and highly individualistic people are more closely bound by marriage than the ordinary folk who claim to believe in it.

The play contains several characters who ridicule and dismiss conventional marriage, and enjoy using a third person to stimulate and review their relationship. Shaw expresses his ideas through the Bishop, a figure of kindly authority who is writing a history of marriage, favours reform of the marriage and divorce laws, and expresses cynical ideas about love, sex and family life. And Sinjon Hotchkiss plays the familiar role of third participant: first as co-respondent in the divorce of Reginald and Leo (when they finally become reconciled he promises to come round and amuse them), and then as a kind of vicarious *cavaliere servente* to the Mayoress, Mrs George, who has lovers to interest her husband as well as herself.

Charlotte (who was fifty-one in 1908) is portrayed in two characters. The Bishop's wife, who is described as 'a quiet happy-looking woman of fifty or thereabouts, *placid*, gentle and humorous, with delicate features and fine grey hair,' entertains her husband by reading aloud the intensely passionate love letters which he receives. And the ironically named Lesbia expresses – in a boastful, smug, selfish and materialistic fashion – Charlotte's defensive justification of maidenhood, preference for dignity and perverse feeling that happiness is vulgar: 'I'm a regular old maid. I'm very particular about my belongings. I like to have my own house, and to have it to myself. I have a very keen sense of beauty and fitness and cleanliness and order. I am proud of my independence and jealous for it.' The pompous, stereotyped General, who unsuccessfully pursues Lesbia, expresses Shaw's complaint: 'You all want geniuses to marry. This demand for clever men is ridiculous.' And the commonsensical grocer Collins suggests some cynical reasons why people like Charlotte and Shaw want to marry though they do not intend to have children and are not fit to have them: there are people (like Charlotte) who want to try a new experience, and people (like Shaw) who want to have done with experiences. Though marriage – in Shaw's play, as in his life – presents great problems, there seems to be no more satisfactory alternative.

Once the sexual question was decided – that is, treated as if it did not exist – the middle-aged Shaws became a most devoted married couple. Charlotte publicly assumed the role of the woman who had domesticated the philandering genius and Shaw meekly submitted to her domination.

Charlotte was a possessive but loyal wife who worshipped Shaw's genius, tolerated his personal eccentricities and satisfied his material needs with lavish generosity. Though unable to create anything herself, she was interested in intellectual things and liked to help Shaw with his work. She learned typewriting, acted as Shaw's secretary in the early years, did research for all his historical plays, protected his privacy, and mediated between her husband and the outside world.

Charlotte urged Shaw to withdraw from the Fabians in 1911 so that he would not waste his intellectual energy in speeches and debates; and involved him in the defence of the Irish patriot, Roger Casement, who was convicted of treason in 1916. Shaw's brilliant *Discarded Defence of Roger Casement*, which was not used in the trial but published as a pamphlet in 1922, convincingly argued that Casement be held as a prisoner of war and not be tried as a traitor. Charlotte also interested Shaw in the revision and publication of *Seven Pillars of Wisdom* and established a surprising intimacy with T. E. Lawrence, who shared her ideas of sexlessness and inviolate virginity, adopted her name in 1925, and made some extraordinary revelations about his family and personal life in his letters to her. The Shaws always regretted that they had given Lawrence the motorcycle on which he had his fatal accident.

Though their sexual problem was repressed it could not be ignored, for it manifested itself in Charlotte's gross eating habits, her obsessive desire to travel and her violent jealousy. Shaw, an abstemious vegetarian, was extremely fastidious about food, liked silence at mealtimes and never spoke to his wife when they were dining alone. Charlotte, by contrast, consumed an astonishing quantity of food at each meal. As Sean O'Casey observed, she 'ate heavily, a great pile on her plate, thickly covered with whatever sauce went with the main dish; she leaned forward determinedly to swallow whenever she filled a forkful, using a sluggish energy to bring it to her mouth and get it down quickly.' Like O'Casey, Shaw must have been silently disgusted by Charlotte's Johnsonian appetite and her compensatory attempt to substitute food for sex.

Charlotte's insatiable urge to travel was also an expression of her inner discontent, her uneasy rootlessness and her lack of serious responsibility for children, family, home or work. In 1908 the exasperated Shaw wrote: 'Every year, the same struggle arises two or three times – the eternal "You must come away" and "Oh, leave me alone: I haven't time: you know I loathe travelling."' Though Shaw was always busy, hated to leave his desk and had a 'cat-like preference' for familiar people and places, Charlotte always had unanswerable reasons why he should take a holiday and absolutely insisted that he accompany her. In 1910, when Shaw tried to persuade Charlotte and her sister to take the car and chauffeur and travel without him, she overruled his objections and forced him to come, and he remained furious and sulky for most of the journey.

Charlotte became very angry when she finally realised that Shaw could not bear her constant company and wanted to get rid of her – at least for a while. For Shaw expressed his irritation about Charlotte's cloying dependence and told Beatrice Webb in 1912: 'I had to force Charlotte to take a holiday *from me*. Being very much in need of me, she quarrelled furiously with me the moment she suspected what I was at, until I wished her at the South Pole; and then she took leave of me (for a month after 14 years continuous adhesion).' Shaw manifested his aggression and took unconscious revenge on Charlotte, while driving in South Africa in 1932, when he lost control of the car, went full throttle over a ditch and barbed wire fence, and crashed through a three-foot bunker. Charlotte, thrown about with the luggage in the back seat, was seriously injured, had a fever of 108° and was forced to spend a month in the hospital 'for repairs.' Shaw,

who escaped unhurt, dwelled on the gory details of the accident and wrote to Lady Astor: 'Her head was broken, her
spectacle rims were driven into her blackened eyes, her left
wrist was agonisingly sprained; her back was fearfully
bruised; and she had a hole in her right shin which something had pierced to the bone!' Neither Shaw nor Charlotte
learned much from this disaster, for the seventy-five-year-old
couple embarked on a round-the-world tour at the end of
the year.

Their most serious problem – Charlotte's intense jealousy
– was constantly provoked by Shaw's frivolous flirtations,
which seemed both natural and inevitable given his extreme
vanity, volatile temperament, enforced celibacy and professional involvement with beautiful actresses. Shaw understood
that Charlotte was jealous of his past and present as well as of
her exclusion from his theatrical life. As he explained in 1903
to the married actress, Janet Achurch, who had inspired
Charlotte's distrust and jealousy:

> She has exactly the same objection to my mother, my sister
> and everybody who forms a part of the past in which she
> has no part. The moment you walk into the room where
> I am you create a world in which you and I are at home
> and she is a stranger. That is the real difficulty of marrying
> at forty; and it must be faced until in the lapse of time the
> new world so grows up and supersedes the old that it need
> no longer be jealous of it.

But the new world could never entirely supersede the old,
and a second major eruption of jealousy occurred in 1910
when Erica Cotterill, a young woman who had conducted
an intimate correspondence with Shaw, became so attached
to him that she took a cottage in his village, Ayot St
Lawrence. In October of that year, when both Charlotte and
Shaw (who had originally encouraged the girl) were weary

of and disgusted with Erica's cloying adoration, Shaw dictated and Charlotte sent an icily dignified letter. They summed up the intolerable situation, chastised Erica's behaviour and banished her from their lives:

> You have made a declaration of your feelings to my husband; and you have followed that up by coming to live near us with the avowed object of gratifying those feelings by seeing as much as possible of him. If you were an older and more experienced woman I should characterise that in terms which would make any further acquaintance between us impossible. As you are young and entirely taken up with your own feelings, I can only tell you that when a woman makes such a declaration to a married man, or a man to a married woman, there is an end of all honourable question of their meeting one another again.

Though the Shaws did not condemn Erica as they would an older woman and attributed her emotions to her youth, there was very little practical difference between making 'any further acquaintance impossible' and putting an end to 'their meeting one another again.'

The gravest threat to Shaw's marriage took place in 1912 when, at the age of fifty-six, he became sexually infatuated with the famous actress, Mrs Patrick Campbell, and Charlotte was again forced to play the agonising role of vicarious participant. Shaw wrote *Pygmalion* for Mrs Pat and then attempted to arouse her interest in the play by writing extravagantly passionate letters. Though Mrs Pat, like Shaw, had a ruthless and calculating side to her character, which had been exaggerated by an unhappy marriage to a man who had left her with two small children, one of her friends felt obliged to warn her that Shaw's 'love is epistolary. He has no respect for the feelings of those who love him. Don't give him affection: he will surely hurt you.'

Though Shaw told Ellen Terry (another vicarious participant) that he had fallen 'head over ears in love with [Mrs Pat]
in thirty seconds,' had a moment's happiness, courted the
oldest illusions, almost condescended to romance and risked
breaking the deepest roots, it seems clear that there was never
any real love on either side. For she merely tried to exert her
power and temporarily triumph over Shaw, while he calculated her utility and pretended to be in love. When Mrs Pat
realised that she had enchanted Shaw but could never hope
to keep him (in this, as in other respects, she was exactly the
opposite of Charlotte), she rejected his half-hearted attempt
to seduce her and sent him back to his wife.

Shaw implicated Charlotte in his love affairs partly for
egoistic and narcissistic reasons and partly to inspire the
jealousy which proved her love and perversely renewed his
affection for *her*. 'I must now go and read this [letter] to
Charlotte,' he told Mrs Pat. 'My love affairs are her unfailing
amusement: all their tenderness recoils finally on herself.
Besides, I love an audience.' Though this remark showed
considerable insight about his own motives, it ignored the
feelings of Charlotte, whose virginity intensified her jealousy. When Charlotte overheard a telephone conversation
between Shaw and the 'middle-aged minx,' Shaw coldly
related that 'she wept and poured out her soul to one or
two young men' – for she also needed an audience. Charlotte's suffering eventually forced Shaw to recognise that his
affair with Mrs Pat was merely an ugly way to torment his
wife and to express his extreme resentment of her denial of
sex and love: 'I must, it seems, murder myself or else murder
her.'

VI

Both Shaw and Charlotte lived to a great age. Though he
remained in good health until he fractured his leg while

pruning a tree in 1950, Charlotte had a nervous breakdown in 1939 and was hopelessly crippled by a painful bone disease, *osteitis deformans*, during the last years of her life. Though Charlotte's suffering made her a difficult invalid until her death in 1943, Shaw always gave her loyal and tender care. But when she died he privately admitted, 'Everybody tells me that I am looking well, and I can't very well say it's relief at my wife's death, but it is you know.'

After Charlotte's death Shaw also expressed his long-standing hostility of her overbearing solicitude, her domineering management of his habits and affairs, her restless urge to travel, and her emotional and sexual frustrations that were expressed in tears and had turned him into a portable wailing wall:

> Even if I cannot enjoy solitude, since the death of my wife I have been my own master, which I find very restful. She was so careful of my privacy that I hardly had a moment to myself. . . . In the last few years of her life she made me sing to her every night, and I had to be in bed by eleven. Since her death I haven't touched the piano and am never in bed before twelve. She made me drive all over Great Britain and the Continent, and travel all over the world. But my real nature is to remain rooted to one spot, like a tree, and since her death my longest journeys have been from Ayot to London and back. . . . She was rather given to tears and would cry all over me, but I got used to it and realised that one of my marital duties was to represent a sort of wailing-body.

And when Shaw read Charlotte's correspondence with T. E. Lawrence after her death, he was extremely surprised by her intimate revelations and confessed: 'I lived with Charlotte for forty years, and I see now that there was a great deal about her that I didn't know. It has been a shock.'

Shaw, who was deprived of maternal love as a child and was terrified of his own emotions, tried to dismiss them in a defensively cynical manner. In his relations with women he affected a theatrical role that demanded a vicarious audience and precluded serious love. Charlotte disguised and justified her pathological fear of sex by attributing it to her unhappy childhood; and unsuccessfully tried to repress her desires, which manifested themselves in her gross appetite, inner discontent and intense jealousy. She was indulged and spoiled in youth, never reached emotional maturity, refused to accept adult responsibility, and denied Shaw the possibility of sex and love – with herself or with other women.

Both Shaw and Charlotte were extremely egoistic people who in middle age repressed their feelings and agreed for selfish reasons to a muffin-like marriage of convenience. Charlotte, for all her wealth, luxuries, travels and reflected glory as wife to a great man, led an unhappy and discontented life. And Shaw, for all his genius, creativity, success and fame, was a superficial thinker with an essentially vicarious view of human relationships.

Joseph and Jessie Conrad
THE CREATOR AS CHILD

'I remember him telling me, in that final way of his,
how much safer it was for a woman to be married to a
roué than to an idealist.'

RICHARD CURLE on Conrad

I

Conrad's biographer, Jocelyn Baines, seems puzzled about his
marriage in March 1896 and writes, 'there is nothing to
show what prompted his desire to marry at this moment nor
why his choice fell on Jessie George.' Baines' reverence for
his subject perhaps obscures the social and practical realities
behind the extraordinary marriage of the Polish sailor and
the suburban typist, who satisfied each other's needs in a

peculiar sort of way. All their friends agreed that Jessie was an admirable wife, and she confirmed this judgment in her lively and anecdotal reminiscences of life with Conrad, published in 1926 and 1935 after his death. Her class and up-bringing were appropriate to Conrad's meagre income and the style of life he could then afford. She was skilled in precisely the domestic arts he needed, and could give him the maternal care and the secure middle-class home he had always lacked. Conrad, who had led a wandering, inde-pendent, solitary and introspective life at sea for twenty years before his marriage, chose Jessie, the opposite of his previous loves, because he needed a safe port in which to create his novels.

But Conrad preserved, within marriage, his solitary inner life. His thought, imagination and resolution of psychological conflicts went into his books. Jessie lived beside him, loved Conrad and was loved by him, but remained essentially unaware of his passionate intellectual and creative existence. She was not equipped to understand it, nor did Conrad want her to share the kind of intense concentration that he devoted to his work. Conrad's major themes – the essential isolation of men (like Kurtz, Decoud and Heyst) and the temptations that threaten the isolated ego – are related to his marriage. Though Jessie relieved Conrad's melancholy concern about his own solitude, she also became a source of anxiety which he treated in his fiction.

Conrad's father, the Polish patriot Apollo Korzeniowski, was arrested for agitating against Russian rule and sent into exile with his family in 1862, when Conrad was four years old. The frozen wastes of Vologda, between Moscow and Archangel, had a disastrous effect on Conrad's delicate mother, Evelina, who became an invalid for several years before she died in 1865, at the age of thirty-two. Exile, illness and the failure of the Polish insurrection of 1863 led Apollo, in his final years, to a despairing mysticism and a morbid cult of his dead wife, which made life unbearably oppressive for the young Conrad. After five and a half years of lonely and bitter exile, the father and son returned to Poland in 1868. Apollo died the following year, and the eleven-year-old orphan was placed in the care of his maternal uncle, Thaddeus.

Conrad spent the twenty years between 1874 and 1894 at sea, mostly in Eastern waters, and became accustomed to a lonely bachelor's life. He attempted suicide in Marseilles in 1878; suffered severe depressions and occasional nervous breakdowns for the rest of his life; and was physically indolent, impractical, absent-minded, moody, nervous and sickly. Jessie softened the truth and compassionately wrote that 'Few people could hope to understand him sufficiently to be happy in constant contact with a nature so charming, yet often hyper-sensitive and broodingly reserved.' But Conrad confessed the truth about himself to Edward Garnett, two months after his marriage: 'I have long fits of depression, that in a lunatic asylum would be called madness. I do not know what it is. It springs from nothing. It is ghastly. It lasts an hour or a day; and when it departs it leaves a fear.' Thus in 1896, when Conrad was thirty-eight, with no money and uncertain prospects as an author (his first novel, *Almayer's Folly*, was published in 1894), he seriously considered returning to sea. He had no relatives or close friends in England; and was foreign, sickly and strange. Who else but Jessie George would have married so unpromising a suitor?

Conrad had had several romantic liaisons in his youth. His suicide attempt in Marseilles was the climax of an unhappy love affair with the beautiful Dona 'Rita de Lastaola,' the head of a Carlist smuggling syndicate, whom he later idealised in *Arrow of Gold*. In Mauritius in 1888, while commanding the *Otago*, Conrad fell in love with and proposed to the charming twenty-six-year-old Eugénie Renouf, and was crushed when he discovered she was engaged to a prosaic pharmacist. He stayed aboard ship for

three days before sailing and swore to Eugénie's brother that
he could never return to the island.

Conrad's third unsuccessful romance concerned
Marguerite Poradowska, the widow of his distant cousin,
whom he met in Brussels in 1890. She was then a famous
beauty in her early forties, and when Jessie met her ten years
later, she called Marguerite 'the most beautiful woman I had
ever seen.' Baines speculates that Conrad may have proposed
to and been rejected by Marguerite, and then married Jessie
on the rebound. But Bernard Meyer, Conrad's psychoanalyt-
ical biographer, believes that though Conrad expressed
passionate feelings for Marguerite in his letters, he maintained a safe distance from his 'Aunt' and never actually
proposed marriage. Eugénie and 'Rita,' who drove him to
despair and self-destruction, were Latin beauties from exotic
locales, while the older Marguerite was a cultivated intellectual and established novelist who shared Conrad's background and interests. Though all of Conrad's early loves were
the exact antitheses of his wife, his relationship with Jessie,
who *wanted* to marry him, was based on reality, not fantasy.
The passionate 'Rita' and pampered Eugénie would never
have been able to cope with Conrad's emotional crises.

Jessie George, the dowerless daughter of a deceased ware-
houseman and bookseller, and the second of nine children,
had been leading a quiet and circumscribed life when she
first met Conrad in November 1894 at the house of a mutual
friend. Jessie, who was sixteen years younger than Conrad,
recalls that 'ours was certainly a strange friendship. Not only
because Conrad was the first foreigner I had ever known
intimately, but he was also the first grown man who appeared
to take a particular interest in me.' She was startled by the
noticeable strangeness, heavy accent and extravagant gestures
of the fastidious aristocrat; and was astounded by his attraction to her. She never understood Conrad until their disastrous trip to Poland in 1914, when they were isolated in the

countryside after the war broke out in August, and had a
dangerous journey through Vienna and Milan before they
reached home in October. In Conrad's homeland 'so many
characteristics that had been strange and unfathomable
before, took, as it were, their right proportions' when Jessie
saw that his temperament was like that of his fellow Poles.

After a year of correspondence and courtship with the girl
of humble birth and little education, Conrad produced his
peculiar proposal of marriage in January 1896. He began,
Jessie writes, 'by announcing that he had not very long to live
and no intention of having children; but such as his life was
(his shrug was very characteristic) he thought we might
spend a few happy years together.' The terrified Conrad
disappeared right after their engagement, causing Jessie
intense humiliation; and when he resurfaced three days later,
he insisted that they marry in six weeks and then go abroad.
Though Mrs George (who had eight other children to
worry about) gave her parental blessing, she could not help
remarking that 'she didn't quite see why he wished to get
married.'

Just before the wedding in March, Conrad wrote an ironic
and defensive letter to his Polish cousin (his Uncle Thaddeus,
the last close link with his family, had died a few months
before Conrad met Jessie), and revealed his profound doubts
and fears. 'I am not frightened at all,' Conrad boasted, 'for as
you know, I am accustomed to an adventurous life and to
facing terrible dangers. . . . [Jessie] is a small, not at all
striking-looking person (to tell the truth, alas – rather plain!)
who nevertheless is very dear to me. . . . The wedding will
take place on the 24th of this month and we shall leave
London immediately so as to conceal from people's eyes our
happiness (or our stupidity).' Conrad's admission of Jessie's
plainness and his own stupidity seemed to prove that he, at
least, had not been duped by love. His morbid proposal, his
need to apologise for normal feelings, and his self-

consciously ironic attitude to Jessie and to marriage, suggest grave misgivings about his transformation from an 'adventurous' to a domestic life.

Conrad nearly accepted the command of a ship two weeks before the wedding – Jessie liked the idea and planned to accompany him but he refused in the end and took her to Brittany instead. She was understandably nervous about leaving her family and country, and adapting herself to the strange moods of her husband. Conrad was intensely irritated when Jessie was mistaken for his daughter on their honeymoon, which was characterised by nervousness, sickness and discomfort.

Jessie appears to have been reasonably attractive in her early photographs; foreign and even Slavic-looking in her middle years; and grotesquely obese, like a dubious medium or a bulging matron in a Chaplin film, in her late pictures. In 1904, when Jessie accidentally fell and seriously damaged her knees, she became a cripple and invalid, and needed a dozen expensive but unsuccessful operations on her legs. After surgery in 1905 Conrad took her to Capri to recuperate in a warm climate. This journey, like all their other trips, was a disaster, for Conrad became helpless when Jessie was incapacitated. The overweight Jessie recalls 'There was great difficulty in getting me on board at Dover. The bearers nearly deposited me in the water between the vessel and the quay. A horrified howl of dismay went up from the passengers when they saw my perilous position.' Conrad always took the darkest view of his wife's condition, and in 1908 sought sympathy for himself and wrote to La Poradowska: 'Poor Jessie can hardly drag herself about. That knee is very bad. I am afraid it will end with amputation one of these days.'

As Jessie's love of food and immobility made her fatter and fatter, Conrad gallantly told a friend, 'it is still impossible for her to claim to be slim'; Jessie confessed, 'I am not and never was a fairy'; and the svelte Virginia Woolf referred to her as

Conrad's 'lump of a wife.' Yet Richard Curle, Conrad's close friend and substitute son during the last twelve years of his life, writes that:

> Conrad's devotion to his wife was obvious to all who stayed with him, and was touching in its completeness. His house was run much more for her comfort and conven- ience, crippled as she was, than for his, and no trouble was beyond his taking where she was concerned. . . . His protective solicitude for her was unceasing, and her perpetual suffering and ill-health caused him infinite distress. He was always thinking about her, from the choosing of a present to the planning of a holiday, and his fondness for her society was touching to witness.

Though it is doubtful that Conrad's house was run more for her comfort than for his (if this were true it would have been difficult for him to do any writing), Curle's eulogy of Conrad's devotion and solicitude is certainly accurate.

While Jessie suffered from physical disability, Conrad was the victim of severe nervous disorders, the result of his painful struggles to create. Just before completing his first great work, *The Nigger of the 'Narcissus'*, in 1897, he lamented: 'I can't eat – I dream – nightmares – and scare my wife. I wish it was over!' Only a self-absorbed engagement of his mind, will and conscience, and a creative effort that obliter- ated the external world and excluded 'all that makes life really lovable and gentle', enabled him to complete *Nostromo*, his finest novel, in 1905. He then wrote with Swiftian irony: 'my sojourn on the continent of Latin America, famed for its hospitality, lasted for about two years. On my return I found (speaking somewhat in the style of Captain Gulliver) my family all well, my wife heartily glad to learn that the fuss was all over, and our small boy considerably grown during my absence.' But the creative agony of *Under Western Eyes* was even more intense and self-destructive, and led to a complete nervous breakdown in 1910. As Jessie wrote to his editor: 'Poor Conrad is very ill and Dr. Hackney says it will be a long time before he is fit for anything requiring mental exertion. . . . There is the M. S. complete but uncorrected and his fierce refusal to let even I touch it. It lays on a table at the foot of his bed and he lives mixed up in the scenes and holds converse with his characters.' Though his creative energy lasted until he had finished the novel, he could neither revise it nor free himself from its imaginative force.

Jessie balanced Conrad's mercurial and meteoric personality with a placid and tolerant temperament that was never shaken by his childish tantrums and frightening breakdowns. Jessie admitted that though she sometimes 'boiled inwardly and my sense of justice was outraged, still I prided myself on my complete self-control, and did not lose my temper.' When her son was gravely ill in Montpellier in 1907 Jessie remained heroic and self-possessed; and as Conrad wrote, was 'always calm, serene, equable, going from one [son] to the other and apparently never tired though cruelly crippled by her leg.'

Jessie, who was an excellent cook, cared for Conrad's home and children, served as his secretary (she became 'quite physically sick' when typing the cannibalistic story, 'Falk'), protected his privacy, and provided a stable and commonsensical foundation for their often impoverished and unsettled existence. Conrad's friends recognised this and praised Jessie's selfless qualities. In his Introduction to Jessie's first book on Conrad, the faithful Richard Curle writes that 'All who knew Joseph Conrad in his home knew how much he relied upon his wife's care and counsel, and how constantly his thoughts centred upon her. Her calm vigilance was ever on the alert to make the material things of existence as easy for him as possible, and to soothe the nervous reactions of his high-strung nature.' Joseph Retinger agrees that 'Jessie was without exception the best and most perfect woman I have ever had the good fortune to know. . . . Her manner was controlled and restful, her good mood never deserted her, and her advice was always of the best.' And David Garnett relates that his mother, Constance, 'often said that Jessie was a woman of amazing physical courage and devotion and, in spite of what one might think, just the wife for Conrad,' who wanted and needed a deeply devoted wife and sacrificial surrogate mother.

Conrad remembered his own mother as a 'loving, wide-browed, silent, protecting presence, whose eyes had a sort of commanding sweetness,' and this nostalgic description applies equally as well to Jessie. Although she was consider-ably younger than Conrad, Jessie relates that from the first days of their engagement she felt a strong maternal feeling for the lonely man who had lost his mother in childhood and never really had a home life: 'In a very short time all my maternal instincts were centred upon the man I was to marry, and he became to me as much a son as a husband.' According to their oldest child, Borys, Jessie called her son by name but always used the word 'Boy' when addressing his father, who rather possessively called Jessie 'Mrs C.'

Conrad's childlike dependence on his protective wife and mother is epitomised by an incident that occurred during their holiday on Capri. Conrad, who was having trouble with his teeth, kept his mouth full of water to relieve the pain:

One night he lay with his poor head on my shoulder and his mouth full of water (I keeping awake and holding the glass ready to pass to him as he wanted it). He would fill his mouth, hand me the glass, and fall asleep, and the water would run all over me. I was soaked before the morning. When he finally roused himself sufficiently to be aware that he was uncomfortable, he declared we had been sleeping in a damp bed.

In this story, like most others told by Jessie, she appears superior to Conrad not only in her altruism but also in her
mature forbearance of his foibles. Despite her reverence for
Conrad, Jessie portrays him as a child-like husband who was
totally dependent on her motherly care and protection.

We have seen that Conrad's bizarre proposal to Jessie
included the warning that he did not intend to have children; he was jealous of her maternal love and wanted to keep
it all to himself. When Jessie first became pregnant in 1897
Conrad, who told Edward Garnett, 'I hate babies,' took no
responsibility for her condition and made it clear that he was
not exactly pleased. He was fearful of losing part of her love
and much of her attention, and felt he had been betrayed: 'It
seemed to him that I had played him false as it were.' When
he announced her first pregnancy to one of his friends, he
tried to conceal his profound feelings under a cavalier indifference, and gloomily suggested that the baby might take
Jessie from him forever: 'There is no other news – unless the
information that there is a prospect of some kind of descen-
dant may be looked upon in the light of something new. I
am not unduly elated. Johnson [the doctor] says it may mend
Jess' health permanently – if it does not end her.'

Conrad was surprised to find that the birth of what he
archly called 'an infant of the male persuasion,' who incon-
veniently made him miss the morning post and caused one
of the frequent attacks of gout that was meant to draw
sympathetic attention to himself, looked 'just like a human
being.' When Borys was two weeks old Conrad once again
felt the call of the sea and imagined he could take Jessie and
the baby with him. But the following month they took a
hilarious train journey instead. According to Jessie, who liked
to portray Conrad as a kind of superior fool:

> He had taken our tickets, first class, and intended travelling
> in the same carriage, but – here he became most emphatic

– on no account were we to give any indication that he belonged to our little party. . . . [He] seated himself in a far corner, ostentatiously concealing himself behind his newspaper and completely ignoring his family. . . . All my efforts to soothe the infant proved unavailing, and the whole carriage re-echoed with his lusty howls. The paper was flung aside and from all sides came murmurs of consternation and sympathy for him – the only man; the stranger in the carriage. . . . Then the whole carriage was convulsed with suppressed merriment when my young sister turned to Joseph Conrad and, forgetting his injunction, demanded that he should reach down the case that contained the baby's bottle.

The brooding genius was thus reduced to the humiliating role of helpful father. It is not surprising that Conrad found his family both irritating and oppressive.

The principal deficiency of Jessie (who humbly served as a representative of the 'average reader'), was her undeveloped mind; and though she understood Conrad's feelings, she could never share his intellectual life. In order to compensate for his inner loneliness and sense of isolation within his own family, Conrad adopted several substitute sons, including Ford Madox Ford and Richard Curle. Ford, the son of *The Times*' music critic and the grandson of a Pre-Raphaelite painter, was closely connected to the artistic and literary establishment of Victorian England. Though Ford frequently shared domestic life with the Conrads, and considered their house his own, he had little in common with Jessie and treated her with a supercilious disdain. This must have caused considerable resentment and intensified her feelings of social and intellectual inferiority. By contrast, Ford's wife Elsie, the daughter of an eminent chemist, was an impressive and well-educated woman.

Jessie relates a number of characteristic and amusing incidents that reveal the kind of burlesque combats that took place between the conventional, house-proud wife and the slovenly bohemian guest. One day Ford washed his Panama hat and put it in Jessie's oven to dry. When the grease from the hatband nearly basted her Sunday roast, she became quite uncommonly enraged. Ford once decided to sleep at the Conrads' house. When he found that the thin curtains let in too much light he took the blanket off his bed to cover the window. He then became cold, searched for another blanket, discovered Conrad's frock-coat and striped trousers, which Jessie had neatly pressed and left in the drawer, and used them to cover himself. The next morning the outraged Jessie found the garments 'crumpled out of all recognition,' and bitterly complained to Conrad about Ford's 'wanton treatment.'

Ford, on his part, mischievously relates how a publisher's harsh rejection of Jessie's cookbook, which refused to buy 'a collection of papers only fit for – I forget what they were fit for,' was sent by mistake to the furious Conrad instead of to Ford. Ford also attacks Jessie on her own territory and brags about his *own* cooking. When Ford secretly replaced the German cook and made dinner, Conrad became ecstatic and said: 'My dear faller. . . . The admirable Johanna has of course surpassed herself. . . . *Une telle succulence, mon cher.*'

These irritating incidents provoked Jessie's jealous attacks on Ford, who had captured the intellectual side of her husband; and she got her revenge in a letter to the editor of *The Times Literary Supplement* which was published in December 1924. This influential letter corrects 'a few of the most fantastic statements' about Conrad in the book that Ford rushed into print just after his friend's death. Jessie emphatically denies that the men were intimate after 1909 and indignantly concludes: 'The author of *A Personal Remembrance* claims to have been Joseph Conrad's literary adviser, also his literary godfather! That claim is, like nearly everything else in that detestable book, quite untrue.' Jessie's version of their relationship has prevailed over Ford's, and her letter hurt his somewhat dubious literary reputation by suggesting that he exaggerated his influence and cashed in on Conrad's prestige. Jessie never forgave Ford for his snubs and boasts, and continued to snipe at him in her books.

Jessie took great pride in her role as guardian of her husband's memory. Though she publicly admired his genius and praised his 'truly lovable nature,' neither of these qualities shine forth in her books. Jessie's oriental patience and infinite capacity for concession finally gave out after Conrad's death, and she portrayed her husband, with considerable resentment and hostility, as an impossibly selfish child who was saved from disaster only by her sacrificial care. She describes his selfish refusal to lift a finger during their frequent moves from house to house and his harsh criticism of her arrangements as she hobbled about the room.

On the return voyage from their ill-fated trip to Capri, Conrad became furious about his lost wallet and exploded when she asked if it was in one of his pockets. When Conrad was sound asleep, the sensible Jessie found the wallet and then went through an elaborate act to avoid hurting his sensitive feelings. Conrad *never* says anything intelligent or interesting in Jessie's memoirs, and constantly mutters epithets like 'Damn jerry-built rabbit hutch.' But Jessie (like Ford) claims to have 'suggested the gist' of 'The Black Mate,' a story Conrad wrote eight years *before* he met her. Despite her genuine virtues, Jessie inadvertently condemns herself in her books and appears as conventional, smug, self-righteous, snobbish and patronising. For she tries too hard to justify her marriage to a genius and attempts to glorify herself at Conrad's expense.

Though Jessie states that a 'wife must be content with reflected glory if married to a famous man,' she pretentiously claimed a glory of her own after Conrad's death. In 1927

Ellen Glasgow noted, 'She has become enormously stout, and so very complacent, poor soul, clinging to the shadow of fame which he shed over her.' And two years later Jessie confided her social and intellectual fantasies to her fellow-invalid, Warrington Dawson: 'My idea would be to have some rooms in New York and be at home there to all Conrad's friends and admirers for a month. . . . I might be able to give talks if not actually lecture.'

II

Jessie never comprehended Conrad's mental life or the meaning of his work, and was serenely unaware that his 'thoughts centred upon her' (though not in the sense Curle suggested). For Conrad projected his hostility to marriage and fear of abandonment in 'Amy Foster' (1903), in *The Secret Agent* (1907) and (to a lesser extent) in *Victory* (1914). These three works deal with a young English wife (or mistress) who is responsible for the death of her older and foreign husband. And Goorall, Verloc and Heyst are all isolated from society, yet doomed by the necessity of contact with other human beings.

Victory portrays Heyst's conflict between a desire for solitude and a need for emotional commitment, and Lena's wish for self-sacrifice that intensifies his own lack of feeling and inability to respond to her. Jessie dressed up as Lena and read her part aloud when the novel was dramatised; and Conrad's erotic fantasy about the painful relations of a brooding intellectual and a grateful, humble and uneducated girl, isolated on a remote island, may have been partly based on their marriage. One reason why Conrad often wrote about the passions of the white man in the tropics, but could never satisfactorily portray a convincing relationship of a European man and woman, was that he never experienced a truly mature and compatible marriage with Jessie George.

Jessie refused to recognise the resemblance between herself and the painfully biographical heroine of 'Amy Foster.' She was even deliberately misleading and wrote that 'The actual character, Amy Foster, was for many years in our service, and it was her animal-like capacity for sheer uncomplaining endurance that inspired Conrad. That and *nothing else*.'

'Amy Foster' characterises the negative aspects of Jessie, describes their intellectual estrangement, and portrays the fierce undercurrent of Conrad's loneliness and despair, his sense of isolation, and fear of being used by a woman and then abandoned – just as his mother had 'abandoned' him when she died in exile. In the story, Yanko Goorall, whose Slavic surname means 'mountain man,' is completely out of his natural element while at sea. He is shipwrecked (Conrad's greatest professional fear) on the south coast of England, and washed ashore in an unknown country. He knows no English, is inarticulate and illiterate, and his indelible foreignness is an object of suspicion, dislike and fear. He 'finds himself a lost stranger, helpless, incomprehensible and of a mysterious origin, in some obscure corner of the earth.' The savage treatment of the castaway by the ordinary Kentish people helps to explain Conrad's desire to marry, acclimatise himself and (despite his strong accent and exotic manners) become an English gentleman.

Amy Foster is a dull, plain and passive creature, the eldest child of a large family, who was put into service at the age of fifteen. The desperate Yanko courts her because she was the only person who pitied his isolation and saved him from suicide. Yet 'It's enough to look at the red hands hanging at the end of those short arms, at those slow, prominent brown eyes, to know the inertness of her mind.' Though Amy's father mistrusts foreigners, who sometimes 'behave very queerly' to women and might want 'to carry her off somewhere – or run off himself' (as Conrad did after his marriage and before his engagement), Yanko eventually marries the gentle and loving Amy.

Jessie writes that during a malaria attack on their honeymoon:

> Conrad raved in grim earnest, speaking only in his native tongue and betraying no knowledge of who I might be. For hours I remained by his side watching the feverish glitter of his eyes . . . and listening to the meaningless phrases and lengthy speeches, not a word of which I could understand.

And during his fever attack in 'Amy Foster' Yanko:

> tossed, moaned, and now and then muttered a complaint. And she sat with the table between her and the couch, watching every movement and every sound, with the terror, the unreasonable terror of that man she could not understand.

Both passages describe the delirious foreigner, watched over by a frightened English wife, who cannot help him or even understand his Slavic ravings.

Though Conrad, who was accused of abandoning his native country, regretted that Borys, despite his Polish name, did not know the language, Yanko maintains contact with his culture by speaking to his son in a 'disturbing, passionate and bizarre' tongue. Yanko gradually alienates Amy, who is repelled and frightened by the strangeness that first attracted her, and whose ignorance makes her behave in a cruel and inhuman way. When she finally abandons Yanko during his fever and runs off with their child, the innocent Yanko is left to die in a miserable condition: sick, helpless and thirsty. His son has stolen his wife's love; and he is 'cast out mysteriously by the sea to perish in the supreme disaster of loneliness and despair.'

Conrad's considerable hostility to his wife and jealousy of his children is also expressed in what he called his 'domestic drama,' *The Secret Agent*. For as Bernard Meyer points out, 'Conrad turned to fiction as a means of effecting a corrective revision of a painful reality.' He began to write the book in February 1906 when his wife was in the early months of her second pregnancy, and completed it in November, about three months after his second son was born. Jessie naively writes of the novel: 'As I did not know in the least what the book was about, I could not account to myself for the grimly ironic expression I used often to catch on his face, whenever he came to give me a look-in. Could it have reference to the expected baby?'

Four months after John was born, during a railway journey in France in December 1906 (which matched the earlier episode with Borys), Conrad impulsively and irrationally opened the train window and, to Jessie's horror, threw out a package containing all the baby's clothes. Jessie bit her lip and then said calmly: 'I am sure the man who finds that bundle will be looking for the baby's corpse.' This symbolic murder of his son John is a striking parallel to a fictional Mr Verloc's destruction of his 'step-son' Stevie. Winnie, who deceives Verloc and marries him for Stevie's sake, represents Conrad's fear of a woman who wants a father for her child rather than a husband for herself.

Winnie's mother is Conrad's fictional portrayal of the placid Jessie, who was especially fat during her pregnancy, and whose crippled condition tried Conrad's limited patience and drained his meagre finances. Winnie's mother 'was a stout, wheezy woman, with a large brown face' whose 'swollen legs rendered her inactive.' There was a 'venerable placidity conferred upon her outward person by her triple chin, the floating ampleness of her ancient form, and the impotent condition of her legs.' All the poignant themes of the novel – the poverty, cruelty, degradation and death-in-life

of the Verloc household, and the sacrifice, displaced maternity and perversion of human emotions that result from it –
are concentrated in the great passage when Winnie's mother
is sent to the poorhouse in a funereal carriage:

> This woman, modest indeed but hardened in the fires of
> adversity, of an age, moreover, when blushes are not
> expected, had positively blushed before her daughter. In
> the privacy of a fourwheeler, on her way to a charity
> cottage (one of a row) which by the exiguity of its dimen-
> sions and the simplicity of its accommodation, might well
> have been devised in kindness as a place of training for the
> still more straitened circumstances of the grave, she was
> forced to hide from her own child a blush of remorse and
> shame.

Conrad's shame at betraying his family responsibilities is
clearly revealed in *The Secret Agent*, which provided a creative
outlet for expressing his ambiguous attitude. For he loved
and cherished his wife and sons at the same time that a part
of him hated them and longed to escape from his domestic
bondage.

Through the artistic sublimation of *The Secret Agent*
Conrad revenged himself on his family by destroying his
unwanted child and abandoning his ungainly and unattractive wife, despite her ironic blush of remorse and shame, to
the deathly existence of an alms house. This is domestic
drama with a vengeance. Despite their overt declarations of
love and respect, the profound and sometimes unconscious
core of hostility that existed in the marriage of Joseph and
Jessie Conrad found expression in his fiction and her
memoirs, and reflected the strains and tensions of their
regressive mother–son relationship.

James and Nora Joyce
THE GENIUS AND THE GODDESS

'I liked him because I saw he understood or felt what
a woman is.'

MOLLY BLOOM in *Ulysses*

The union of James Joyce, one of the most subtle intellects
of the twentieth century, with Nora Barnacle, a simple and
uneducated girl from the west of Ireland, both complemented and completed him. It represented the marriage of
mind and body, of art and life, for Joyce had the 'luminous
certitude' that his was 'the brain in contact with which she
must think and understand' and his was 'the body in contact
with which her body must feel.' The earthy Nora allowed
Joyce to abandon his masks and disclose his inner self, what
he called 'those boundless ambitions which are really the
leading forces of my life. . . . A man whose brain is on fire
with hope and trust in himself *must* tell someone of what he
feels. Whom should I tell but you?'

Despite their difference in intellect and character, Joyce and Nora had some important things in common. They both came from an Irish Catholic background; both had weak fathers who were failures and families which had decayed and disintegrated, leaving them cut off and isolated. They fell in love when they were both very young (Joyce was twenty-two and Nora twenty), defied caution and public opinion, and left for Europe without money or married respectability. Nora, with no work or intellectual interests to sustain her, and no knowledge of Italian, felt frightened and depressed in Pola. Joyce, though absorbed in his writing, had to spend long and boring hours teaching classes and private pupils in order to support his family. Though their life was plagued by poverty, alcoholism, illness and frequent changes of houses, cities and even countries, their exile drew them together. Though Joyce became more aloof as he grew older, they were devoted to each other and remained constant in adversity and in love.

Nora took Joyce out of his loneliness and put him in closer touch with physical reality; stabilised, strengthened and protected him; provided family life and children, who were so important to him; gave him a sense of adult responsibility; and as he later told her: 'made me a man.' She became the symbol of Ireland whom Joyce took with him into exile, who provided a connection and continuity with his past, and who always remained faithful when others betrayed him. Nora liberated him from repression and frustration, and enabled him to fuse his spiritual with his debased view of women. 'One moment I see you like a virgin or madonna,' Joyce told her, 'the next moment I see you shameless, insolent, half-naked and obscene.' Nora, who once said that Joyce 'knows nothing at all about women,' revealed the complexities of the female psyche to him. Joyce even recorded Nora's dreams, with his own interpretations, and used them in his work. She embodied his physical desires and sexual fantasies;

inspired the creation of Molly Bloom; and helped transform Joyce from the icy and arrogant intellectuality of Stephen Dedalus to the warm and compassionate humanity of Leopold Bloom.

Joyce's letters to Nora, written during their courtship in 1904 and their separate trips to Ireland in 1909, 1912 and 1922, reveal one of the deepest sources of his imagination: his heightened sense of the physical and his fascination with the body, not as a beautiful or divine form, but as a gross substance that sweats, pisses, farts, shits, ejaculates and bleeds. Joyce's theme of the cultured intellect martyred by the physical reflects his Irish Catholic obsession with the beastly man who strives for the divine.

Joyce was born in Dublin in 1882, educated in Jesuit schools and graduated at the age of twenty from University College. He studied medicine in Paris for a short time, but was recalled to Dublin during his mother's fatal illness in 1903. In *A Portrait of the Artist* Joyce describes the decline of his talented but superficial father from vague promise to a kind of nostalgic bankruptcy, and calls him 'A medical student, an oarsman, a tenor, an amateur actor, a shouting politician, a small landlord, a small investor, a drinker, a good fellow, a storyteller, somebody's secretary, something in a distillery, a taxgatherer, a bankrupt and at present a praiser of his own past.'

The death of Joyce's mother led to the disintegration of the rather shabby family, and he felt isolated from them by what he called his 'restless shame and rancour.' During the following year Joyce lived an idle and impoverished life about town, moved into the famous Martello tower at Sandycove, taught school for a while, and began to write *Stephen Hero* and *Dubliners*. Joyce was a sensitive, gifted, intellectual and artistic rebel. He defiantly used the weapons of 'silence, exile and cunning' in his secret war against family, country and church, and achieved his victory over them in his works.

Joyce first met Nora Barnacle on Nassau Street in Dublin on 10 June 1904, which became the date of the action of *Ulysses* and was subsequently celebrated as 'Bloomsday.' Nora's father, a baker and heavy drinker, could barely support his large family and she had been farmed out to relatives, sent as a girl to work in a convent in Galway and was presently employed as a chambermaid in Finn's Hotel. Nora was a tall, blue-eyed, auburn-haired beauty, who had considerable vivacity and wit. Robert McAlmon, a publisher and Paris friend, said that though Joyce's eyes were supposed to be weak, they had not affected his choice of a wife, for Nora 'was very pretty, with a great deal of simple dignity and a reassuring manner.' Though Nora had virtually no comprehension of literature, especially of Joyce's kind, she had a good understanding of music and was a talented amateur actress. Nora was outspoken, affirmed the superiority of women, failed to recognise his artistic genius, and was often indifferent or rude to her 'Simple-minded Jim,' who once begged her not to call him an 'imbecile.' But Padraic and Mary Colum state that 'Joyce was markedly devoted to Nora; her personality was full of interest to him, and he delighted in her sayings and snappy remarks.' And Sylvia Beach, who published *Ulysses*, agrees that 'Joyce enjoyed being called a good-for-nothing by Nora; it was a relief from the respectful attitude of others. He was delighted when she poked and pushed him.'

When Nora failed to appear for their first meeting, Joyce assumed the conventional role of dejected suitor and humbly begged for a second rendezvous: 'I may be blind. I looked for a long time at a head of reddish brown hair and decided it was not yours. I went home quite dejected. I would like to make an appointment but it might not suit you. I hope you will be kind enough to make one with me – if you have not forgotten me!' But Joyce made swift progress and only a week later she was addressing him passionately as 'My Precious Darling.'

The following month Joyce took a jaunty tone and begged the 'Little Pouting' Nora to '*Please* leave off that breastplate as I do not like embracing a letter-box'; and in August he expressed his dependence on and need for her while he poked fun at the Catholic Church: 'I have been in such a whirl of trouble that I want to forget everything in your arms. . . . In virtue of apostolic powers vested in me by his Holiness Pope Pius the Tenth I hereby give you permission to come without skirts to receive the Papal Benediction.' Nora, who lacked grammar and did not write I with a capital, relied on a letter-writing book to elevate the style and tone of her correspondence.

By the end of August Joyce was speaking of more serious matters and confessed that he totally rejected the conventional ideas about morality, society and the church, and did not believe in bourgeois virtues, the social order or established religion. In practical terms this meant that he would refuse to submit to the absurdity of a marriage ceremony. When Nora asked why Joyce did not express his love for her, he replied with a mixture of affection, respect and lust that committed him in a qualified sort of way: 'Surely you must believe I am very fond of you and if to desire a person wholly, to admire and honour that person deeply, and to seek to secure that person's happiness in every way is to "love" then perhaps my affection for you is a kind of love.' In early October Joyce, who had been assured of a job with the Berlitz School in Zurich, asked Nora to elope with him to the Continent. When she bravely agreed, he borrowed from all his family and friends. They left Dublin on 8 October 1904, less than four months after their first meeting, with just enough money to get to Paris.

When they arrived in London Joyce left Nora in a park for two hours while he went to see the English poet, Arthur Symons. She became frightened that he would not return, but was soon reassured. Two months later Joyce reaffirmed his faith in Nora and wrote to his aunt: 'I have not been able to discover any falsehood in this nature which had the courage to trust me. It was this night three months ago that we left the North Wall. Strange to say I have not yet left her on the street, as many wise men said I would.' Joyce's father observed that Miss Barnacle would always stick to him.

The Joyces consummated their marriage in a dingy Zurich hotel on 11 October. But Joyce was shocked to find there was no job in that city; was sent to the Trieste school, which also had no job for him; and finally accepted a teaching position at the Berlitz School in Pola. That town, southeast of Trieste on the Adriatic coast, was then an Italian-speaking port in the Austro-Hungarian Empire. Since the Joyce children grew up in Trieste, where Joyce transferred after a few months, the family usually spoke Italian at home.

In February 1905 Joyce wrote to his younger brother Stannie that Nora's 'disposition, as I see it, is much nobler than my own, her love also is greater than mine for her. I admire her and I love her and I trust her.' There is no doubt that their physical relationship was passionate and intense. Joyce shocked and disturbed Nora with descriptions of his sexual experience with prostitutes, and took pleasure from her confession that she practised the 'gentle art of self-satisfaction.' As Richard Ellmann, Joyce's excellent biographer, observes, Joyce insisted that Nora 'recognise all his impulses, even the strangest, and match his candour by confiding in him every thought she has found in herself, especially the most embarrassing. She must allow him to know her inmost life, to learn with odd exactitude what it is to be a woman.'

The Joyces experienced the first of three great marital crises in the second half of 1905. Despite their sexual and psychological intimacy, Nora could not adapt to the penurious life in their tiny room, and felt alienated and cut off from her family in the 'queer old place.' In Pola, and then in Trieste (where they moved in March 1905 when a spy ring was discovered and all foreigners were expelled from Pola) she had nothing to occupy her time, frequently cried and was often silent all evening. As Joyce told Stannie, 'I can see no prospect of her being happy if she continues to live this life here. . . . She is really very helpless and unable to cope with any kind of difficulties.' The birth of their son Giorgio, in July 1905, which prompted Joyce's college friend Vincent Cosgrave to announce in Dublin: 'Mother and bastard doing well,' did not improve matters.

The increased economic responsibility drove Joyce to excessive drinking, Nora was never sure when he would turn up, and one evening a friend found him lying in the gutter. When Joyce sought alcoholic oblivion, Nora threatened the atheist with the worst thing she could think of: 'Yes, go now and get drunk. That's all you're good for. Cosgrave told me you were mad. Faith I tell you I'll have the children baptised tomorrow.' Many years later, after a drunken binge with McAlmon in Paris, the exasperated Nora screamed: 'Jim, you've been doin' this for twenty years, and I'm tellin' you it's the end. Do you understand? You've been bringin' your drunken companions to me too long, and now you've started McAlmon in the same way.' But her most desperate and draconic manoeuvre was to tell Joyce she had torn up his manuscript. This made him instantly sober and he remained that way until he found his work was safe.

Joyce was so depressed after the birth of Giorgio that he thought of leaving Nora and wrote rather formally to his aunt: 'I imagine the present relations between Nora and myself are about to suffer some alteration.' Joyce complained that Nora did not appreciate his superior qualities and 'does not seem to make much difference between me and the rest of the men she has known.' But Joyce saved the marriage by finding a job in Pola for the patient and sacrificial Stannie, who joined their household, provided extra funds, acted as a friendly mediator and deflected their hostility on to himself. As the crisis gradually subsided Joyce recognised Nora's redeeming qualities and praised her warm, impulsive and life-giving love.

Their second marriage crisis occurred in August 1909, two years after the birth of their daughter Lucia and a year after Nora's miscarriage. When Joyce returned to Ireland with Giorgio he accidentally met Cosgrave who told him that Nora had been unfaithful when he was courting her in 1904 and had been seeing Cosgrave on alternate nights. Joyce was shattered by this revelation, which seemed to desecrate and destroy his love for Nora, and without reflecting on Cosgrave's motives or on the improbability of the story, he immediately wrote to her about the pain of his betrayal: 'I have heard this only an hour ago from his lips. My eyes are full of tears, tears of sorrow and mortification. My heart is full of bitterness and despair. I can see nothing but your face as it was then raised to meet another's. . . . I loved you only: and you have broken my faith in you.'

His jealous torments increased during the night and the following day, before Nora could reply to him, he masochistically wrote to her about intimate details and even questioned Giorgio's paternity: 'Were you lying down when you kissed? Did you place your hand on him as you did on me in the dark? . . . Is Georgie my son? The first night I slept with you in Zurich was October 11th and he was born on July 27th. That is nine months and 16 days. I remember there was very little blood that night.'

A few days later, when Stannie read Joyce's letters to Nora (who remained restrained and dignified throughout the crisis), he confirmed her innocence and revealed that in 1904 Cosgrave swore him to secrecy, confided that he had tried to steal Nora from Joyce and admitted that she had rebuffed him. Cosgrave's Iago-like revelation to Joyce was thus an attempt to avenge himself. Joyce meanwhile had asked the advice of John Byrne, another college friend, and learned the truth when Byrne defended Nora and stated that Cosgrave had lied. Joyce castigated himself in the next letter to Nora, asked her to fight with him against their enemies, begged absolution for his crazed jealousy and swore to be worthy of her love:

> I have spoken of this affair to an old friend of mine, Byrne, and he took your part splendidly and says it is all a 'blasted lie.' What a worthless fellow I am! But after this I will be worthy of you, dearest. . . . My sweet noble Nora, I ask you to forgive me for my contemptible conduct but they maddened me, darling, between them. We will defeat their cowardly plot, love. . . . My darling, forgive me. I love you and this is why I was so maddened only to think of you and that common dishonourable wretch. Nora darling, I apologise to you humbly. Take me again to your arms. Make me worthy of you. . . . I am absurdly jealous of the past.

The profound effect of Nora's 'betrayal' made Joyce painfully aware of the fascinating possibilities of portraying this theme in his writing. Once he was sure of her fidelity, Joyce derived satisfaction from studying her attraction to other men. He was both intrigued and amused when in 1911 his friend and pupil, the Venetian journalist Roberto Prezioso, attempted and failed to become Nora's lover. Many years later Nora tearfully confessed to the English painter, Frank Budgen, that Jim wanted her to 'go with other men so that he would have something to write about.' In Joyce's play *Exiles* (1918), the hero Richard Rowan declares to his wife in his final speech: 'It is not in the darkness of belief that I desire you. But in restless living wounding doubt.' Joyce frequently portrayed the relation of desire and doubt, and the heroes of *Exiles*, 'The Dead' and *Ulysses* are all obsessed by their jealousy and fear of betrayal.

After two months in Ireland, Joyce returned to Trieste in August 1909, bringing one of his sisters to keep Nora company. But he went back to Dublin the following month and, with the backing of film producers in Trieste, opened the first cinema in the capital and signed a contract for the publication of *Dubliners*. (Unfortunately, the cinema failed and had to be sold at a loss, and the Dublin firm never published the book.) Once he had recovered from the pain of Cosgrave's plot Joyce felt that every veil of shame had fallen from them and that nothing could ever come between them. The 'betrayal' had intensified his craving for his wife, and he begged Nora to love him fiercely and violently so that he would forget his wound. Joyce used the fantasy of Nora's 'betrayal' to revive his first passionate desires, and prolonged them in life so that he could savour them and record them in art. In *Ulysses*, Bloom spends the entire day trying (without success) to avoid Molly's lover, Blazes Boylan, and his sexual fantasies focus on what Blazes is doing with his wife. Joyce's letters from Dublin to Nora during the autumn of 1909 anticipate the fantastic and scatological parts of *Ulysses*, and reveal how closely Bloom's experience with and reveries about Molly are based on his own sexual relationship with Nora.

Joyce wanted to build their spiritual love on a physical reality. He urged Nora to hide herself in a dark closet and to use his letters to masturbate. But Joyce took his own fantasies too seriously and was afraid she would become over excited and give herself to someone else in his absence. In their bizarre correspondence Joyce deliberately regresses to a kind of infantile dependence and craving for gratification ('O that I could nestle in your womb like a child born of your flesh and blood'), blames himself for his obscenity, begs for punishment and wishes to be flogged while Nora's eyes blaze with anger. Joyce is both fascinated and horrified by certain aspects of adult sexuality, which he describes as 'brief, brutal, irresistible and devilish.' He deliberately degrades physical love by emphasising the excremental element, and his 'wild beast-like craving for every inch of [Nora's] body, for every secret and shameful part of it, for every odour and act of it.' Because Joyce was intellectually isolated from Nora, he had to break down all her physical resistance and possess her totally. Nora's body became an intellectual concept for Joyce, who wanted to anatomise and explore it as he analysed every aspect of human experience.

Joyce begins the correspondence in September 1909 with suggestions and allusions, and coyly writes: 'There is a place I would like to kiss you now, a *strange* place, Nora. *Not* on the lips, Nora. Do you know where?' And he urges her to 'take that cocoa every day and I hope that little body of yours (or rather *certain* parts of it) are getting a little fuller. I am laughing at this moment as I think of those little girl's breasts of yours.' In another letter Joyce (like Bloom) wishes that his wife were strong, with a big bosom and fat thighs, so she could beat him; and he states that he is a 'filthy wretch' because (again like Bloom) he is attracted to the brown stain on her girlish white drawers.

The rhythm, fantasy, excess and delight in the obscene language of three even 'madder and dirtier' letters (first published in 1975), which Joyce wrote to Nora in early December, clearly anticipate Bloom's dreams in Nighttown and Molly's nocturnal soliloquy. The first rather startling letter (so different from his priestly propriety of speech) expresses the squalor of Joyce's body and the riot of his mind, his attraction to anal smells and desire for sodomy:

[I'd like to] fuck you up behind, like a hog riding a sow, glorying in the very stink and sweat that rises from your arse . . . with you feeling your fingers fondling and tickling my ballocks or stuck up in me behind and your hot lips sucking off my cock while my head is wedged in between your fat thighs, my hands clutching the round cushions of your bum and my tongue licking ravenously up your rank red cunt.

In the second letter Joyce returns to the themes of brown stains and buggery; and reveals his attraction to whorish gestures, obscene words and bodily smells, which would stimulate him to spill sperm on Nora's face:

> The smallest things give me a great cockstand – a whorish movement of your mouth, a little brown stain on the seat of your white drawers, a sudden dirty word spluttered out by your wet lips, a sudden immodest noise made by your behind and then a bad smell slowly curling up out of your backside. At such moments I feel mad to do it in some filthy way, to feel your hot lecherous lips sucking away at me, to fuck between your two rosy-tipped bubbies, to come on your face and squirt it over your hot cheeks and eyes, to stick it up between the cheeks of your rump and bugger you.

The third quite hilarious letter concerns the relation of fucking and farting (with its symphonic variations) and Joyce's unerring recognition of Nora's fetid fragrance:

> If I gave you a bigger and stronger fuck than usual fat dirty farts came spluttering out of your backside. You had an arse full of farts that night, darling, and I fucked them out of you, big fat fellows, long windy ones, quick little merry cracks and a lot of tiny little naughty farties ending in a long gush from your hole. It is wonderful to fuck a farting woman when every fuck drives one out of her. I think I would know Nora's fart anywhere. I think I could pick hers out in a roomful of farting women. It is a rather girlish noise not like the wet windy fart which I imagine fat wives have.

The gross candour of these letters – which were meant to shock, amuse and excite Nora – suggests that Joyce had a profound desire and need to overcome the extreme sexual repression of his childhood and to break down his physical restraints by the verbal expression of his fantasies. Joyce felt that if the corrupt, the filthy, the polluted and the obscene could be freely and openly expressed (if only in private letters), then their shame could be burnt out, they could return to and revive the spiritual element in marriage, and as he said in *Exiles*, be united in body and soul and utter nakedness. Joyce sought and achieved the spiritual not, like St Paul, by denying the physical, but by embracing and transcending the physical. Unlike Swift, who was revolted by the terrible paradox that man is born between urine and faeces, that (in Yeats' words) 'Love has pitched his mansion in/ The place of excrement,' Joyce was intensely excited by this fact, which made a woman's body more fearful and more fascinating to him.

Three years later, in July 1912, Nora took Lucia on a visit to Dublin. When she failed to write Joyce complained: 'It is a monstrous thing to say that you seem to forget me in five days and to forget the beautiful days of our love' – and he followed her to Ireland with Giorgio. Nora was triumphant at his touching concern and obvious dependence upon her, and boasted to his sister: 'Well what have you to say to Jim now after all our little squabbles he could not live without me for a month.'

The year 1914 was the great turning point in Joyce's literary career and the beginning of his international reputation. After nearly ten years of frustration *Dubliners* was finally published in London; *A Portrait of the Artist*, with the help of Ezra Pound, was serialised by *The Egoist*; and Joyce began to write *Ulysses*. In January 1915, a few months after the outbreak of the Great War, Stannie was interned by the Austrians; and in July Joyce moved to Zurich (where he lived for the next five years), gave up teaching, and received money from several English literary institutions and from two wealthy patrons: Harriet Shaw Weaver and Edith Rockefeller McCormick.

At the end of 1918 Joyce began a brief flirtation with his neighbour, Marthe Fleischmann, which included a candle-light *soirée* on Joyce's birthday at the studio of the painter, Frank Budgen. But the affair did not get very far because, as Richard Ellmann notes, Marthe's lover was vigilant, she was extremely coy, and Joyce shy and ailing. In *Ulysses* Molly suspects 'some little bitch or other he got in with somewhere or picked up on the sly if they only knew him as well as I do,' but Nora, fortunately, did not discover Joyce's harmless dalliance with Marthe.

The Joyces' third marriage crisis occurred in April 1922, two years after they had moved from Zurich to Paris and two months after the publication of *Ulysses*. After a quarrel with Joyce, Nora left for Ireland with the children and threatened not to return. A few days later the repentant Joyce wrote: 'It is impossible to describe to you the despair I have been in since you left. . . . O my dearest, if you would only turn to me even now and read that terrible book [*Ulysses*] which has now broken my heart in my breast and take me to yourself alone to do with me what you will.' In Galway Nora was caught in the fighting of the Civil War when soldiers entered her bedroom to take up a firing position. She was naturally terrified and left immediately for Dublin by train, which was then fired on by both sides as it pulled out of the station. Nora was glad to get back to her husband in Paris; and this incident, like the false betrayal of 1909, strengthened and solidified their marriage. As Robert McAlmon noted, 'Joyce is lonely, desolate and an anxious husband, parent, brother, and son, if home and family and a degree of loving and admiring friends are not about.'

Joyce had suffered from poor eyesight since childhood; but beginning in 1917 he became what he called an 'interna-tional eye sore,' suffered acutely from iritis, glaucoma and cataracts, and had to endure eleven costly and painful eye operations. He wrote in 1924 to Harriet Weaver, who gave him moral as well as financial support, 'My wife is in a weak state of nerves and I believe the operation will cause her more pain than it will cause me.' Three years later he lamented his ocular and literary troubles, and mentioned the endless obstacles that plagued him as he struggled through the monumental task of *Finnegans Wake*: 'The last five years with three violent eye attacks, seven operations – the last particularly bad – nine editions of *Ulysses*, the piracy, protest, lawsuit and Pen dinner with its sequel and the French and German translations are quite enough to say nothing of the completion of Pts I & III amid all sorts of changing domiciles etc.' In 1928 Joyce stayed in the hospital with Nora when she underwent an operation for cancer; and she had to have radium treatments and a hysterectomy before she finally recovered the following year.

Though Joyce suffered from extreme poverty, drunkenness, marital problems, lack of artistic recognition and even blindness, the greatest tragedy of his life was the madness of his daughter, Lucia, who had been born in the pauper ward of Trieste in 1907 and had led a strange and nomadic existence. She had begun school in Italian in Trieste, lost a year while she learned German in Zurich, and then had to learn French when the Joyces moved to Paris in 1920. Lucia wanted to become a ballerina, studied under Egorova (who also taught Zelda Fitzgerald) and had worked six hours a day for three years on dance. But in 1929 Lucia decided that she did not have the physique for a strenuous dancing career, refused an offer to dance at Darmstadt (just as Zelda turned down an offer at Naples), and then wept bitterly at the sacrifice of her talent and the waste of so much work.

Joyce, who was totally absorbed in his writing, took an indulgent and *laissez-faire* attitude toward his children, and failed to provide the element of stability that was so clearly lacking in their lives. Though Joyce (according to the Colums) believed that Nora's neglect of Lucia in childhood was partly responsible for her mental breakdown just after her engagement in 1932, he also felt that 'Whatever spark of gift I possess has been transmitted to Lucia and has kindled a fire in her brain.'

Harriet Weaver reports that after Nora had called Lucia a bastard, she 'had shouted "And who made me one?" She then refused to speak to her mother for several days and would say nothing to her father except the same thing. . . . It certainly upset Mr. Joyce considerably, and I think it was one of his reasons for going through a ceremony of marriage,' in May 1931. Lucia's illness aroused Joyce's intense family feelings and he refused to accept a negative diagnosis. 'The poor child is just a poor girl who tried to do too much, to understand too much,' Joyce told Harriet Weaver.' Her dependence on me is now absolute and all the affection she repressed for years pours itself out on both of us.'

Lucia was put under the care of Dr Oscar Forel (who had also treated Zelda for schizophrenia) at Prangins in Switzerland in July 1933. Joyce's friend, Paul Leon, told Harriet Weaver: 'The opinion of this doctor is that she ruined her nervous system by five years of dancing strain, something which [Joyce] always combatted and tried to discourage as far as he could while recognising her great talent.' Lucia's illness persisted despite many consultations and treatments, devoured most of Joyce's income, interrupted his writing for extended periods and drove him to excessive drinking. In 1935 Joyce lamented that despite the faithful support of his patrons, his friends and his wife, 'there are moments and hours when I have nothing in my heart but rage and despair, a blind man's rage and despair.' Joyce suffered similar agonies in 1939 when Giorgio's wife Helen had a series of nervous breakdowns, which led to the collapse of their marriage.

Though Nora was loyal and compassionate about Joyce's

problems, he realised from the first that she had absolutely no understanding of his intellectual and creative life. Nora cared nothing for his art, and frequently expressed resentment and hostility toward the totally absorbing work which seemed to seal him off from her, but never brought in any money. Nora grumbled that Joyce never stopped writing, reached down while half-awake in the morning for the pencil and paper that lay beside his bed, and never even knew the time of day. 'Look at him now!' she exclaimed to Sylvia Beach, 'Leeching on the bed, and scribbling away.' When Nora saw him making a second draft of *Dubliners* she asked: 'Will all that paper be wasted?'; and when he was composing *Ulysses* she confided to a Swiss friend in vivid Anglo-German: 'My husband is writing a book; I tell you *das Buch is ein Schwein*.' Despite Joyce's pleading, Nora refused to read through *Ulysses*, and in 1922 he told his aunt: 'I think Nora will beat you in all the competition. She has read as far as page 27 counting the cover.' McAlmon reports that when someone in Paris once asked Nora if she had read her husband's work, she replied '"Sure, why would I bother? It's enough he talks about that book and he's at it all the time. I'd like a bit of life of my own."' She later admitted that she had read the last pages of *Ulysses* in which Molly Bloom's thoughts are portrayed. Her comment was short but to the point. 'I guess the man's a genius, but what a dirty mind he has, hasn't he?'

Nora, who called *Finnegans Wake* 'chop suey,' urged Joyce either to write sensible books that people could understand or to abandon literature for a singing career. She was extremely impressed that Joyce had once been on the same stage as the Irish tenor, John McCormack. When the Hemingways invited them to dinner, Joyce said that he feared his writing was 'too suburban and that maybe he should get around a bit and see the world.' Nora, who had contempt for her husband's weaknesses, agreed with him and told Hemingway, 'Jim could do with a spot of that lion-hunting.'

Though Nora was indifferent and even hostile to Joyce's art, she directly inspired his greatest short story, *The Dead*. For as early as 1904 Joyce, who admitted he was 'absurdly jealous of the past,' told Stannie 'she has had many love-affairs, one when quite young with a boy who died. She was laid up at news of his death.' And during their marriage crisis of 1909, two years after writing the story, Joyce tenderly asked Nora, 'Do you remember the three adjectives I have used in *The Dead* in speaking of your body. They are these: "musical and strange and perfumed."' He might have added that in the story these physical qualities 'sent through him a keen pang of lust.'

In *The Dead* (which influenced *The Stranger*, Katherine Mansfield's story on the same theme), a husband's jealousy is aroused, his complacency shattered, his desire extinguished, and his life embittered when he discovers that his wife's emotions are more closely attached to a dead youth than to himself.

> 'It was a young boy I used to know,' she answered, 'named Michael Furey. He used to sing that song, "The Lass of Aughrim". He was very delicate. . . . I used to go out walking with him when I was in Galway. . . . He is dead. He died when he was only seventeen. Isn't it a terrible thing to die so young as that?' . . . Gabriel felt humiliated by the failure of his irony and by the evocation of the figure from the dead, a boy in the gasworks. While he had been full of memories of their secret life together, full of tenderness and joy and desire, she had been comparing him in her mind with another.

The rather pretentious and vulnerable Gabriel Conroy is astonished, angered and humiliated to find that his wife's impalpable though 'vindictive' lover, who 'died for her sake,' still has power over their life: 'He thought of how she who lay beside him had locked in her heart for so many years the image of her lover's eyes when he had told her that he did not wish to live.' Gretta's confession forces Gabriel to painfully reinterpret their marriage, and to realise that he has never aroused her love in the way the foolish boy had when he called to her in the rain before his death. In an important sense, Gabriel is more dead than his rival.

The theme of retrospective jealousy in 'The Dead' suggests Joyce's need to possess Nora's heart and mind as well as her body, and his fascination with the intensely personal themes of jealousy and betrayal. When Joyce followed Nora to Ireland in 1912, their visit to the grave of her Galway sweetheart was both a tribute to his literary inspiration and a final attempt to exorcise the influence of the dead.

In an interview published a year after her death in 1951, Nora (who had scarcely read Joyce's novel and preferred the work of the aptly named Paul de Kock) stated 'I have heard people think I am Molly Bloom in *Ulysses*, but I'm not; Molly Bloom was much fatter.' Nora, like Molly, had a gift for concentrated, pungent expression, was uneducated and anti-intellectual, and attached to her husband without being awestruck. Joyce once asked Stannie, 'Do you notice how women [i.e., Nora] when they write disregard stops and capital letters?' and Molly's last speech is characterised by a lack of punctuation that suggests her release from social and sexual convention. Yet Nora had good reasons for her ingenuous disclaimer. Though many specific details about Molly were undoubtedly inspired by Nora, her commonness, squalor, sensuality and sloth are exaggerated in Molly, who lacks Nora's affection and tenderness as well as her fidelity.

The Joyces, like the Blooms, actually slept '"lying opposed in opposite directions," the head of one toward the tail of the other.' Joyce urged Nora 'to wear drawers with three or four frills one over the other at the knees and up the thighs and great crimson bows in them,' and Bloom is also 'mad on the

subject of drawers that's plain to be seen.' Like Joyce, Bloom
is excited by shit-stains, and Molly thinks 'the ironmould
mark the stupid old bundle burned on them he might think
was something else.' And just as Joyce wanted his 'hands
clutching the round cushions of your bum,' so Bloom 'kissed
the plump mellow yellow smellow melons of her rump.'

But Molly's notorious obscenity and prodigious sexual
appetite are (as his published letters reveal) much more a
projection of Joyce's fears and fetishes than of Nora's. Joyce
said that Nora practised the 'gentle art of self-satisfaction,'
and Molly confesses 'I tried with the Banana but I was afraid
it might break and get lost up in me somewhere.' Joyce asked
'Did you place your hand on him as you did on me in the
dark?' and Molly recalls 'I touched his trousers outside the
way I used to Gardner after with my ring hand to keep him
from doing worse where it was too public.' Joyce noticed
'there was very little blood' on their wedding night, and
Molly says 'they always want to see a stain on the bed to
know you're a virgin for them.' Joyce hoped that '*certain* parts
of [your body] are getting a little fuller,' and Molly agrees to
'take those eggs beaten up with marsala to fatten them out
for him.'

Molly also expresses *Joyce's* fantasies. She thinks of cutting
off her pubic hair to look like a young girl and startle Bloom
the next time he pulls up her skirt. Joyce is aroused by 'a
sudden dirty word spluttered out by your wet lips,' and Molly
plans to 'let out a few smutty words smellrump or lick my
shit or the first mad thing comes into my head.' Joyce imag-
ines Nora's 'hot lips sucking off my cock,' and Molly idealises
this crudely expressed desire when she dreams about
seducing Stephen Dedalus, who has been rescued from a
drunken brawl in a whorehouse and brought home by
Bloom: 'I often felt I wanted to kiss him all over also his
lovely young cock there so simply I wouldn't mind taking
him in my mouth if nobody was looking as if it was asking

you to suck it so clean and white.' And Joyce's witty obsession with farts is expressed by Molly as a natural and eupho-
nious relief: 'give us room even to let a fart God or do the
least thing better yes hold them like that a bit on my side
piano quietly sweeeee theres that train far away pianissimo
eeeeeeee one more song that was a relief wherever you be
let your wind go free." Molly is less a fictional portrayal of
Nora than a representation of Joyce's erotic desires, which are
severely suppressed in Stephen but freely expressed by both
Bloom and his wife.

Joyce's tribute to Nora is expressed in Molly's assertion: 'of
course hed never find another woman like me to put up
with him the way I do.' Sylvia Beach, who agreed with
McAlmon, the Colums, Budgen and Harriet Weaver,
observed that Joyce was extremely lucky to find Nora and
that his marriage was the happiest of any writer she knew.
Nora's attitude toward her husband reflected his reputation,
for she never recognised Joyce's genius until after his death.
When asked about André Gide, Nora proudly exclaimed:
'Sure, if you've been married to the greatest writer in the
world, you don't remember all the little fellows'; and she
admitted: 'Things are very dull now. There was always something doing when he was about.' And Lucia, who was in a
maison de santé in Vichy when her father died in 1941, affec-
tionately asked: 'What's he doing under the ground, that
idiot? When will he decide to come out? He's watching us
all the time.'

Virginia and Leonard Woolf
MADNESS AND ART

'We both of us want a marriage that is a tremendous living thing, always alive, always hot, not dead & easy in parts as most marriages are.'

VIRGINIA to Leonard, May 1912

I

The life of the brilliant and beautiful Virginia Woolf was scarred by a series of crises, breakdowns and suicidal impulses. She was born in 1882, had a nervous illness in childhood, and suffered mental breakdowns after the sudden death of her young mother in 1895; after the slow death of her father, Leslie Stephen, in 1904; soon after her marriage, in 1913; and just after completing *Between the Acts* in 1941. She tried to kill herself in 1904 and in 1913, and finally succeeded in 1941. Though she always lived in a state of perilous tension, there were long periods of relative calm

when she shone in her circle of illustrious friends, travelled
to Greece and to Spain, and enjoyed a rich quarter-century
of creative life. But Virginia's years of happiness and creativity
– despite the tragedy of her mental illness – would never
have been possible without the sacrifice and devotion of her
husband. Though Leonard Woolf accomplished a great deal
in his long life, he was sufficiently self-assured to surrender
his masculine prerogatives and give first priority to Virginia's
career. He gave up his sexual life, had no children, and strictly
curtailed his political activities and literary work. His greatest
achievement, the five volumes of autobiography published
between 1960 and 1970, were written after Virginia's death.

In the last year of her life Virginia recorded, in a letter to
the composer Ethel Smyth, one of her earliest and most trau-
matic memories which had occurred in 1888 and concerned
her stepbrother George Duckworth: 'I still shiver with shame
at the memory of my half-brother, standing me on a ledge,
aged about 6 or so, exploring my private parts.' This sexual
exploration was not mere child's play for George was then in
his twenties, and it produced a more profound effect than
shameful shivers, for George continued to molest and terrify
her throughout her childhood. Virginia was entering the
crucial and hypersensitive years of adolescence when her
mother died in 1895, and George chose this dark moment to
console her with surreptitious fraternal embraces that both
disguised and expressed his incestuous desires. As her biographer Quentin Bell writes; 'Virginia felt that George had
spoilt her life before it had fairly begun. Naturally shy in
sexual matters, she was from this time terrified back into a
posture of frozen and defensive panic.'

George continued to pet and probe Virginia until as late as
1904, when she was twenty-two but still as innocent and
chaste as a child, and she later described how 'George would
fling himself on my bed, cuddling and kissing and otherwise
embracing me in order, as he told Dr. Savage later, to comfort

me for the fatal illness of my Father – who was dying three or four storeys lower down of cancer.' Virginia's earliest sexual experiences were inevitably associated with death, disgust, shame and horror. Though her half-sister Laura Stephen and her cousin James Stephen were both mad, and she inherited the melancholia and insomnia of her stern, irascible and tyrannical father, George's behaviour was partly responsible for her sexual fears and frigidity as well as for her severe mental collapse, three months after the death of Leslie Stephen, in May 1904. Quentin Bell gives a vivid account of her nightmarish grief, fear, frenzy, delusion and madness:

In the breakdown that followed she entered into a period of nightmare in which the symptoms of the preceding months attained frantic intensity. Her mistrust of [her older sister] Vanessa, her grief for her father became maniacal, her nurses – she had three – became fiends. She heard voices urging her to acts of folly; she believed that they came from overeating and that she must starve herself. In this emergency the main burden fell upon Vanessa; but Vanessa was enormously helped by [their maternal friend] Violet Dickinson. She took Virginia to her house at Burnham Wood and it was there that she made her first attempt to commit suicide. She threw herself from a window, which, however, was not high enough from the ground to cause her serious harm. It was here too that she lay in bed, listening to the birds singing in Greek and imagining that King Edward VII lurked in the azaleas using the foulest possible language.

When Virginia began to recover in late September, she felt resurrected and told Violet Dickinson: 'It is the oddest feeling, as though a dead part of me were coming to life.'

The precarious, delicate and ethereal quality of Virginia's mind was reflected in her striking beauty, what Christopher

Isherwood calls her forlorn eyes, her high-shouldered and strangely tense figure, and 'the eggshell fragility of her temples.' Leonard Woolf recalled that when he first saw the Stephen sisters at the turn of the century, in the Cambridge college of their brother Thoby and his friend, 'in white dresses and large hats, with parasols in their hands, their beauty literally took one's breath away, for suddenly seeing them one stopped astonished.' Dora Carrington, the painter and companion of Lytton Strachey, agreed that 'few women since the beginning of the world have equalled her for wit and charm, and a special rare kind of beauty.' And Carrington's sometime lover, Gerald Brenan, observed that Virginia's facial 'bones were thin and delicately made and her eyes were large, grey or greyish blue, and as clear as a hawk's. In conversation they would light up a little coldly while her mouth took an ironic and challenging fold, but in repose her expression was pensive and almost girlish.'

Virginia's cold irony, satiric wit, spiteful sarcasm and malicious jealousy, which reflected an awareness of her superior birth and brains, and her place in the intellectual aristocracy of England, were essentially an aggressive defence of her own fearful sensitivity. The haughty Lady Ottoline Morrell, who was hurt as well as deceived by Virginia's self-protective arrogance, wrote 'Her swiftness of mind astounded me. She sat as if on a throne and took it for granted that we must worship. She seemed to feel certain of her own eminence. It is true, but it is rather crushing, for I feel she is very contemptuous of other people.' But Gerald Brenan, who was Virginia's host in Spain in 1923, was more acute when he related her vanity and scorn to her personal instability: 'She was tied to her set by her birth, her social proclivities, her craving for praise and flattery, and could only throw distant and uneasy glances outside it. Her sense of the precariousness of things, which gives her work its serious-ness, came from her private life – from the shock of her brother Thoby's death [in 1906] and from her experience of madness.'

Virginia's ethereal fragility attracted a number of Thoby's Cambridge friends who fell in love and proposed to her before Leonard Woolf finally triumphed in 1912. Even the confirmed homosexual, Lytton Strachey, was momentarily carried away in 1909, and informed his brother James: 'On Feb. 19th I proposed to Virginia, and was accepted. It was an awkward moment, as you may imagine, especially as I realised, the very minute it was happening, that the whole thing was repulsive to me. Her sense was amazing, and luckily it turned out that she's not in love. The result was that I was able to manage a fairly honourable retreat.' Virginia thought Strachey so physically grotesque that the idea of marriage was nearly as repulsive to her as to him. She also received and rejected proposals from the lawyer, Hilton Young, in May 1909; the teacher, Walter Lamb, in July 1911; and the Cambridge intellectual, Sydney Waterlow, in November 1911.

Leonard Woolf, the son of a distinguished Jewish barrister, was born in 1880 and entered Trinity College in 1899 with Thoby Stephen, Lytton Strachey and Clive Bell, who married Vanessa Stephen in 1907. Leonard was rational, definite and emphatic, very steady and very masculine, with a rabbinical seriousness and intensity. In November 1904, when Virginia was recovering from her first suicide attempt and second breakdown, Leonard sailed for Ceylon. He became chief administrator of a southern province of the country, and like George Orwell in Burma and Joyce Cary in Nigeria, was road builder, policeman, magistrate, hangman and head of state. And his seven long years of isolation and self-imposed chastity must have intensified his vision of the beautiful Stephen sisters on that summer afternoon.

Leonard had, as Virginia wrote, 'ruled India, hung black men, shot tigers' and, like herself, written a novel. This extensive experience of action and responsibility, in a 'different universe' from Virginia, was a strangely apt preparation for marrying and caring for her. He was used to celibacy and solitude, was independent and decisive in emergencies, and was thoroughly imbued with the imperial ethic of duty and self-sacrifice. He returned from the East to Bloomsbury in June 1911, the very month Virginia lamented to Vanessa: 'I could not write, & all the devils came out – hairy black ones. To be 29 & unmarried – to be a failure – Childless – insane too, no writer.'

Leonard once again met Virginia at Clive and Vanessa Bell's home in July, saw a great deal of her during the next six months, took rooms at the top of her house in Brunswick Square in December, and proposed to her in January 1912. He realised the depth of his love when he thought of going back to Ceylon; but Virginia did not yet know her feelings and needed an indefinite amount of time to see more of him and make up her mind. Leonard then asked the Secretary of State for Colonies to extend his home leave; and two days after the proposal told Virginia, with considerable injustice to himself: 'I see the risk of marrying anyone & certainly me. I am selfish, jealous, cruel, lustful, a liar. . . . Your qualities [are] magnificence, intelligence, wit, beauty, directness.' But even these qualities could not strengthen and protect Virginia; and undermined, this time, by a crisis of love, she had a minor breakdown and spent most of February in a nursing home. In March she promised Leonard: 'I shall tell you wonderful stories of the lunatics. By the bye, they've elected me King.'

Virginia, who had written on a voyage to Spain in 1905, 'There are a great many Portuguese Jews on board, and other repulsive objects, but we keep clear of them,' described Leonard as 'a penniless Jew.' And on 1 May she sent him an extremely disturbing letter, frankly expressed her fears about his religion, race, lust and love, and about her own instability, frigidity and impossibly idealistic hopes for marriage:

I feel angry sometimes at the strength of your desire. Possibly, your being a Jew comes in also at this point. You seem so foreign. And then I am fearfully unstable. . . . I want everything – love, children, adventure, intimacy, work. . . . Is it the sexual side of it that comes between us? As I told you brutally the other day, I feel no physical attraction in you. There are moments – when you kissed me the other day was one – when I feel no more than a rock. And yet your caring for me as you do almost over-whelms me. It is so real, and so strange. . . . I feel I must give you everything; and that if I can't, well, marriage would only be second-best for you as well as for me.

Instead of becoming disheartened or frightened by this letter, Leonard, who was madly in love, somehow managed to find it encouraging. When his extension of leave was refused, he abandoned a brilliant career and resigned from the Colonial Service. Virginia was as intrigued, impressed and excited by his risky sacrifice as by his origins, character and exotic experience, which were so different from her own. As she wrote of Leonard to her friend Madge Vaughan: 'First he is a Jew: second he is thirty-one; third, he spent 7 years in Ceylon, governing natives, inventing ploughs, shooting tigers, and did so well that they offered him a very high place the other day, which he refused, wishing to marry me, and gave up his entire career there on the chance that I would agree.'

While trying to decide about Leonard, Virginia complained to another friend, Molly MacCarthy, about the timidity and boredom of both marriage and spinsterhood, and expressed her desire for a truly exciting man: 'The extreme safeness and sobriety of young couples does appall me, but then so do the random melancholy old maids. I began life with a tremendous, absurd, ideal of marriage, then my bird's eye view of many marriages disgusted me, and I thought I must be asking for what was not to be had. But that has passed too. Now I only ask for someone to make me vehement, and then I'll marry him!' At the end of May Virginia was finally moved by Leonard's combination of vehement intellect and strength, confessed that she loved him, and agreed to the marriage which Quentin Bell justly calls 'the wisest decision of her life.' The civil wedding took place in the St Pancras Registry Office on 10 August, and Leonard's outraged mother was not asked to attend.

II

Night and Day (1919), Virginia's second book, which belongs in the classical tradition of Jane Austen, is a novel of self-discovery which reveals many of her doubts and fears about marriage, and portrays the most negative aspects of Leonard's character and courtship. But unlike the heroines of Jane Austen, who assume the validity and desirability of wedlock, Virginia's autobiographical heroine, Katharine Hilbery, is extremely sceptical about making a total emotional commitment to the 'very queer business' of marriage. She prefers friendship but does not know how to avoid marriage, becomes engaged to William Rodney whom she does not love, contemplates with horror a prosaic and loveless union, yet is afraid to renounce such a vital part of life and to become one of the 'eccentrics, undeveloped human beings, from whose substance some essential part had been cut away.'

Katharine Hilbery, like Virginia (and Vanessa), is 'very tall and distinguished and rather absent-minded,' egoistic, impersonal and severe, who 'never made any attempt to spare people's feelings.' Her self-respect forbade emotional surrender, and her aloofness and force of character checked all of William's 'natural methods of attack.' Though her emotions are 'absolutely unruffled' by William's passion, she accepts his momentous proposal in a listless monotone and then tells her mother: 'It will make no difference. I shall always care for you and father most.'

Virginia portrays Leonard as the able but fussy, vain and emotional William Rodney, 'half poet and half old maid,' whose 'lips perpetually formed words that remained unspoken' and whose eyes, when he was angry, 'protruded more than ever, and his face had more than ever the appearance of being covered with a thin crackling skin, through which every flush of his volatile blood showed itself instantly.' William's hot blood impels him to plead with Katharine: 'Make me feel that you care for me!'; and when he takes her arm and impulsively exclaims, 'We might be so happy,' she withdraws it immediately and coldly replies, 'As long as you let yourself feel like this we shall never be happy.' Despite William's authoritative answers to intelligent questions, his firmness and sympathy, and his profound love for Katharine, she rejects him at the very end of the novel for the poor but brilliant lawyer, Ralph Denham. Though Katharine and Ralph are promised happiness, they do not actually experience it in the book, which is mainly concerned with her gradual rejection of William. For Ralph belongs to the world of dreams and William to the world of reality.

Though Katharine chooses Ralph, she is still torn by the perpetual conflict, expressed in the title of the novel, between the solitary life of thought and art, madness and creativity, and the social life of marriage and action, sanity and normality: 'this astonishing precipice on one side of which the soul was active and in broad daylight, on the other side of which it was contemplative and dark as night.' As Virginia, who led a twilight existence in which night dominated day, explained to Ottoline Morrell, the theme of the novel which attempts to unite emotion and intellect, dreams and reality, 'is that we all live in some dream world of our own with some occasional rocks of real life emerging, but the dream is the ether round us.' Though most people do *not*

live in a dream world, Virginia certainly did. She was fundamentally adrift and perilously close to drowning, and clung
to Leonard – who embodied intellect, order and reason – as
a life-saving rock of reality.

Though Lytton Strachey enjoyed the book and 'longed to
return to it,' Virginia admitted that she wrote it as a kind of
exercise to prove she could create a classical novel before she
transcended the prosaic conventions of literary realism. But
the novel was a therapeutic as well as a literary exercise in
which Virginia, during her long period of adjustment to life
with Leonard, attempted to purge herself of marital fears by
expressing them in her fiction. *Night and Day* was Virginia's
only novel about Leonard; and her rejection of him in art
helped her to accept him in life. She learned to love Leonard
by admiring his origins (Katharine states 'Robert Browning
used to say that every great man has Jewish blood in him')
and by recognising his human weaknesses as well as his
impressive strengths.

III

The effects of George Duckworth's childhood molestation
of Virginia, and the fears about Leonard's passion and her
sexual frigidity, were manifested during her honeymoon
when she wrote to her friend, Ka Cox (who was having an
affair with Rupert Brooke): 'Why do you think people make
such a fuss about marriage & copulation? Why do some of
our friends change upon losing chastity? Possibly my great
age [thirty] makes it less of a catastrophe; but certainly I find
the climax immensely exaggerated.' Virginia was of course
confessing that she could not physically respond to Leonard;
and their sex life, as Vita Sackville-West wrote in 1926, 'was
a terrible failure, and was abandoned quite soon.'

Vanessa tried to console Leonard by saying that Virginia
had never understood or sympathised with sexual passion in

men; and Vita, who later became Virginia's lover, emphatically stated: 'She dislikes the possessiveness and love of domination in men. In fact she dislikes the quality of masculinity.' In the early 1930s, when Stephen Spender asked, 'How much importance do you attach to sex in marriage?' Leonard replied, 'It depends on how much importance you attach to cocks and cunts.' Though Spender admired the 'candour' of this answer, it was actually evasive and defensive; for Leonard, who was used to chastity and had virtually no sexual life, suggested that others put an excessive emphasis on physical love. His fanatical capacity for work was clearly a sublimation of his sexual drive just as his passionate attachment to dogs was a compensation for his lack of children.

Shortly after their marriage, when Leonard began to understand more about Virginia's physical frigidity and mental frailty, he doubted whether she could stand the strain and responsibility of childbearing. And his fears were confirmed in the spring of 1913 when Virginia's doctors strongly advised them *not* to have children. Though Leonard was undoubtedly right to follow the doctors' advice, Virginia's frustrated maternity intensified her sense of being 'incomplete' and became a permanent cause of sorrow. She always envied Vanessa's children, who never diminished her ability to lead an adventurous and adulterous sexual life, and wrote: 'I always measure myself against her and find her much the largest, most humane of the two of us.' Whenever Virginia analysed the reasons for her melancholy, she always mentioned her lack of children. In October 1920 she recorded in her diary: 'It's having no children, living away from friends, failing to write well, spending too much on food, growing old'; and in 1929, when she was forty-seven, she listed and then rejected various anodynes: 'Work, reading, writing are all disguises; and relations with people. Yes, even having children would be useless.' Eventually Virginia, who needed constant care and attention, became Leonard's child;

and her books became her own symbolic children. Their births were long and difficult, their lives painful and precarious, and they always remained part of herself.

Virginia's revulsion against 'the quality of masculinity,' which derived from her father's rigidity and repression, her stepbrother's covert lechery and her husband's repressed passion, was complemented by her attraction to women, which reflected the loss of her mother during her adolescent sexual awakening. Quentin Bell writes that her early letters to Violet Dickinson and Madge Vaughan clearly show 'that she was in love and that her love was returned.' Virginia's intense yet ambiguous relationship with Katherine Mansfield had lesbian overtones, while her friendship with Vita Sackville-West was inspired by Vita's physical passion.

In July 1916 Lytton Strachey met Katherine Mansfield at Garsington, the home of Ottoline Morrell. Virginia wrote that Katherine 'was decidedly an interesting creature . . . very amusing and sufficiently mysterious,' and arranged an introduction at the end of the year. Though Katherine was six years younger than Virginia, she had published her first book of stories in 1911, four years before the appearance of Virginia's first novel, *The Voyage Out*. Both women shared a passionate devotion to their 'precious' art, for as Katherine wrote: 'We have got the same job, Virginia, and it is really very curious and thrilling that we should both, quite apart from each other, be after so very nearly the same thing.' They were both sensitive, poetic, impressionistic and lyrical writers, concerned with vivid visual details and subtle nuances of emotion, who relied on their 'inner voices' to achieve stylistic purity and perfection.

But they were also intense artistic rivals who deeply distrusted one another. Leonard, who explains Virginia's contradictory feelings about Katherine, writes that 'A curious friendship, with some deep roots, did spring up between them. When they did not meet, Katherine regarded

Virginia with suspicion and hostility and Virginia was irritated and angered by this, and supercilious towards Katherine's cheap scent and cheap sentimentality. But when they met, all this as a rule fell away and there was a profound feeling and understanding between them.' But Virginia never really knew about the early life of Katherine, who had been deeply wounded by her love affair with Garnet Trowell, her miscarriage and her abortion, and who manifested her vulnerability in suspicion and hostility.

Virginia, who thought that Katherine 'dressed like a tart and behaved like a bitch,' was truly shocked by her self-conscious bohemian life and reckless sexual adventures. But in October 1917 the far more snobbish and conventional Virginia felt that Katherine's appearance and character were redeemed, as Strachey had suggested, by her cleverness and wit: 'I'm a little shocked by her commonness at first sight; lines so hard and cheap. However, when this diminishes, she is so intelligent and inscrutable that she repays friendship.'

In the spring of 1919, Virginia noted the queer mixture of amusement and annoyance in her attitude toward Katherine, recognised that Katherine's 'hard composure is much on the surface' and saw that it was, like her own defiant stance, essentially defensive. Both women were high-strung and delicate invalids, childless, lonely, bitter and caustic. But the insecure Colonial, who was frightened by the intellectual aristocrat, pretended to be hard and tough. In May 1920 Virginia wrote in her diary that though Katherine was rather cautious and withdrawn, she found in her an ease and interest lacking in other clever women, shared some of her deepest feelings and values, and could speak to her in a frank and free fashion:

She is of the cat kind; alien, composed, always solitary – observant. And then we talked about solitude and I found her expressing my feelings as I never hear them expressed

. . . . A queer effect she produces of someone apart, entirely self-centred; altogether concentrated upon her 'art': almost fierce about it. . . .

Once more as keenly as ever I feel a common under-standing between us – a queer sense of being 'like', not only about literature, and I think it's independent of grat-ified vanity. I can talk straight out to her.

Katherine's intense observation and egoistic concentration may have alarmed Virginia, but they were absolutely essential to Katherine's art.

Virginia was seriously disappointed in Katherine's story 'Bliss,' which appeared in 1918, rather harshly condemned her superficiality, limited vision and poor style – and then attempted to relate her literary to her personal weaknesses:

Her mind is a very thin soil, laid an inch or two deep upon very barren rock. For Bliss is long enough to give her a chance of going deeper. Instead she is content with super-ficial smartness; and the whole conception is poor, cheap, not the vision, however imperfect, of an interesting mind. She writes badly too. And the effect was as I say, to give me an impression of her callousness and hardness as a human being. . . . Or is it absurd to read all this criticism of her personally into a story?

Virginia, whose view of the story contradicted her earlier view of Katherine's intelligence, realised she was being unfair and expressed a far more generous opinion in her review of Katherine's posthumously published *Journal*, which appeared in 1927, in the *Nation and Athenaeum*: 'No one felt more seri-ously the importance of writing than she did. In all the pages of her journal, instinctive, rapid as they are, her attitude toward her work is admirable, sane, caustic, and austere. There is no literary gossip; no vanity; no jealousy.' It is significant that

Virginia praised Katherine's freedom from the vices frequently associated with Bloomsbury: gossip, vanity and jealousy.

Virginia never realised the agony Katherine suffered when poor health frequently forced her to live apart from Middleton Murry, whom she was unable to marry until 1918. For as Katherine wrote to Murry in November 1919: 'Oh, God, let us try to make this our last separation. At any rate it will be. I'd never bear another. They are too terrible.' Katherine always envied Virginia's happy marriage much more than her artistic genius, and exclaimed: 'No wonder she can write. There is always in her writing a calm freedom of expression as though she were at peace – her roof over her, her posssessions round her, and her man somewhere within call.' Though Virginia certainly had a secure home and devoted husband, Katherine seriously misunderstood the superficial calmness and peace that disguised her internal chaos.

Virginia saw Katherine for the last time in August 1920; and when Katherine died of tuberculosis at the age of thirty-four, Virginia's reaction was insensitive and malicious. She compared herself to Katherine as she had compared herself to Vanessa, admitted that Katherine had aroused her artistic jealousy, egoistically judged Katherine by coldly calculating her fidelity, and wrote in her diary of 16 January 1923:

At that one feels – what? A shock of relief? – a rival the less. . . . Did she care for me? Sometimes she would say so – would kiss me – would look at me as if (is this senti-ment?) her eyes would like always to be faithful. She would promise never never to forget. That was what we said at the end of our last talk. . . . I was jealous of her writing – the only writing I have ever been jealous of. . . . I have the feeling that I shall think of her at intervals all through life. Probably we had something in common which I shall never find in anyone else.

Virginia met Vita Sackville-West the year after Katherine died and was intimate with her throughout the late 1920s, for Vita did not share Katherine's profound commitment to her art and to her husband. She found in Vita, who was also beautiful, arrogant and talented, a woman whose noble birth, aristocratic manner and dashing character were far more impressive than her own. 'Since Virginia's marriage, no-one save Katherine Mansfield had touched her heart at all,' observes Quentin Bell, but toward Vita 'Virginia felt as a lover feels – she desponded when she fancied herself neglected, despaired when Vita was away, waited anxiously for letters, needed Vita's company and lived in that strange mixture of elation and despair which lovers – and one would have supposed only lovers – can experience. All this she had done and felt for Katherine.'

Virginia knew that Vita, though married to the diplomat Harold Nicolson and the mother of two children, was an unequivocal lesbian who had fallen passionately in love with her. And she recorded in her diary of December 1925, with considerable excitement and envy: 'These Sapphists *love* women; friendship is never untinged with amorosity. . . . [She is] in short (what I have never been) a real woman. Then there is some voluptuousness about her.' Vita, who was fascinated by the force of Virginia's spiritual beauty, wrote to her husband, with disarming frankness, in 1926: 'I am scared to death of arousing physical feelings in her, because of the madness. . . . I *have* gone to bed with her (twice) but that's all.' Their physical passion, most probably, neither excited Virginia nor satisfied Vita. Virginia felt it was all rather a bore for Leonard but that he could – and did – tolerate her liaison. And Harold, who could afford to be generous because he was homosexual, told Virginia he was delighted that she and his wife were such great friends.

IV

Though Leonard never felt sorry for himself nor complained to anyone, he had even greater problems than Virginia's sexual frigidity, inability to bear children and lesbian love affairs. For he had willingly undertaken the care of a woman who had been mad and suicidal. He frequently had to neglect his own work as a journalist, editor, publisher, author and politician; and had to bear the intense and continuous strain of regulating Virginia's life, guarding her genius and protecting her sanity. Leonard was forced to assume the role of family ogre, and had to make certain that Virginia followed a perfectly regular routine, ate and slept properly, was not tired by social life and travel, or subject to emotional strain. As he wrote in the third volume of his autobiography, *Beginning Again* (1964): 'If Virginia lived a quiet, vegetative life, eating well, going to bed early, and not tiring herself mentally or physically, she remained perfectly well. But if she tired herself in any way, if she was subjected to any severe physical, mental or emotional strain, symptoms at once appeared which in the ordinary person are negligible and transient, but with her were serious danger signals.'

Many of their friends noticed and admired Leonard's self-less and vigilant concern. William Plomer was 'aware that she was being watched, perhaps with a touch of anxiety, by her husband'; and John Lehmann reports that if Virginia went out for a walk in London without telling him, 'he would become completely distraught.' Alix Strachey, who observed that Leonard strictly laid out Virginia's hours of work and recreation, and attempted to minimise her anxiety, remarked: 'I think she needed someone as firmly anchored mentally as he was and I am sure that he was the only person who could have kept her going.' And Nigel Nicolson thought Leonard behaved 'as if he were looking after a very precious Ming vase which was known once to have been slightly cracked

and which must be handled with immense care.' Though
Virginia submitted to Leonard's firm yet benign rule, she
naturally disliked the feeling 'that I'm always taking care, or
being taken care of.' But she did not have the courage to
venture against his will, for Leonard was at once gentle and
devoted, wise and sympathetic. Virginia respected and loved
him, and believed that Leonard was her superior in every
respect.

Toward the end of 1916, when Leonard decided it would
be good for Virginia to have a manual occupation that would
distract her completely from the intense strain of writing
Night and Day, they both began to learn printing. They
bought a small hand press the following spring, and with the
aid of an instruction pamphlet, published the first book of
the Hogarth Press – Virginia's *The Mark on the Wall* together
with Leonard's *Three Jews* – in July 1917. Their second work
was Katherine Mansfield's *Prelude* (1918); they also printed
and published Eliot's *Poems* (1919) and *The Waste Land*
(1923) as well as works by Forster and Gorky. The Hogarth
Press also published Quentin Bell's biography of Virginia.

John Lehmann, who worked at the press in the early
1930s, failed to realise he had become the innocent victim
of Leonard's repressed anxiety, frustration and hostility, and
saw the worst side of his character. For Leonard had a
'dangerous passion' for efficiency, and treated Lehmann as he
had treated his underlings in Ceylon. Lehmann writes that
he 'could be a very exacting taskmaster, nervy and obstinate
in petty argument,' and he criticised Leonard's 'repeated
invasions of the office, anxious examinations of work being
done, nagging tirades and unnecessary alarms and impa-
tience about what is progressing steadily.' Other friends
mention Leonard's obsessive care with money, which irritated Virginia, for her father, though well off, also suffered
from agonising financial insecurity. After the success of
Orlando in 1928 she noted in her diary: 'For the first time

since I married, 1912–1928 – 16 years, I have been spending money . . . and yet have an agreeable luxurious sense of coins in my pocket beyond my weekly 13/- which was always running out, or being encroached upon.' But she also wrote in 1924, 'Leonard thinks less well of me for powdering my nose and spending money on dress. Never mind, I adore Leonard.'

V

Though Leonard was extremely careful and vigilant, no routine of 'rest' could protect Virginia from the perpetual menace of insanity, for it seemed to him 'as if deep down in her mind she was never completely sane.' Her creativity and genius were closely connected to her fantasies and insanity, and the terrible strain of completing a book would always drive her to the verge of a mental breakdown. She recognised that 'the dark underworld has its fascinations as well as its terrors,' and described her fearful *furor divinus*, or divine madness, on the day she finished *The Waves*: 'having reeled across the last ten pages with some moments of such intensity and intoxication that I seemed only to stumble after my own voice, or almost, after some sort of speaker (as when I was mad) I was almost afraid, remembering the voices that used to fly ahead.'

Virginia was totally dependent on Leonard's judgment of and reassurance about her work; and Leonard, knowing her pathological sensitivity to criticism and her perilous mental balance at the end of an exhausting period of creativity, had to make his appraisals seem rational and impersonal as well as positive and convincing. Virginia, who carefully preserved his cautious and considered opinions in her diary, accepted them with a healthy mixture of scepticism and trust:

L. read it; thinks it my best – but then has he not *got* to think so?

(on *Mrs. Dalloway*, January 1925)

'It's a masterpiece,' said L., coming out to my lodge this morning. 'And the best of your books.'

(on *The Waves*, July 1931)

The miracle is accomplished. L. put down the last sheet about 12 last night; and could not speak. He was in tears. He says it is 'a most remarkable book' – he likes it better than *The Waves*.

(on *The Years*, November 1936)

Though Leonard was certainly impressed by the succession of novels which clearly revealed his wife's artistic genius, he realised that Virginia's very sanity depended upon his opinion of *The Years*. For in June 1936 Virginia had felt the wind of the wing of madness and wrote in her diary: 'Two months dismal and worse, almost catastrophic illness – never been so near the precipice to my own feeling since 1913.' And Leonard affirmed: 'I knew that unless I could give a completely favourable verdict she would be in despair and would have a very serious breakdown. . . . To Virginia I praised the book more than I should have done if she had been well, but I told her exactly what I thought about its length. This gave her enormous relief and, for the moment, exhilaration.' Fortunately, the public liked Virginia's return to the traditional novel much better than Leonard did, and when it was published in America in the autumn of 1937 it became a best-seller and made her really wealthy for the first time in her life.

But there were times when even Leonard's encourage-ment and care could not save Virginia, and she had a nervous breakdown after completing seven years' work on *The Voyage*

Out in 1913 and another after finishing *Between the Acts* in 1941. One of the horrors of her madness was that she was always sufficiently sane to recognise her own insanity. Her attacks usually began with what she called 'the horrors of the dark cupboard of illness': headaches, inability to concentrate, racing pulse, back pains, nervous excitement, exhaustion, insomnia, sedatives, digitalis, recoveries and relapses. Her breakdowns were divided into two distinct manic–depressive phases. In the manic phase she talked incessantly and inco-herently for several days, had delusions, heard voices and was oblivious of everyone. In the depressive stage, writes Leonard: 'she was in the depths of melancholia and despair; she scarcely spoke; refused to eat; refused to believe that she was ill and insisted that her condition was due to her own guilt: at the height of this stage she tried to commit suicide, in the 1895 attack by jumping out of a window, in 1913 by taking an overdose of veronal; in 1941 she drowned herself in the River Ouse.'

During the second phase, when Virginia thought of food as repulsive matter that had to be excreted in a disgusting way, every meal took one or two hours; and Leonard, with paternal patience, had to sit next to her, hand her a fork, quietly encourage her to eat and even move her arm. Though he took every precaution against the possibility of suicide, he could not guard her every moment of the day and night; and on 8 September 1913, a year after her marriage, she swallowed a mortal dose of veronal. As Lytton Strachey wrote to the painter Henry Lamb: 'Virginia tried to kill herself last Tuesday, and was only saved by a series of acci-dents. She took 100 grains of veronal and also an immense quantity of an even more dangerous drug – medinal. The doctors at one time thought there was very little hope. But she recovered, and is apparently not seriously the worse for it. Woolf has been having a most dreadful time for the last month or so, culminating in this.' The doctors wanted to certify Virginia as insane, but Leonard persuaded them that he could care for her.

Virginia's third mental breakdown lasted in an acute form from mid-1913 to late 1915. In the last year, when her condition was at its worst, she needed as many as four nurses in the house for months on end, was constantly visited by specialists and spent more than £500 on medical bills. In many ways, Leonard writes, '1914 and 1915 were years which we simply lost out of our lives, for we lived them in the atmosphere of catastrophe or impending catastrophe.' When she began to recover and heard Leonard bringing her breakfast in bed, Virginia bravely tried to 'simulate, for myself as well as for him, great cheerfulness.' It is hardly suprising that Leonard, who had always suffered from trembling hands that sometimes prevented him from filling teacups or signing his name, finally broke under the strain, and in March 1914 he also had a nervous breakdown 'in a mild way.'

VI

In 1940, Leonard and Virginia agreed to asphyxiate them-selves with the fumes of their car if Germany invaded and defeated England. Though they were never forced to this extreme, Virginia, for entirely different reasons, experienced a terrible depression and despair, had her fourth serious breakdown early in 1941, and drowned herself in a Sussex river on 28 March. That morning she wrote Leonard a poignant, final letter in which she diagnosed her own help-less madness, expressed her intense guilt about ruining his life and work, explained that her suicide was a sacrifice to save him from another struggle against insanity, and thanked him for the devotion and happiness he had given her:

Dearest,
I feel certain that I am going mad again. I feel we can't go

through another of those terrible times. And I shan't recover this time. I begin to hear voices, and I can't concentrate. So I am doing what seems the best thing to do. You have given me the greatest possible happiness. You have been in every way all that anyone could be. I don't think two people could have been happier till this terrible disease came. I can't fight any longer. I know that I am spoiling your life, that without me you could work. And you will I know. You see I can't even write this properly. I can't read. What I want to say is I owe all the happiness of my life to you. You have been entirely patient with me and incredibly good. I want to say that – everybody knows it. If anybody could have saved me it would have been you. Everything has gone from me but the certainty of your goodness. I can't go on spoiling your life any longer. I don't think two people could have been happier than we have been.

Her body was recovered three weeks later when some children saw it floating in the River Ouse.

Leonard, who had great patience, courage, strength of character and personal integrity, was the moral hero of the Bloomsbury Group; and E. M. Forster rightly felt he was undervalued by Virginia's friends. Though his personality was very different from Virginia's, their complementary unity and personal harmony were extraordinary, their sympathies extremely close, and their love profound. As Virginia wrote to Leonard in April 1923, when they were separated for a few days: 'I lie & think of my precious beast, who does make me more happy every day & instant of my life than I thought it possible to be. There's no doubt I'm terribly in love with you. I keep thinking what you're doing, & I have to stop – it makes me want to kiss you so.' It does not in any way detract from Virginia's achievement to say that she never could have realised her potential and accomplished her work without

Leonard's code of duty, faith in her art, and belief in his ability to encourage, sustain and even cure her.

When their friend William Plomer observed, 'Those who have known Leonard and Virginia Woolf have known civilisation,' he suggested their contrast to the ethos of Bloomsbury, whose love was predominantly homosexual and whose marriages were adulterous. The Woolfs' marriage was certainly characterised by rationalism, order, mutual respect, tolerance, kindness, devotion, sacrifice and courage. But it was also besieged, like a doomed and isolated fortress, by frigidity, barrenness, perversity, illness, madness and suicide. The 'wisest decision' of Virginia's life was not the wisest of Leonard's, for she was never able to unite the world of dreams and of reality, and remained, as she had feared, an 'eccentric and emotionally undeveloped human being.'

Katherine Mansfield and
John Middleton Murry
NAUSICAA AND POLYPHEME

'We have a relationship which is unique but it is not
what the world understands by *MARRIAGE*.'

KATHERINE to Murry

Katherine Mansfield was a passionate and tragic woman who
controlled her art but could not regulate her life. Aldous
Huxley perceived that 'she was an unhappy woman, capable
of acting any number of parts but uncertain of who, essentially, she was.' And he portrayed these contradictory characteristics – the conventional and bohemian sides of her
personality – when he satirised her as Mary Thriplow in
Those Barren Leaves (1925): She 'was at once oldfashioned and
tremendously contemporary, school-girlish and advanced,
demure and more than Chelsea-ishly emancipated. . . . He
liked her combination of moral ingenuousness and mental

sophistication, of cleverness and genuineness.' Katherine's
good friend, S. S. Koteliansky, believed that her character was
more interesting than her work. Though Bertrand Russell
agreed with Kot, he emphasised the malicious and sometimes frightening side of her character: 'Her talk was marvellous, much better than her writing, especially when she was
telling of the things that she was going to write, but when
she spoke about people she was envious, dark and full of
alarming penetration in discovering what they least wished
known and whatever was bad in their characteristics.'

Lytton Strachey, who also had a cruel wit, called Katherine
'an odd satirical woman . . . very difficult to get at'; Ottoline
Morrell thought her 'very envious and jealous'; and to
Virginia Woolf she seemed 'an unpleasant but forcible &
utterly unscrupulous character.' Even the adoring Dorothy
Brett, who speaks with the authority of a victim, mentions
her biting anger, her 'ironic ruthlessness toward small minds
and less agile brains. . . . Katherine had a tongue like a knife,
she could cut the very heart out of one with it.' But most of
Katherine's friends failed to realise that her black rages and
cruel speeches were the outward expression of the constant
pain of her disease. Only after Katherine's death did Virginia
Woolf admit, 'I never gave her credit for all her physical
suffering and the effect it must have had in embittering her.'
The central conflict in both the character and work of
Katherine Mansfield was between the remote, restrained and
forbidding figure who frightened people and the lonely,
isolated and often helpless child who was herself frightened
of life and of death; between the savage satirist of German
crudity and marital cruelty, and the nostalgic sentimentalist
of childhood life in New Zealand.

Katherine's bizarre relationship with John Middleton
Murry, literary critic and editor of the *Athenaeum*, was the
central event of her life. Murry accurately characterised
himself as 'Part snob, part coward, part sentimentalist,' as if the

confession justified the failings. Katherine called him 'a monk without a monastery' and said he 'couldn't fry a sausage without thinking about God.' He had an endless capacity for self-deception, a total egocentricity behind his mock saintliness and was always eager to display his stigmata before the public. As Katherine impatiently exclaimed: 'When you know you are a voice crying in the wilderness, *cry*, but don't say "I am a voice crying in the wilderness."' The conflict between Katherine's fierce independence and her need for Murry's emotional support continued until the end of her life; and she could never fully engage Murry's feelings until, after her death, he invented the cult of Katherine and transformed her into a convenient and manageable symbol.

Katherine's ambiguous attitude toward her provincial yet exotic New Zealand background was characterised by an early desire to escape its restrictions and a late longing to return to the primary source of her creative inspiration. She was born in Wellington in 1888 and attended school there until she was fifteen, when she was sent to London to complete her education. Her cosmopolitan experience seemed to emphasise the philistine vulgarity of her native land when she returned there in 1906; and she decided to be as obnoxious as possible in order to force her stern and taste-less parents to allow her to return to England. As she complained in her schoolgirl prose:

They are worse than I had even expected. They are prying and curious, they are watchful and they discuss only the food. They quarrel between themselves in a hopelessly vulgar fashion. My Father spoke of my returning as damned rot, said look here, he wouldn't have me fooling around in dark corners with fellows. His hands, covered with long sandy hair, are absolutely cruel hands. A physically revolted feeling seizes me. He wants me to sit near.

He watches me at meals, eats in the most abjectly blatantly vulgar manner that is describable. . . . *She* is constantly suspicious, constantly overbearingly tyrannous.

Katherine's rather crude strategy eventually succeeded; and in 1908 her father agreed to provide an allowance of £100 a year and she left New Zealand for ever.

Katherine's attitude toward her father, a self-made tycoon whom she called 'the richest man in New Zealand, and the meanest,' influenced her attitude toward men just as his financial support (which provided money instead of love) led to emotional insecurity. 'I feel towards my Pa-man like a little girl,' she wrote in 1913. 'I want to jump and stamp on his chest and cry "You've got to love me."' When her father visited her in November 1919 in Ospedaletti, where she was seriously ill and living in impoverished circumstances, she was tempted by the luxurious life she had abandoned to become a writer: 'I was, I am, just a little corrupted, Bogey darling,' she told her husband. 'That big soft purring motor [car], the rugs and cushions, the warmth, the delicacy, all the uglies so far away.' She had counted on her father's generosity and after she had served him lunch, he criticised her villa, complained of the cold and left her five cigarettes.

Her father first stopped, and then reduced, her allowance when she received the first small royalties for 'Bliss' in 1921; and after she died of tuberculosis, which was exacerbated by the poverty that could easily have been eliminated by her father, he bequeathed £6000 (more than four times the amount he had given his daughter) towards the establishment of a National Picture Gallery in Wellington. In *The Little Girl* (1912) she wrote that the father 'was a figure to be feared and avoided', and she was determined to shape her life and marriage so that it would not, like her invalid mother's, be dominated by a powerful male ego.

While still at school in Wellington Katherine developed a passion for a beautiful half-caste Maori girl named Maata, who was the subject of her unfinished novel, and (as an entry from her journal reveals) her feelings were roused again in 1907:

Do other people of my age feel as I do I wonder so absolutely powerful *licentious* so almost physically ill – I alone in this silent clock filled room have become powerfully – I want Maata I want her – and I have had her – terribly – this is unclean I know but true. What an extraordinary thing – I feel savagely crude – and almost powerfully enamoured of the child.

Katherine's guilt-ridden lesbianism continued throughout her adult life, most notably with Ida Baker, the daughter of a London doctor, whom she had met at Queens College in 1903 and renamed 'Lesley Moore.' Ida worshipped Katherine, quite literally devoted her life to her and was at once lover, friend, nurse, slave and scapegoat. She became a buffer between Katherine and the harsh world of men, and cared for her during the long periods of sickness and separation from Murry. Katherine inevitably came to resent her dependence on the rather dull-witted and gluttonous Ida (who was literally starved for affection) and deflected her anger at Murry on to her friend, who reciprocated Katherine's bitter cruelty with a cringing self-abasement. As Katherine complained to Murry:

Meal times and walk times are quite enough to exasperate me and lash me into fury beyond measure. 'Katie mine, who is Wordsworth? Must I like him? It's no good looking cross because I love you, my angel, from the little tip of that cross eyebrow to the *all* of you. When am I going to brush your hair again?' I shut my teeth and say 'Never!' but

I really *do* feel that if she could she'd EAT me. . . . It is impossible to describe to you my curious hatred and antagonism to her – gross, trivial, dead to all that is alive for me, ignorant and *false*.

Katherine truly claimed Ida as 'the person I flew to with bad tempers, worries, depressions, money troubles, wants, rages, silences' and admitted 'I take advantage of you – demand perfection of you – crush you.' But Ida, who could not bear to be separated from her beloved, apologised for her abusive behaviour and sympathetically explained: 'It must have been dreadful for the poor darling, banging away on putty.'

Katherine portrayed Ida in 'Psychology' (1918) in which the heroine fails to re-establish an intimate rapport with her all-too-'spiritual' lover and has the unsatisfactory compensation of 'an elderly virgin, a pathetic creature who simply idolised her (heaven knows why) and had this habit of turning up and ringing the bell and then saying, when she opened the door: "My dear, send me away!" She never did.' In the *Scrapbook* Katherine projects on to Ida some of her own guilt about the conflict between the spirit and the flesh, and writes, 'Her body was obedient [to the touch], but how slowly and gravely it obeyed, as though protesting against the urge of her brave spirit.' Katherine could never bring herself to send Ida away because she desperately needed the love that she failed to get from her father and her husband.

While still in New Zealand Katherine recorded, 'Does Oscar now keep so firm a stronghold in my soul?'; and once in Wilde's bohemian London 'the little Colonial' revolted against her family's Victorian respectability ('he wouldn't have me fooling around in dark corners with fellows') with a self-punishing sexual extremism that both craved and repudiated men. In 1908 she was deeply wounded by a passionate and pathetic love affair with Garnet Trowell, the brother of a New Zealand musical prodigy who had rejected her. When she got pregnant, Garnet abandoned her and she became panic-stricken and permanently embittered. Then, quite suddenly in March 1909, she dressed entirely in black and married George Bowden. Though ten years older than Katherine, he naively believed 'Her mind would be somewhere above her body.' But she was completely frigid on her wedding night and left Bowden the very next morning. She satirised Bowden, who was a singing teacher, in 'Mr. Reginald Peacock's Day'; and explained her impulsive one-day marriage in a *Scrapbook* sketch of 1915:

> 'Then I got ill, and my voice went – and a hard time came,' she said. 'And then you know, out of pure cowardice – yes, really – I couldn't fight any more and I hadn't the courage to – I married.' Louise turned her grave glance to her. 'I didn't love him a bit,' said Nina, shaking her head, – 'just because I was afraid'. . . . 'And then – oh well, it served me right – he was a brute and my –' she hesitated a second, 'my baby died and I left him.'

Bowden was, in fact, tolerant rather than brutish, and she left him *before* rather than after the baby died. Katherine's mother was alarmed when the news of the marriage reached New Zealand, sailed to London, and found that her daughter had joined the chorus of a travelling light-opera company, and was destitute and pregnant. In order to avoid a scandal, she sent her daughter to Bad Wörishofen, a fashionable but conveniently obscure spa, fifty miles west of Munich. There Katherine miscarried and convalesced; and in these miserable circumstances wrote the bitterly satiric sketches, *In a German Pension* (1911), which emphasised the gruesome details of childbirth. Katherine felt guilty about the sordid squandering of her 'inward purity,' and while 'doing her stunts' (as the painter Mark Gertler called it), she would weep and throw herself about wailing: 'I am a soiled woman.'

Most of Katherine's friends had never seen her confessional 'Russian' moods, for she was usually quiet, controlled, cautious and, according to Leonard Woolf, 'perpetually on her guard against a world which she assumed to be hostile' – and which frequently was. In *Those Barren Leaves*, Huxley describes her features as 'small and regular, the eyes dark brown; and their arched brows looked as though they had been painted on to the porcelain mask by an oriental brush. Her hair was nearly black. . . . Her uncovered ears were quite white and very small. It was an inexpressive face, the face of a doll, but of an exceedingly intelligent doll.' After Katherine's death in 1923 her friend and rival, Virginia Woolf, condescendingly recorded in her diary: 'Hers were beautiful eyes – rather dog-like, brown, very wide apart, with a steady slow rather faithful and sad expression. Her nose was sharp, a little vulgar. Her lips thin and hard.' Frieda Lawrence called her 'exquisite,' Frank Swinnerton also mentioned her 'porcelain delicacy' and, like Frieda, emphasised her sweetness, sympathy and capacity for affection. Victor Pritchett, misled by the qualities that Katherine often chose to emphasise rather than conceal, quite mistakenly calls her 'the exquisite colonial, the prim exile, who belongs neither to England nor to New Zealand.' Though illnesses gave her a frail and delicate appearance, her character was more tough than exquisite, more like Simone Weil's than like Camille's. She was cynical, amoral, ribald and witty – not prim; and she belonged very much to New Zealand as well as to England.

Murry's weakness, insecurity, dependence, timidity and naivety aroused Katherine's maternal feelings when they first met in 1912, after he had requested one of her stories for his avant-garde magazine, *Rhythm*. She immediately assumed the dominant role, invited him to live with her and eventually seduced him. When she asked Murry: 'Why don't you make me your mistress?' he primly replied: 'I feel it would spoil – everything'; and when she added: 'So do I,' he missed her subtle irony. 'I had been the man and he had been the woman,' she wrote in her *Scrapbook*, 'and he had been called upon to make no real efforts. He had never really "supported" me. When we first met, in fact, it was I who kept him.' Yet Katherine needed the protection and support Murry was never able to give her, for he guarded his personality against her emotional onslaughts and developed his tendency to resist and withdraw from her. When she was ill, she frequently condemned Murry for his selfishness, and lack of warmth and responsiveness; but when relatively healthy she tended to be understanding and to blame herself for the burden she imposed upon him. As she wrote to her friend, Violet Schiff:

[I am a woman] who instead of 'looking after' the other has made demands upon a man who confesses he has very little vitality to spare and doesn't ultimately care for people except as symbols. Who finds that after all, he doesn't in the least desire her kind of life – but wants to be a scholar and live quietly, remotely, writing poetic drama, growing learned – and feeling that she is by and sympathetic but does not interfere. . . . Oh how well I understand this jealous passionate love of himself, this absorption and tenderness – which comes from his wretched childhood and poor stifled youth.

The Murrys' emotional problems were exacerbated by their impoverished and itinerant life. Katherine earned almost nothing from her writing and Murry had no adequate salary until he became editor of the *Athenaeum* in 1919; and they had nearly a dozen addresses during their first two years together. When Murry's lively but short-lived *Rhythm* collapsed under a debt of £400, Katherine agreed to pay her next four years' allowance to the printers. Yet Murry, who grew up in poverty and was miserly, insisted that they keep their finances separately, and he rarely contributed anything to his wife's support. When Katherine was seriously ill in 1920 and wired Murry for £10, he sent the money as an advance against her book reviews, and she angrily replied: 'I would perfectly understand your *money is tight* had I NOT consumption, a weak heart, and chronic neuritis in my lower limbs.' The following spring she wrote an exasperated yet witty letter to Ida Baker in which she compared Murry's stinginess and lack of decent feelings with her father's:

> Just now – making out the week's bills he asked me for 11 francs for the carriage – half – plus a 2 franc tip! I think it's awful to have to say it. But fancy not paying for your wife's carriage to and from the surgery! Is that simply extraordinary or am I? I really am staggered. I think it is the meanest thing I ever heard of. It's not the fact which is so queer but the lack of fine feeling. I suppose if one fainted he would make one pay 3d for a 6d glass of salvolatile and 1d on the glass. That really does beat father.

Katherine, who wrote about childhood and cultivated childishness, sought refuge from the unpleasant realities of poverty and illness in a fantasy world of pet names (Bogey and Wig), favourite pets and dolls (Wingley and Ribni) and unreal plans for a permanent home (The Heron) and for a baby, which she believed would solve all their problems. Murry was inept in bed – his biographer describes their sex life (such as it was) as a climax without a crescendo – and when they finally realised they could not have a child, Katherine, who was anxious to hide her past life, put the blame on Murry. He accepted it; and never found out about the abortion she had had in 1911, which may have led to her sterility (he later had several children) until the publication of Katherine's biography in 1954.

The husband in 'A Married Man's Story' (1923) says: 'Though one might suspect her of strong maternal feelings, my wife doesn't seem to me the type of woman who bears children in her own body.' But the dream – and the symbol – of the baby persisted. In 1915 she dreamed of having a dead baby; and two years later told Murry, 'we shall have to have all our babies in pairs so that we possess a complete set in either place' – for security. In November 1919 Katherine insisted, 'We *must* have children – we *must*'; and when Murry sent one of his cruellest letters the followmg month, the deeply wounded Katherine translated it into the metaphor of a dead child: 'I'd say we had a child – a love-child, and it's dead. We may have other children, but this child can't be made to live again. J. [her cousin] says: Forget that letter! How can I? It killed the child – *killed* it *really* and *truly* for ever as far as I am concerned.' And as late as 1922, during the terminal phase of her disease and the last year of her life, she combined her fantasies about Russia, Chekhov (her literary father) and babies into an impossible but revealing wish: 'I want to adopt a Russian baby, call him Anton, and bring him up as mine, with Kot for a godfather and Mme. Tchehov for a godmother. Such is my dream.' Katherine, who had briefly adopted a child in Germany after her miscarriage in 1909, felt a child would help to ease the anguish of disease and solitude.

Though Murry recognised that Katherine was his moral, artistic and intellectual superior, he was totally self-absorbed, took the best study for himself and left all the household affairs to his wife. When they travelled together and Murry made the arrangements, he was more a hindrance than a help. En route to Switzerland in 1922, Murry gave away a 500 franc note instead of a 50, and allowed Katherine to get thoroughly drenched on the way from the station to the hotel. Katherine, who was disgusted by the squalid atmosphere of their dingy flats, told him, 'You don't want my love

– not my living love – you only want an "idea."' And Murry weakly confessed, 'I feel that the kind of unearthly love I'm inclined to ends inevitably in disaster.'

Though Katherine was dreadfully lonely during the winter of 1917–18, counted the days until she could come home, and then was trapped in Paris for three weeks during the German bombardment of the city, Murry was insensitive and indifferent to her feelings when she finally returned to England to marry him in April 1918, and packed her off to Cornwall after their wedding. 'Our marriage,' she tried to explain to him, when the sea stank and grey crabs scuttled on the rocks and the paths had been fouled by human excrement,

> Our marriage. . . . You cannot imagine what that was to have meant to me. It's fantastic – I suppose. It was to have shone – apart from all else in my life. And it really was only part of the nightmare, after all. You never once held me in your arms and called me your wife. In fact, the whole affair was like my silly birthday. I had to keep on making you remember it.

The only time they were really happy, when they were living together in a lovely place and both working well, was at the Villa Pauline in Bandol in the early months of 1916; and the only time Katherine ever had a home of her own was at 'The Elephant' in Hampstead in 1919.

Though Katherine was sustained by these happy moments and retained her belief in marriage, she had left Murry in the spring of 1915 when she thought she was in love with Francis Carco. Carco, born Carcopino-Tusoli in 1886 on the Pacific island of New Caledonia (north of New Zealand), was a popular novelist of low-life in Montmartre. Murry had first met him during his student days in Paris in 1910, and had introduced him to Katherine during their brief, disastrous stay in that city just before the War. Katherine was attracted to Carco's bohemianism, his self-confidence and his warm, sensational life – so different from Murry's priggish repression. She carried on a highly charged correspondence with Carco during 1914, when she was unhappy with Murry, who admits he 'did not need Katherine in the way she then believed she required to be needed. . . . She wanted me to remain an innocent lover: and then got bored [and frustrated] with me for being an unexciting one.' In January 1915 she dreamed of Carco while in bed with Murry, and wrote in her *Journal*, 'I deliberately drugged myself with Jack and made it more bearable by talking French.' During a party at Gilbert Cannan's the same month, the handsome Mark Gertler recorded, 'Katherine and myself – both very drunk – made passionate love to each other in front of everybody!' D. H. Lawrence, who was one of the guests, was furious at Murry's shameless indifference, pulled him into the corner and exclaimed: 'Are you blind? If not, how dare you expose yourself?'

Carco had joined the French army when the war broke out and wrote Katherine passionate letters from Grey, between Dijon and Besançon, where he was ignobly serving as postman to a bakery unit. He urged Katherine to visit him, and in February 1915 (without any protest from Murry) she made her way to Paris and then into the war zone, where women were forbidden. The trip was agonising, for the train passed slowly through stations where the wounded were waiting to be rescued. Katherine had some brief but ecstatic moments with Carco, and on 20 February wrote a suggestive passage in her *Journal*: 'And F. quite naked – making up the fire with a tiny poker – so natural, so beautiful. . . . Then he was gone. This is a terrible moment for a woman.' But Carco, whom she imagined would be her 'deliverer,' turned out to be as selfish as Murry, and only three days later she returned home, deeply disillusioned and

bitterly hurt by both the egoism of Carco and the indifference of Murry.

In Carco's novel, *Les Innocents* (1916), Winnie (Katherine)
is portrayed as a lesbian who has an affair with Beatrice
(Beatrice Hastings) and as a 'poule de luxe' who lives with
Milord (Carco), pays for everything and parasitically uses him
as raw material for her writing: 'Elle n'aimait pas le Milord,
mais se sentait amoureuse, pour son livre, de tout ce qui
formait sa vie mystérieuse. Elle vivait ce qu'elle écrivait et,
peut-être, était-elle jalouse de ce qui détachait le Milord de
sa malsaine curiosité.' Though Carco later softened his
description of Katherine in *Mémoires d'une autre vie* (1942),
to fit the rather sentimental French legend that had developed after her death, there is no doubt that his earlier
portrayal is the more accurate reflection of his feelings.

Katherine's bitter and personal story, 'Je ne parle pas
français' (1919), expresses her profoundest fears, and settles
some scores with both Carco and Murry. The first-person
narration is essentially a revelation of the loathsome and
epicene character of Raoul Duquette (Carco), who egoistically confides, 'without my clothes I am rather charming.
Plump, almost like a girl, with smooth shoulders, and I wear
a thin gold bracelet above my left elbow.' He is the author of
the rather sinister-sounding *False Coins, Wrong Doors* and *Left
Umbrellas* and is, by his own admission, superficial, impudent
and cheap, boastful, cynical and calculating.

Dick Harmon (Murry) has a 'dreary half smile on his lips'
that barely disguises his weak and treacherous character. He
runs away to Paris with the frail and exquisite, childlike and
terribly vulnerable Mouse (Katherine), and is met at the
station by Duquette, who takes them to their hotel. Dick then
abandons Mouse, leaving a letter that feebly explains, 'I can't
kill my mother! Not even for you' (shades of D. H. Lawrence!).

When Mouse tells Raoul that it is impossible to go home
because all her friends think she is married, he ambiguously

promises to come back the next morning to 'take care of you a little.' But he thinks better of it when he realises how little he can get out of it for himself. Mouse, abandoned by both men and quite helpless – 'Je ne parle pas français' – is in a desperate state and may even be forced to give herself to some 'dirty old gallant' whose promises would match those of Raoul and Dick. The story, as Katherine told Murry, is *a cry against corruption. . .* I mean corruption in the widest sense of the word' – a protest against moral perversion that leads to personal betrayal.

A second emotional crisis, and one of the major turning points in Katherine's life, occurred in the autumn of 1915. Her younger brother, Leslie (who was born in 1894), had joined the British Army in New Zealand and come to England for training en route to the war in France. Though they had not been very close as children, their meetings were happy and largely nostalgic, and they spent most of their time reminiscing about their early life in New Zealand.

On 7 October, a week after he arrived at the front, Leslie was blown to bits while giving a hand grenade demonstration. This particularly horrible, meaningless and even ludicrous death had a profound effect on Katherine. She developed a fanatical cult of her brother in which she longed to join him in death: 'First, my darling, I've got things to do for both of us, and then I will come as quickly as I can . . . . The present and the future mean nothing to me. . . . The only possible value anything can have for me is that it should put me in mind of something that happened or was when he was alive.' Though Leslie's death turned her thoughts back to her native country and inspired some of her finest stories, Katherine also carried her posthumous adoration to the pathological extreme of rejecting Murry for Leslie, as if they were interchangeable. In one of her frequent *Journal* entries addressed to her brother she said: 'You know I can never be Jack's lover again. You have me. You're in my flesh as well as in my soul. I give Jack my "surplus" love, but to you I hold and to you I give my deepest love. Jack is no more than . . . anybody might be.' Murry, reduced to insignificance by Leslie's ghost, was more confused and helpless than ever, and he admitted that her brother, 'though dead was far more real and near to her than I was now; and that was anguish to me.'

Despite Katherine's genuine grief, there was something false as well as morbid about it, for her adoration of Leslie really exemplified the way she wanted Murry to love *her*. (She adopted Leslie's second name, Heron, as the name of their private press and their never-to-be-found dream house.) Though Katherine criticised Viginia Woolf's *Night and Day* (1919) for leaving the war out, her own works do not deal with or reflect the war either. She was oblivious to the cataclysm until it affected her personal life – and even afterwards. Though the battle of Verdun was raging while the Murrys lived blissfully in Bandol in the spring of 1916, they never once mention it. As Huxley shrewdly writes of Katherine in *Those Barren Leaves*: 'She was proud of being able to suffer so much; she encouraged her suffering. This sudden recollection of Jim [Leslie], when he was a little boy . . . was a sign of her exquisite sensibility.' It is ironic that Katherine made, or pretended to make, a deeper emotional commitment to her dead brother than she ever made to Carco or Ida (who was also called Lesley) or even to Murry.

The winter of 1915 was the first that Katherine spent in a warmer climate, outside England. These annual separations put an almost intolerable strain on her, for she could not stand either the solitude or the essential companionship of Ida, who always seemed to make things worse. Murry's fourth wife, Mary, attempted to answer one of the central questions of their marriage – why Murry left her alone and ill in a foreign country – by explaining 'It was of paramount importance that her lover should earn some money.' But since Murry rarely gave Katherine any money, it would be more accurate to say that though he recognised her genius, he was unaware of her fears, hopes and needs, and was unwilling to make the inconvenient sacrifices that were necessary to sustain her. As Katherine wrote in her *Scrapbook*:

> We were not *pure*. If we had been, he would have faced coming away with me. And that he would not do. He would not have said he was too tired to earn enough to keep us here. He always refused to face what it meant – living alone for two years on not much money. He said, and three-quarters of him believed: 'I couldn't stand the strain of it with you ill.' But it was a lie, and a confession that all was not well with us.

Katherine, who seemed to spend 'half of my life arriving at strange hotels. And asking if I may go to bed immediately,' recognised that Murry 'has not this same great devouring need of me that I have of him. He *can* exist apart from me . . . . He will never realise that I am only WELL when we are "together."' She quoted Marlowe's 'Lone women like to empty houses perish,' and Keats' prophetic letter to Fanny Brawne: 'They talk of my going to Italy. 'Tis certain I shall never recover if I am to be so long separate from you.' She reminded Murry of her invalid mother whose illness was palliated by family, friends, home and possessions – 'and I've not one of these things. I have only my work.' And she envied Virginia Woolf who was sustained, in her work and her phases of madness, by the devotion and constant companionship of her husband. Katherine often felt, thinking of all the times they had sworn never to part again, that she would rather come back to England and die there than remain alone.

The darkest moment in their marriage came in December 1919 when Murry responded with characteristic indifference to Katherine's desperate *cri de coeur*. She then sent him her most moving poem, a ballad called 'The New Husband,' in which she is a helpless child abandoned by Murry and 'rescued' by death:

> Someone came to me and said
> Forget, forget that you've been wed.
> Who's your man to leave you be
> Ill and cold in a far country?
> Who's the husband – who's the stone
> Could leave a child like you alone?

Fortunately, Katherine was rescued by her wealthy Catholic cousin who recognised her condition and took her from Ospedaletti (where she had been firing a revolver to give herself courage) to her luxurious villa in Menton:

I have got away from that hell of isolation, from the awful singing at night, from the loneliness and fright. To tell you the truth, I think I have been *mad*, but really, medically mad. A great awful cloud has been on me. . . . It's nearly killed me. Yes. When J[ennie] took me in her arms today she cried as well as I. I felt as though I'd been through some awful deathly strain, and just survived – been rescued from drowning or something like that.

Though Katherine, who compared her hellish state to madness and drowning, knew the truth of their relationship – 'it's only on the rarest occasions that we have any confidential intercourse' – she nevertheless believed 'on my death bed, I shall regret the time we didn't have together.'

The following winter, when Katherine returned to Menton, Murry appears to have had an affair with Princess Elizabeth Bibesco, the married daughter of the wartime prime minister, Herbert Asquith. While Katherine felt 'I have to be physically faithful because my body wouldn't admit anyone else – even to kiss *really*, you know,' Murry complained to Elizabeth: '*How* one is starved for [feminine warmth] when one has spent years tending, and anxious for, a sick wife!' When Katherine discovered his infidelity she was deeply shocked at 'the lack of sensitiveness as far as I am concerned – the selfishness of this staggers me.'

Katherine told Murry to act as he pleased as long as he did not tell her about it, but Elizabeth, in a desperate effort to win Murry (who remained passive, as usual) wrote accusingly to Katherine and asked how 'a sick woman, away in France and quite unable to make any kind of happiness for Murry, how dared she try to hold him?' Katherine tried to remain dignified and replied in a rather arch tone: 'I have no desire to come between them only she must not make love to him while he is living with me, because that is undignified,' but her attempt at objectivity merely revealed the depths of her bitterness.

But the greatest trial for Katherine as well as for Murry was her tuberculosis. Murry was more than half in love with *Katherine*'s easeful death, which he dispassionately regarded 'not merely as a foregone conclusion, but as part of a necessary educative experience'. 'You see Jack "accepts" it,' Katherine told Ida, 'it even suits him that I should be so subdued and helpless. And it is deadly to know he NEVER tries to help.'

> I cough and cough. . . . Life is – getting a new breath. . . . And J. is silent, hangs his head, hides his face with his fingers *as though* it were unendurable. 'That is what she is doing to me! Every fresh sound makes *my* nerves wince.' I know he can't help these feelings. But, oh God! how wrong they are. If he could only for a minute, serve me, help me, give *himself* up. . . . It's like having a cannonball tied to one's feet when one is trying not to drown.

Katherine quite naturally resented Murry's 'romantic' feeling that she was doomed to die (so he could 'learn'), his self-pity and his lack of love and understanding, but her independent spirit felt guilty about imposing herself upon him.

Katherine's problems in living *with* Murry when she had tuberculosis were as great as those when living apart from him. She had been forced to leave a hotel in San Remo because of her disease and had to pay to have the room disinfected; and says she understands Shakespeare's line – 'To *rot* itself with motion' – 'better than I care to. I mean – alas! I have proof of it in my own being.' Despite this self-disgust, she tried to reassure Murry by quoting a doctor who said that tuberculosis transferred from a wife to a husband 'was so rare as to be absolutely left out of account.' This, of course, runs counter to all medical evidence, for as Dr Benjamin Goldberg writes in *Clinical Tuberculosis*: 'Husbands and wives in marital contact with tuberculosis . . . are infected five to nine times as often as persons with no known contact with the disease.' It is not surprising, therefore, that Murry was frightened and even disgusted by Katherine, as she was quick to perceive: 'Do you remember when you put your handkerchief to your lips and turned away from me? . . . You are always pale, exhausted, in a kind of anguish of set fatigue when I am by. Now I feel in your letters this is lifting and you are breathing again. "She's away and she is famously 'all right.'" Now I can get on.' Murry's fourth wife testifies to the 'lack of any physical expression of their love which her illness imposed upon them.'

Murry weakly acquiesced in Katherine's self-deception about her disease and by doing so hastened her death. In Katherine's time the only treatment for tuberculosis was similar to the regimen described in *The Magic Mountain* (1924) and consisted of rest cure, proper diet, fresh air and collapse therapy (pneumothorax). X-rays were not widely used for diagnosis until the thirties, and advanced techniques in pulmonary surgery and chemotherapy (especially the discovery of streptomycin in 1944) were not employed until the late forties. In October 1918, eight months after her first haemorrhage, which followed her second acute attack of pleurisy, an English doctor told her the truth, recommended the only possible treatment that might save her life, and warned her about what would happen if she did not follow his advice: 'Climate means nothing. Discipline everything. If she will go somewhere for a year and submit to discipline, then she has about an even chance. If not, she has two or three years to live – four at the outside.' Murry then relates their conversation:

> 'He says I must go into a sanatorium,' she said. 'I can't. A sanatorium would *kill* me.' Then she darted a quick, fearful glance at me. 'Do you want me to go?'
> 'No,' I said dully. 'What's the good?'
> 'You do believe it would kill me?'
> 'Yes, I do,' I said.
> 'You do believe I shall get well?'
> 'Yes,' I said. . . .
> Did I really believe that she would get well? I did not know. What I did know was that I must say so, again and again – for ever.

Katherine, who never even gave up smoking, not only believed that the sterile regimen of a sanatorium would kill her ('It's a 2nd lunatic asylum to me . . . being alone, cut off, ill with the other ill'), but that it would also extinguish her creative inspiration. Though Arthur Koestler writes of George Orwell, who died of tuberculosis in 1950, 'Had he followed the advice of doctors and friends and lived in the self-indulgent atmosphere of a Swiss sanatorium, his master-piece [*1984*] could not have been written – nor any of his former books,' Orwell wrote most of *1984* in British sanatoria, and Robert Louis Stevenson, John Addington Symonds and James Elroy Flecker all continued to write while being treated for tuberculosis in Davos.

Katherine's medical history from 1918 to 1923 was marked by a steady deterioration of her disease combined with a desperate and pathetic search for a medical, a 'miraculous' and finally a mystical cure for tuberculosis. Her ineffectual daily routine in the 'mild' winter climate of the French and Italian Rivieras, which were often bitterly cold with rain, wind, fog and air like acid, was to rise at noon, lie down on a sofa till six, and then take a hot-water bottle to bed.

In 1919 Dr Foster said she stood a reasonable chance. In 1920 the vividly alive Dr Bouchage, who also had the disease and seemed like a plant the frost had laid a finger on, recommended paraffin and iodine, a procedure, writes Dr Goldberg, 'to be condemned and never employed.' No wonder, then, that Katherine wrote to Ottoline Morrell in May 1921: 'I've just paid little B[ouchage] 2,000 francs for looking after me and I'm 50 times worse than I was at Christmas.' In the spring of 1921 she went to Montana, in Switzerland, to try the Spahlinger treatment, which attempted to stimulate the patient's antibodies with vaccines and serums, but this was also useless. In 1922 she heard from Koteliansky about the Russian doctor, Manoukhin, who tried to cure tuberculosis by the application of x-rays to the spleen. Like most 'revolutionary' treatments of that time, it did much more harm than good because the powerful x-rays could neither be precisely focussed nor controlled.

In a letter to Beatrice Campbell, Murry unfairly blamed Kot for his 'quite pernicious' influence on Katherine and for encouraging her in 'the dangerous dream of being completely cured by the Russian, Manoukhin.' Like most doctors, Manoukhin had had some success, and Kot had the best intentions when he told Katherine about it. The fault, in fact, lies much more with Murry for not insisting that she have proper treatment in 1918 and for allowing her to leave the salubrious quiet of Montana for the Russian's clinic in Paris. Katherine found Manoukhin 'a tall formal rather dry man (not in the least an "enthusiast") who speaks scarcely any French and has a lame Russian girl for his interpreter.' The doctor rashly said: 'I can promise to cure you – to make you as though you had never had this disease ... It will take 15 séances – then a period of repose preferably in the mountains for 2–3–4 months just as you like. Then 10 more.'

The effect of all these treatments ('Saw two of the doctors – an ass, and an ass') is reflected in the letters and journals of Katherine's last years:

One wants to weep; one thinks of death; the seagulls fly into the infinite – and one wonders why on earth one should be cursed with this perpetual ill health! (1918)

All these two years I have been obsessed by the fear of death. This grew and grew and grew gigantic, and this it was that made me cling so, I think. (1919)

I cough and cough, and at each breath a dragging, boiling, bubbling sound is heard. I feel that my whole chest is boiling. . . . Life is – getting a new breath. Nothing else counts. (1920)

Both my lungs are affected; there is a cavity in one and the other is affected through. My heart is weak too. Can all this be cured? Ah, Koteliansky – wish for me! (1921)

My cough is so much worse that I *am a* cough – a living, walking or lying down cough. (1922)

She was haunted, every day of her life, by the nearness and inevitability of death and realised – finally, in 1922 – 'No treatment on earth is any good to me, really. . . . The miracle never came near happening.'

Katherine's tubercular haemorrhage reaffirmed her emotional and artistic bonds with Marie Bashkirtseff, Keats and Chekhov; affected her attitude to her work; and turned her first toward a flirtation with the Catholic Church, and then toward a self-destructive mysticism. Influenced by Murry's view of her as a doomed genius, she saw herself in the great tradition of tubercular artists: 'I do not see how we are to come by knowledge and love except through pain,' she wrote, 'I, being what I am, had to suffer *this* in order to do the work I am here to perform.'

Like the Russian painter, Marie Bashkirtseff (1860–84), whom she had read as a girl in New Zealand, Katherine sensed the first flowering of her mature talent (she published 'Prelude' and 'Bliss' in 1918) at the very moment she was threatened by death. Marie had written in the last months of her life: 'I have spent six years working ten hours a day to gain what? The knowledge of all I have yet to learn in my art – and a fatal disease. . . . Here it is at last, then, the end of all my miseries! So many aspirations, so many hopes, so many plans – to die at twenty-four, on the threshold of everything.' And Katherine, with less self-pity, bravely faced the truth at the same time that she tried to avoid it: 'I *must* know from somebody how I am getting on, i.e., I must be cheered up. Ten years passed this morning as I sat in my darkish little room. I am now 41 and can't lose a moment. I must know.'

Katherine also saw Keats' tragedy reflected in her own life and quite consciously echoed his last letters about the effect of tuberculosis on the nerves, the tenuous line between life and death, and the relation between disease and creativity (the great theme of Nietzsche and Thomas Mann):

A person in health as you are can have no conception of the horrors that nerves and a temper like mine go through. (Keats)

I get so irritable, so nervous that I want to *scream*, and if many people start talking I just lose my puff and feel my blood getting *black*. (Mansfield)

How horrid was the chance of slipping into the ground instead of into your arms. (Keats)

That is the fearful part of having been near death. One knows how easy it is to die. The barriers that are up for everyone else are down for you, and you've only to slip through. (Mansfield)

How astonishingly does the chance of leaving the world impress a sense of its natural beauty upon us! (Keats)

My fever makes everything 100 times more vivid, like a nightmare is vivid. (Mansfield)

Katherine was morbidly fascinated by Keats' and Chekhov's striking descriptions of their haemorrhages and by Chekhov's beautiful objective statement (in Katherine and Kot's translation) that 'there is something ominous in blood running from the mouth: it's like the reflection of a fire.' Katherine's comments on Chekhov apply to herself as well as to her Russian master. She felt that in his last letters 'He had given up hope. If you de-sentimentalise those final letters they are terrible. There is no more Chekhov. Illness has swallowed him.' She is also quite revealing about the difference between her artistic aspirations and achievement when discussing the effect of disease on Chekhov's art: 'For the last 8 years he knew no *security* at all. We know he felt his stories were not half what they might be. It doesn't take much imagination to picture him on his death-bed thinking "I have never had a real chance. Something has been all wrong."' In Chekhov and in Mansfield, the self-protective cynicism of an over-sensitive artist scarcely had sufficient time to ripen into compassion.

Until the last six months of her life Katherine's disease seemed to stimulate her creativity and she burned with a brighter, if ephemeral, flame. But her illness inevitably intensified her egocentric introspection which limited both the range and the depth of her stories. She was caustic and austere about her own work, aware of her lack of education and tendency to superficial smartness as well as her clinical rather than sympathetic attitude toward the people who inspired her fictional characters: 'I am a writer who cares for nothing but writing – that's how I feel. When I am with people I feel like a doctor with his patients – very sympathetic – very interested in the case! very anxious for them to tell me all they can – but as regards myself – quite alone, quite isolated – a queer state.' Katherine's themes are those of a lonely, frightened and sensitive invalid who wants to escape from the oppressions of adult reality into the fantasies of childhood, and concern abandonment, solitude and a profound fear of sex and death.

A group of her most important stories – 'Bliss,' 'Marriage a la Mode,' 'The Stranger,' and 'The Man Without a Temperament' (all written between 1918 and 1921) – concern her relationship with Murry and provide a fictional portrayal of their marriage that complements the grim reality of her *Journal* and *Letters*. 'Bliss' (1918) describes the destruction of Bertha's false euphoria about her too perfect marriage, complete with the baby, money and home that Katherine never possessed. The smugness and falsity of the dinner party merely intensifies her self-deception, though she seems to experience an epiphany with her guest, Pearl Fulton, a beautiful woman who had 'something strange' about her. The spell is shattered at the end of the story when Bertha discovers that her husband, whom she really desires for the first time in her marriage, is having an affair with Pearl. The *dénouement*, like the pear tree which symbolises deception (as in Chaucer's tale of January and May), is too obvious. But the theme of the worm in the bud, what Katherine called 'the snail under the leaf,' and her belief that one can never count on happiness, are basic to her life and work, for they were nurtured by her early unhappiness as well as by her insecurity with Murry.

'Marriage à la Mode' (1921) portrays the shell of a marriage in the modern, bohemian mode, after the core of meaning has been taken out of it. William, the rather plodding yet providing husband, disturbed by premonitions, comes home, like Ulysses, to a houseful of suitors and an indifferent Penelope. He is estranged from his wife and mocked by her arty friends who eat the fruit that he bought for his children – whom he barely managed to see. He is left isolated, with only the idyllic memories of their earlier life when 'he hadn't the slightest idea that Isabel wasn't as happy as he.' When poor William returns to the city and sends Isabel a love letter to set things right again, she reads it to her friends who become hysterical with laughter. This, curiously enough, recalls the famous incident in the Café Royal when Katherine interrupted a group of Lawrence's acquaintances who were reading his poems aloud and mocking them, loyally snatched the book away and symbolically rescued her friend from their scorn. Though Isabel suffers a moment of conscience, guilt and recrimination – 'what a loathsome thing to have done' she chooses to swim with her friends (who had previously excluded William from this pleasure) rather than answer his pathetic though well-meaning letter.

Though it is difficult to identify with – or even care about either William or Isabel, and the satire is far too facile, the story does concern a significant conflict of loyalties between what really matters – her marriage and her family – and what (though she cannot see it) is essentially trivial and meaningless. Her friend's joking suggestion that William is 'sending you back your marriage lines as a gentle reminder,' reminds the reader if not Isabel, of the sacramental aspect of marriage in which Katherine deeply believed: 'I believe in marriage. It seems to me the only possible relation that is really satisfying. And how else is one to have peace of mind to enjoy life and to do one's work? To know *one other* seems to me a far greater adventure than to be on kissing acquaintance with dear knows how many.'

In 'The Stranger' (1921) John Hammond, wealthy, successful, self-important, pompous yet terribly insecure, waits impatiently for his wife's ship to dock in New Zealand. He is desperately eager to regain and possess her, and childishly jealous of her friends aboard ship, of the doctor and the captain, and even of his children's letters to their mother – of anything that distracts her attention from himself. Yet when he finally embraces his wife, 'again, as always, he had the feeling he was holding something that never was quite his . . . that would fly away once he let go.'

Mansfield subtly conveys the intense strain on Hammond because of the difference in their feelings for each other – his wife responds coolly to his caresses – for he has great difficulty in re-establishing intimacy with her and 'never knew for dead certain that she was as glad as he was.' When he finally discovers (and all discoveries in these stories are shattering) the reason for the ship's delay and his wife's preoccupation – that a man has died in his wife's arms – he immediately understands that his wife has achieved an emotional connection with the stranger far stronger than he has ever achieved with her. Despite her half-hearted reassurance, 'It's nothing to do with you and me,' he is destroyed by this recognition: 'They would never be alone together again.'

Hammond's jealousy of the dead stranger, whose emotional hold on his wife can never be broken, is stronger than anything he could feel for a living man, and it reveals the superficiality and meaninglessness of their entire marriage.

'The Man Without a Temperament' (1920), the most revealing and intimate of Mansfield's marriage stories, describes her fears about how Murry would feel if he had given in to her pleas and followed the advice of her doctor – and of D. H. Lawrence, who urged him to 'save yourself, and your self-respect, by making it complete between Katherine and you' – and lived abroad with her for the two years that she needed to recover her health. The boredom and trivial irritations of life *en pension* and the longing for a more meaningful existence in England are vividly evoked. Katherine lamented in her *Journal* that her 'typically English husband' (unlike Lawrence and Carco) seemed to lack a 'temperament' and was 'not warm, ardent, eager, full of quick response, careless, spendthrift of himself, vividly alive, [or] *high-spirited*.' In this story, the woman, though an invalid, is far more intense and vital than the man, who is forced to suppress his temperament under an ox-like passivity and obedience. But he fails to conceal his bitterness and resentment about the inevitable sacrifice of his career and his independent life.

Though they live in constant intimacy, the couple are divided by an abyss of unspoken hostility which she feels will lead to the dreaded separation. The story is far more subtle than 'Bliss' or 'Marriage à la Mode,' and succeeds because Katherine has understood Murry's needs and feelings as well as her own, and dramatised the central and insoluble dilemma of their marriage: 'It is *anguish* to be away from him but as my presence seems to positively torture him – I suppose it's the better of the two horrors.'

Katherine's marriage stories reflect her own fear of abandonment and fear of betrayal, her self-destructive jealousy and guilt about invalidism. They emphasise the isolated heroine who needs sympathy and love, and the lack of understanding and basic honesty in marital relations. As she told Murry in 1920: 'I have hiding places – so have you. They are very different ones. We do though emerge from them strange to each other, and it's only when the strangeness wears off that we are together. This must ever be so.'

Katherine never found a doctor who could dominate and discipline her will during the long period of physical recuperation, and when Manoukhin failed to perform his 'miraculous' cure her fantasy of an omnipotent and magical physician, who would protect her against the dreadful consequences of her illness, was shattered: 'I had made him my "miracle." One must have a miracle. Now I'm without one and looking round for another.' Katherine, who had a desperate need to believe in *something*, had flirted with conversion to the Catholic Church while under the care and propaganda of her wealthy cousin in Menton. Though she found it impossible to believe in God, her cousin's influence ironically prepared her for her final conversion to mysticism.

Disgusted by the futility of medical treatment, Katherine came to believe that her illness was more spiritual than physical. She wanted to escape from the prison of her flesh, to pretend her disease did not exist and to 'cure her soul.' She therefore turned for her salvation to mysticism, to the psychic control of tuberculosis and to the persuasive Caucasian, George Gurdjieff, whom she supposed to possess the same powers in the psychic sphere that she had once attributed to the doctors in the realm of the physical. Gurdjieff, she said, 'is the only man who understands there is no division between body and spirit.'

When she and Murry had found bugs in their bed in 1914, three years after Diaghilev and Nijinsky's triumphant debut in London, she bravely declared: 'Let's imagine we are Russians.' Gurdjieff was the fatal culmination of 'Yékaterina's' lifelong infatuation with Russians: with Dostoyevsky, Bashkirtseff, Chekhov, Gorki, Bunin, Koteliansky and Manoukhin.

Murry, the future author of *God*, did not enter his own mystical phase until after Katherine's death, and disapproved of her commitment to Gurdjieff, whom she had heard about from A. R. Orage, her former editor at the *New Age* and the Caucasian's leading disciple in England. But Murry was, as usual, too weak, confused and indecisive to influence Katherine positively, and they drifted apart during the last year of her life. Murry admits that 'we now had a depressing effect upon one another, and [agreed] that we ought not to live together until one or other of us had found a faith to live by.' Katherine, in October 1922, put it much more strongly: 'I remember what we really felt there – the blanks, the silences, the anguish of continual misunderstanding. Were we positive, eager, real, alive? No, we were not. We were a nothingness shot with gleams of what might be.'

Gurdjieff, who was supposed to have studied in 'mysterious' Mongolian and Tibetan monasteries, had set up temporary 'Institutes for the Harmonious Development of Man' in Moscow, Tiflis, Constantinople, Berlin and Dresden before settling in 'The Priory' at Fontainebleau. Katherine could not speak directly to either Manoukhin or Gurdjieff, for the Teacher's native languages were Armenian and Greek, and he spoke only broken Russian. One follower described him as 'altogether Eastern in appearance, short, swarthy, almost bald, but with long black moustaches, a high brow and piercing eyes'; and Katherine, in one of her more lucid moments, thought he looked 'exactly like a carpet dealer from the Tottenham Court Road.'

Gurdjieff demanded and received absolute obedience from his disciples and ruled as a despot over devoted slaves. Though his exuberant and dynamic personality was forceful and attractive, he had a violent temper, a shameless greed for money, a personal extravagance and a megalomania that scarcely reflected the Wisdom of the East. Gurdjieff emphasised the harmonious integration of the physical, emotional and mental centres; and C. E. Bechhofer writes that:

> The aim of the institute is the development of the innate faculties of its members by first breaking down the artificial barriers of their personality and then by developing and harmonising their various mental and physical centres, the means of doing this being self-observation; a practical course of dancing; manual and physical exercise; psychical analysis of every kind; and a series of tests, mental and physical, applied by Gurdjieff to fit each individual case.

Gurdjieff had about fifty Russian disciples, with some English, mostly of the theosophical type, who spent their time 'breaking down the artificial barriers' by doing hard manual labour, looking after the farm animals and practising the Master's special kind of dancing which, according to Llewelyn Powys, who saw a performance in New York in 1924, seemed 'like a hutchful of hypnotised rabbits under the gaze of a master conjuror.'

The dying Katherine arrived at the damp and chilling Priory in October 1922, and deliberately endured the physical discomforts of hard work, poor diet, little sleep, cold rooms and bad air. Though she noted in her *Journal* that 'the corridors are like whistling side-streets to pass down – icy cold,' she tried to justify her meagre and miserable existence in her letters and speaks quite seriously of 'the monkey [Gurdjieff] has bought which is to be trained to clean the cows.'

Gurdjieff, not to be outdone by the doctors, decided to give Katherine the benefit of the traditional peasant remedy for tuberculosis. He told the workers to build a special platform for her above the cow-byre and ordered her to spend several hours each day inhaling the fetid exhalations of the beasts. One disciple explains that the tiny wooden balcony, 'artistically designed,' was constructed so Katherine could 'renew her strength through the radiation of animal magnetism, or perhaps simply for the *health*y smell of fresh manure'; and another female follower insists that 'Katherine simply adored that place. She never ceased to express her gratitude to Gurdjieff for all that he had done for her.'

This same woman, Olgivanna (the future wife of Frank Lloyd Wright), also told Katherine: 'There is no death for one like you who perceives the possibility of sweeping death aside when the time comes as a necessary phase to go through.' And Katherine agreed that 'the only thing to do is to get the dying over – to court it, almost. . . . And then all hands to the business of being reborn again.' Katherine, who understood death far better than rebirth, lasted six weeks in this salubrious regimen and soon achieved her wish. On the very day that Murry came to visit her, as she slowly climbed the long staircase to her room, she was seized by a fit of coughing, gasped out 'I believe I'm going to die,' and put her hand over her mouth as the bright flame of blood gushed fiercely from her lungs and through her fingers. A few minutes later she was dead at the age of thirty-four. It is ironic that Katherine's death at Fontainebleau and her dismal burial in a cheap coffin first attracted public fame and attention to Gurdjieff's Institute.

In one of his books on Keats, who with Christ and Katherine formed his holy trinity, Murry writes with appalling egoism that 'Nothing more powerfully prepares a man's instinctive and unconscious nature for passionate love than prolonged contact with hopeless illness in a loved one.' A year after Katherine's death in 1923, Murry married his second wife, Violet Le Maistre, who looked astonishingly like Katherine and self-consciously imitated her dress, hair-style, handwriting and mannerisms. Murry was still in love with the *idea* of Katherine, and since Violet wanted nothing more than to replace Katherine, they seemed well suited to each other. Murry, with his incredible obtuseness, took three years to discover that Violet was not Katherine, and admitted: 'It never struck me for a moment that there was a great difference between Katherine when I first met her, and Violet now.'

Murry encouraged Violet's pathological attachment to his dead wife and the spirit of Katherine hovered over their marriage. Murry, who was not exactly generous when Katherine was alive, gave Violet Katherine's engagement ring, bought their house with the £1000 royalties on Katherine's books, lived on the £500 a year that Katherine's posthumously published books brought in, named their daughter Katherine, and published Violet's stories, as well as Katherine's, in the *Adelphi*. When Violet contracted tuberculosis, she exclaimed: 'O I'm so *glad*. I wanted this to happen. . . . I wanted you to love me as much as you loved Katherine – and how could you, without this?' Just as Katherine had turned away from Murry to Gurdjieff at the end of her life, so Violet fell in love with his friend, Max Plowman. After Violet died of tuberculosis in 1931, Murry pitifully asked: 'Am I attracted only by two kinds of women – one that I kill, the other that kills me?'

Though Murry's treatment of Katherine had been shabby and irresponsible, he began an egoistic enshrinement after her death, and became the high priest of the powerful cult of Katherine which overshadowed her literary reputation until after the Second World War and which still survives in France. Huxley (who was Murry's editorial assistant on the *Athenaeum*) undoubtedly exaggerated this aspect of Murry, whom he characterised as Burlap in *Point Counter Point* (1928), but he is worth quoting for his wit as well as for the essence of truth in the satire, which recalls Katherine's cult of her dead brother.

When Susan died Burlap exploited the grief he felt, or at any rate loudly said he felt, in a more than usually painful series of those always painfully personal articles which were the secret of his success as a journalist . . . pages of rather hysterical lyricism about the dead child-woman. . . .

At the end of some few days of incessant spiritual masturbation, he had been rewarded by a mystical realisation of his own unique and incomparable piteousness ... Frail, squeamish, less than fully alive and therefore less than adult, permanently underaged, she [Katherine] adored him as a superior and almost holy lover . . . [who would] roll at her feet in an ecstasy of incestuous adoration for the imaginary mother-baby of a wife with whom he had chosen to identify the corporeal Susan.

Huxley quite accurately perceives not only the falseness of the cult and Murry's pitiful exploitation of his grief, but also the emotional immaturity and childish role-playing of both Katherine and Murry, and he describes the destructive aspect of Murry's 'spiritual' love in the metaphor of sexual perversion.

Despite the instructions in Katherine's will that Murry should 'publish as little as possible and tear up and burn as much as possible,' and his own statement that 'I am old-fashioned enough to believe that it is almost a crime to make public fragments of an author's manuscripts which he obviously did not mean to show the world,' Murry undertook the publication of her (frequently unfinished) work – she featured in every issue of the *Adelphi* for two years – and deliberately created a false and misleading picture of her character and their marriage.

Though Murry knew, for example, about Katherine's bitter and self-destructive sexual experiences, he falsely stressed her 'inward purity' ('a condition of soul essential to writing') and angered her friends. Kot maintained that when Murry published her letters and journals he left out all the jokes to make her an English Tchekov. In 1928 Lawrence wrote to Dorothy Brett, 'I hear Katherine's letters sell largely, yet Murry whines about poverty and I hear he *inserts* the most poignant passages himself. Ottoline declares that in the letters to her, large pieces are inserted, most movingly.' Lawrence criticised Murry for assuming the role of the acolyte chosen to bear the chalice of her fame, for he told Murry – who was fond of comparing Katherine to his beloved Keats – 'You are wrong about Katherine. She was *not* a great genius. She had a charming gift, and a finely culti-vated one. But *not more*. And to try, as you do, to make it more is to do her no true service.'

Though Murry's biographer claimed 'The greatest [of his virtues], and the least conventional, was his honesty,' the Mansfield manuscripts now in Wellington reveal that Murry deliberately changed the dates and distorted the texts, which he skilfully but silently compiled from fifty different note-books and fragments, in order to present his own sentimental image of his wife and to create the Mansfield myth which attracted infinitely more readers than did the stories she had published in her lifetime. Thus, after her death as during her life, as Leonard Woolf (who knew them well) perceived,

> Murry corrupted and perverted and destroyed Katherine both as a person and as a writer. She was a very serious writer, but her gifts were those of an intense realist, with a superb sense of ironic humour and fundamental cynicism. She got enmeshed in the sticky sentimentality of Murry and wrote against the grain of her own nature. At the bottom of her mind she knew this, I think, and it enraged her.

Despite Katherine's female emancipation – her cigarettes, bobbed hair, lesbianism and abortion – she was a classic example of the woman in transition from convention to liberation. Katherine, who was frustrated in motherhood, craved an orthodox and secure marriage with a powerful and intelligent husband, an equal partnership like that of George Eliot and George Henry Lewes or Virginia and Leonard Woolf. She was attracted to Murry, who had a basically female temperament and was emotionally dependent and sexually passive, because of her revulsion against her aggressive and domineering father. But Katherine did not realise that when she rejected masculine authority she also gave up the hope of the emotional support she rightly felt was essential for the development of her artistic gifts. Murry's selfish response to Katherine's illness proved that Lawrence was right when he said they were not 'complete.' Though Murry was extremely weak, he subtly dominated Katherine in a way that hurt both of them, and continued to exercise his power after her death when he transformed her into the docile wife that he had always wanted.

Though Murry was a charming and attractive man, he was also insensitive and remarkably stupid. He encouraged Katherine's childish fantasies and failed her at every critical moment of her life: when she left him for Carco; when her brother was killed; when she was lonely and isolated in Ospedaletti; when she contracted tuberculosis; when she left Switzerland for Manoukhin; and when she became infatuated with Gurdjieff. Despite her emotional dependence on Murry, Katherine's *Journal* entry of October 1922 shows that she saw with a penetrating clarity the fundamental falsity of their marriage:

What have you of him now? What is your relationship? He talks to you – sometimes – and then goes off. He thinks of you tenderly. He dreams of a life with you *some day* when the miracle has happened. You are important to him as a dream. Not as a living reality. For you are not one. What do you share? Almost nothing. . . . Life together, with me ill, is simply torture with happy moments. But it's not life.

D. H. and Frieda Lawrence
A GENIUS FOR LIVING

'I think the real tragedy is in the inner war which is waged between people who love each other, a war out of which comes knowledge.'

D. H. LAWRENCE

I

D. H. Lawrence, who believed the relation between men and women was '*the* problem of today,' was an important theoretician and practitioner of modern marriage. In *Women in Love* (1920), his most important novel, he rejected 'the old way of love [which] seemed a dreadful bondage, a sort of conscription. What it was in him he did not know, but the thought of love, marriage, and children, and a life lived together, in the horrible privacy of domestic and connubial satisfaction, was 'repulsive.' Birkin, the autobiographical hero of the novel, strives for a more ambitious and individualistic relationship of two free beings who balance and complement each other, and transcend the conventional bonds of marriage. As he tells Ursula (who is modelled on Frieda):

> What I want is a strange conjunction with you ... an equilibrium, a pure balance of two single beings: – as the stars balance each other. . . . He wanted a further conjunction, where man had being and woman had being, two pure beings, each constituting the freedom of the other, balancing each other like two poles of one force, like two angels, or two demons.

Lawrence conceived of marriage as a living and enduring connection of man and woman, which would not limit their personalities nor prevent them from forming other relationships.

In *John Thomas and Lady Jane* (written in 1927), the second version of *Lady Chatterley's Lover*, Lawrence described marriage in the metaphor of two ships, connected by an invisible thread of magnetic vitality, and sailing skilfully and independently to the same port:

> So it must be: a voyage apart, in the same direction. Grapple the two vessels together, lash them side by side, and the first storm will smash them to pieces. That is marriage, in the bad weather of modern civilisation. But leave the two vessels apart, to make their own voyage to the same port, each according to its own skill and power, and an unseen life connects them, a magnetism which cannot be forced. And that is marriage as it will be, when this is broken down.

In both these passages, as in his major novels, Lawrence attempts to resolve his desire for individual freedom and self-determination with his need for the strengthening security of permanent marriage. He did not want a joining of two halves nor a total submergence of one in the other, but a union in which both husband and wife would retain their individual integrity. But in Lawrence's marriage and in his novels about marriage this concept was essentially idealistic. He and Frieda constantly fought for domination, and the independent and sensitive women in his books are nearly always placed under the control of powerful men.

In a letter of 1916 to the painter, Mark Gertler, who was suffering love agonies with his sometime mistress, Dora Carrington, Lawrence offered the kind of good advice he was himself incapable of following: 'If you could only really give yourself up in love, she would be much happier. You always want to dominate her, which is no good. One must learn to relinquish oneself, not to bother about oneself, but to love the other person. You hold too closely to yourself, for her to be free to love you.' Though Lawrence advocated selfless love and wanted to surrender himself to Frieda (what he called 'a passing of the self into a pure relationship with the other'), he also valued individuality and felt that sexual relations threatened his personal identity. He expressed this ambivalence in his early poem, 'Wedlock':

And how I am not all, except a flame that mounts off you.
Where I touch you, I flame into being; – but is it me, or you?

Though Lawrence-Birkin yearned for a starlike 'equilibrium, a pure balance of two single beings,' Frieda-Ursula recognised that what he really wanted was a satellite, a woman submissive to his will.'I do think a woman must yield some

sort of precedence to a man,' Lawrence explained to
Katherine Mansfield in 1918:

> and he must take this precedence. I do think men must go
> ahead absolutely in front of their women, without turning
> round to ask for permission or approval from their
> women. Consequently the women must follow as it were
> unquestioningly. I can't help it, I believe this. Frieda
> doesn't. Hence our fight.

At the turn of the century, when male dominance was the
rule, Lawrence had seen his gifted mother fight to achieve
the bitter and self-righteous conquest of his weak but brutal
father; and he portrayed this struggle in *Sons and Lovers*.
Throughout his entire life Lawrence felt threatened by
possessive women: his mother, Jessie Chambers, Alice Dax,
Ottoline Morrell, Dorothy Brett, Mabel Luhan, and, most
important, Frieda. And from his experience with them he
learned to see marriage as an endless struggle of clashing
wills in which man either maintains a precarious dominance
or is overcome by humiliating defeat. Though Lawrence kept
up his end of the battle, as his poems of marriage, *Look! We
Have Come Through!* (1917), testify, he had much to fear from
Frieda, whose strengths seemed to match his own weaknesses. She was of noble birth, richer, older, stronger and
healthier than the sickly Lawrence; she was sexually liberated
and had had a number of love affairs before, during and after
her marriages to Ernest Weekley and the puritanical
Lorenzo. He resented his dependence on Frieda, was awed
by her sexual experience and sexual demands, was fiercely
jealous of the longing for her three abandoned children (they
had no children of their own), hated her wilful refusal to
submit to him, and was alternately enraged, depressed and
resigned to her flirtations and liaisons. As he wrote in
'Tortoise Shout':

The cross,
The wheel on which our silence first is broken, [is]
Sex, which breaks up our integrity, our single inviolability,
  our deep silence,
Tearing a cry from us.

Lawrence's theoretical attempt to resolve the conflict between submission and dominance is explained by his friend and biographer, Catherine Carswell: 'Lawrence asserted himself on the strength of his power. And he asserted the male principle, which he believed was destined to lead. But there was no egoism in it, and it left Frieda the utmost liberty of her female assertion, so long as she did not try to "put across" mere female egoism.' Though Lawrence was not always successful, his effort to transcend his personal ego left Frieda 'the freest woman he had ever met,' for he had chosen a wife who seemed to give him the special submission he required and at the same time to assert the female principle and triumph in her womanhood.

The marriage of Lawrence and Frieda expressed the conflict between man and woman, English and German, proletarian and aristocrat, travel and home, freedom and children. But they never compromised their principles and always did what they really wanted to do: they travelled around the world and lived a free, proud and intensely creative life in the most beautiful parts of Europe.

In 1912 Lawrence told W. E. Hopkin, an old friend in Eastwood, that he was certain about Frieda and was inspired by her emotional and intellectual challenge to his ideas: 'Some of my acquaintances seem to think Frieda and I are wrongly mated. She is the only possible woman for me, for I must have opposition – something to fight or I shall go under.' He then added that it would have been a fatal step to marry his first love, the clinging and submissive Jessie Chambers: 'I should have had too easy a life, nearly everything my

own way, and my genius would have been destroyed.' Frieda
also thrived on the violent but open and honest quarrels that
so frequently shocked their friends, and affirmed in her
autobiography, *Not I, But the Wind*: 'It was a long fight for
Lawrence and me to get at some truth between us; it was a
hard life with him, but a wonderful one. . . . I think the
greatest pleasure and satisfaction for a woman is to live with
a creative man, when he goes ahead and fights.' Lawrence's
struggle for truth in his marriage was directly related to his
opposition to society and his struggle to conceive and
express his beliefs.

II

Frieda von Richthofen, the beautiful and passionate
daughter of a German baron, was born in Metz in 1879 and
grew up in the society of the Prussian Imperial Court. Violet
Hunt called her a charming, 'handsome, golden-haired, tall
woman with a magnificent figure, like a Teutonic goddess.'
Cynthia Asquith described her as 'exuberant, warm,
burgeoning, she radiated health, strength and generosity of
nature.' And Brigit Patmore wrote that Frieda shone 'in a
sun-drenched way, wild, blonde hair waving happily, grey-
green eyes raying out laughter, her fair skin an effulgent pale
rose.'

In 1896, when Frieda was seventeen, she met Ernest
Weekley, a thirty-two-year old English teacher at Freiburg
University, during a walking tour of the Black Forest. Two
years later the wild girl blundered into marriage with
Weekley, whom Aldous Huxley called 'possibly the dullest
Professor in the Western hemisphere,' and went to live in the
gloomy industrial city of Nottingham where he had been
appointed Lecturer at the University. Frieda had three children (a boy and two girls, born between 1900 and 1904) and
numerous lovers, including Otto Gross, a brilliant pupil of

Freud, who later became a hopeless drug addict. She was extremely bored, after twelve years of stifling marriage, when Lawrence, her husband's former pupil, was invited to their home in April 1912. Later that month Lawrence, the son of a coalminer, described Weekley as 'a middle class, gentlemanly man, in whom the brute can leap up. He is forty-six, and has been handsome, is usually ironic, pessimistic and cynical, nice, I like him. He will hate me, but really he likes me at the bottom.'

Lawrence, who was six years younger than Frieda and had published his first novel, *The White Peacock*, in 1911, was then at a critical period of his life. His mother, to whom he was deeply attached, had just died; he had resigned his teaching position at Croydon; and was completing his first major work, *Sons and Lovers*. Lawrence's love affairs with Jessie Chambers, Alice Dax, Louie Burrows and Helen Corke had been compromised and limited by his intense love for his mother. But her death liberated his emotions and allowed him to respond fully to Frieda, to whom he later confessed: 'If my mother had lived I could never have loved you, she wouldn't have let me go.'

In her vivid autobiography, Frieda relates that Lawrence 'came to see me one Sunday [in April]. My husband was away and I said: "Stay the night with me." "No, I will not stay in your husband's house while he is away, but you must tell him the truth and we will go away together, because I love you."' 'She is ripping – she's the finest woman I've ever met – you must above all things meet her,' Lawrence wrote to his friend and confidant, Edward Garnett, on 17 April. 'She is the daughter of Baron von Richthofen, of the ancient and famous house of Richthofen – but she's splendid, she is really. How damnably I mix things up. Mrs Weekley is perfectly unconventional, but really good – in the best sense. I'll bet you've never met anyone like her.' On 3 May, three weeks after their first meeting, they left England together.

'Oh there has been *such* a to-do,' Lawrence told Garnett on 21 May. 'Weekley was suspicious. He wrote to her saying he thought she had deceived him recently. When we came back from the Cearne [Garnett's house], F. told him about two *other, earlier* men, but not about me.' But Lawrence insisted on complete honesty and told Frieda that he wanted 'no more dishonour, no more lies. Let them do their – silliest – but no more subterfuge, lying, dirt, fear. I feel as if it would strangle me. . . . I love you. Let us face anything, do anything, put up with anything. But this crawling under the mud I cannot bear.'

They were met at the station of Metz, in Lorraine, where Frieda's father had been the Prussian governor after the war of 1870, by her younger sister, Johanna. She immediately liked Lawrence and told Frieda: 'You can go with him. You can trust him.' A few days later, as they were walking on the fortifications of Metz, Lawrence was arrested by a German guard who suspected him of being an English spy; and Frieda had to use her father's influence to free her lover.

This unpleasant incident (which partly inspired 'The Prussian Officer') forced Lawrence to leave Metz on 8 May. During his three-week separation from Frieda (who remained with her father to celebrate the fiftieth anniversary of his entrance into the army), they conducted a passionate but painful correspondence about their most serious problems: the possibility of having children, Frieda's profound attachment to her own children, and her desire for sexual freedom. Though at first Frieda may have thought of Lawrence as a temporary lover, he was absolutely determined to marry her against all obstacles. As Frieda later said: 'I had to be his wife if the skies fell, and they nearly did.' Though nearly penniless, Lawrence did not believe in birth control, was pleased at the idea of having a child, was willing to undertake the responsibility of an infant, and made the important distinction between sexual passion and the calmer love of permanent marriage:

Never mind about the infant. If it should come, we will be glad, and stir ourselves to provide for it – and if it should not come, ever – I shall be sorry. I do not believe, when people love each other, in interfering there. It is wicked, according to my feeling. I want you to have children to me – I don't care how soon. I never thought I should have that definite desire. But you see, we must have a more or less stable foundation if we are going to run the risk of the responsibility of children – not the risk of children, but the risk of the responsibility. . . . It is a great thing for me to marry you, not a quick, passionate coming together. I know in my heart, 'here's my marriage.'

Frieda's divided loyalty to her lover and her children was similar to Anna Karenina's anguished conflict between Vronsky and her son, Seriozha; and like Vronsky, Lawrence could not sympathise with or understand his mistress' attachment to her children. Frieda writes that when they were living in the Isartal, near Munich, in June 1912, Lawrence refused to recognise her anguish and rather defensively said: '"You don't care a damn about those brats really and they don't care about you." I cried and we quarrelled. "What kind of unnatural woman would I be if I could forget my children?" Yet my agony over them was my worst crime in his eyes.' Lawrence remained jealous of Frieda's love for her children, even after they had grown up, and this intense conflict persisted throughout their marriage.

Though Ernest Weekley tried to use the children to make Frieda return to him, Lawrence's pride would not allow him to assume a conventional sexual role and beg her to stay. As he wrote to Edward Garnett in July 1912:

The children are miserable, missing her so much. She lies on the floor in misery – and then is fearfully angry with me because I won't say 'stay for my sake.' I say 'decide what you want most, to live with me and share my rotten chances, or go back to security, and your children – decide for *yourself* – choose for yourself.' And then she almost hates me, because I won't say 'I love you – stay with me whatever happens.'

When they returned to England in the summer of 1913, Frieda (despite Lawrence's disapproval) waited outside her children's school to get a brief glimpse of or word with them; and Katherine Mansfield acted as a friendly liaison: 'She was a perfect friend and tried her best to help me with the children. She went to see them, talked to them and took them letters from me.' Another friend, S. S. Koteliansky, told Leonard Woolf that a few months after their marriage in July 1914:

> Frieda began lamenting how much she missed her children. . . . Kot said: 'Frieda, you have left your children to marry Lawrence. You must choose either your children or Lawrence – and if you choose Lawrence, you must stop complaining about the children. . . . [Katherine Mansfield then appeared and said:] "Lorenzo, Frieda has asked me to come and tell you that she will not come back." "Damn that woman," shouted Lawrence in a fury, "tell her I never want to see her again."'

Their third problem, Frieda's desire for sexual freedom, also plagued Lawrence throughout their marriage, for she did not believe in restraining her passionate impulses. When Frieda was still married to Weekley but had run off with Lawrence, she tormented her lover by describing her desire for a young German. In a letter from Waldbröl, written a week after he had left her in Metz, Lawrence contrasted his own monogamy with Frieda's belief in free love: 'If you want H—, or anybody, have him. But I don't want anybody, till I see you. But all natures aren't alike. But I don't believe that

even *you* are at your best, when you are using H— as a dose
of morphia – he's not much else to you.' Lawrence's reasonable and objective tone did not disguise his jealousy and wish
to keep Frieda for himself.

Though Frieda may have used this incident to arouse
Lawrence's possessive jealousy, she also slept with other men
to punish him and revive her self-esteem. Edward Garnett's
son, David, who lived with the Lawrences in the summer of
1912, reports that 'after they had had a row, she had gone
down to the Isar and [like Leander] swum over to where a
woodcutter was working, had made love with him and had
swum back – just to show Lawrence she was free to do what
she liked.' Though Lawrence theoretically admired her
freedom, it was actually torture to him; and he suffered when
Frieda was unfaithful with Middleton Murry in 1923 and
with Angelo Ravagli in 1928.

Frieda's wedding night with Weekley had been a disaster.
When she undressed, climbed upon a cupboard and waited
to be carried down, he was shocked at her behaviour. 'She
had expected unspeakable bliss,' Frieda wrote of that night,
'and now she felt a degraded wretch.' And in 'First Morning,'
Lawrence admitted his own sexual repression and the failure
of their first night together:

> In the darkness
>   with the pale dawn seething at the window
>   through the black frame
>   I could not be free,
>   not free myself from the past, those others –
>   and our love was a confusion,
>   there was a horror,
>   you recoiled away from me.

But this problem was short-lived, and by early June Lawrence
was writing enthusiastically to Edward Garnett about

Frieda's incredible beauty – and her somewhat alarming character:

> Frieda is awfully good-looking. You should see her some-times. She is getting the breakfast. We are both a bit solemn this morning. It is our first morning at home. You needn't say things about her – or me. She is a million times better than ever you imagine – you *don't* know her, from litera-ture, no, how can you? *I* don't. She is fond of you. I say she'd alarm you. She's got a figure like a fine Rubens woman, but her face is almost Greek.

Lawrence, who gained enormous confidence as he lived with Frieda, boasted to Garnett at the end of June about his sexual performance: 'Love rather suits me. I am getting fat, and look awfully well. You don't know how surprised I am, considering the rate we go at it.' He records this passion in 'Gloire de Dijon,' describes Frieda bathing in the sunbeams and compares her generous breasts to glorious yellow roses:

> When she rises in the morning
> I linger to watch her;
> She spreads the bath-cloth underneath the window
> And the sunbeams catch her
> Glistening white on the shoulders,
> While down her sides the mellow
> Golden shadow glows as
> She stoops to the sponge, and her swung breasts
> Sway like full-blown yellow
> Glorie de Dijon roses.

Both Lawrence and Frieda were extremely vital and respon-sive, and derived great pleasure from ordinary things. 'I believe the chief tie between Lawrence and me was always the wonder of living,' Frieda wrote, 'every little or big thing that happened carried its glamour with it.' Lawrence was delighted with the wonder of Frieda, and in August wrote ecstatically to Mrs Hopkin: 'Whatever happens, I do love, and I am loved. I have given and I have taken – and that is eternal. Oh, if people could marry properly; I believe in marriage.'

Though happy, they could not ignore the practical difficulties of Frieda's adjustment to poverty. (She later attempted to alleviate this problem in a characteristically frank yet naive fashion. When introduced to the author of *Peter Pan* she said: 'How do you do, Sir Barrie. I hear you make an income of fifty thousand a year. . . . Why shouldn't you give Lorenzo enough money to pay for our passage to Australia?') But in August 1912, the same month that Lawrence had described his marital happiness, he also quoted Frau von Richthofen's condemnation of her daughter's primitive life: 'Who was I, did I think, that a Baronesse should clean my boots and empty my slops: she, the daughter of a high-born and highly-cultured gentleman? . . . No decent man, no man with a common sense of decency, could expect to have a woman, the wife of a clever professor, living with him like a barmaid.' Lawrence reproduced this criticism, and many others, in his play about their early life together, *The Fight for Barbara* (1912).

The totally impractical Frieda, who had never done any housework before she lived with Lawrence, relates, 'The first time I washed sheets was a disaster. They were so large and wet, their wetness was overwhelmlng. The kitchen floor was flooded, the table drenched, I dripped from hair to feet.' Maria Huxley was quite right when she said, 'Frieda is silly. She is like a child, but Lawrence likes her *because* she is a child.' Lawrence was delighted to rescue Frieda from her watery fate, and helped her with the household chores in the same way that he had once helped his mother. 'He regarded no task as too humble for him to undertake,' Aldous Huxley observed, 'nor so trivial that it was not worth his while to do it well. He could cook, he could sew, he could darn a stocking and milk a cow, he was an efficient wood-cutter and a good hand at embroidery, fires always burned when he had laid them and a floor, after Lawrence had scrubbed it, was thoroughly clean.'

At the end of 1912 Lawrence confided to Mrs Hopkin: 'We've had a hard time, Frieda and I. It is not so easy for a woman to leave a man and children like that. And it's not so easy for a man and a woman to live alone together in a foreign country for six months, and dig out a love deeper and deeper.' Lawrence's sequence of love poems, *Look! We Have Come Through!*, reveals their successful attempt to dig out a deeper love and 'the intrinsic experience of a man during the crisis of manhood, when he marries and comes into himself.' Though Bertrand Russell objected to Lawrence's intimate revelations and wittily remarked, 'They may have come through, but I don't see why I should look,' the poems go beyond the merely personal, and illuminate the connection of Lawrence's emotional and creative maturity.

When Frieda asked him, 'What do I give you, that you didn't get from others?', he answered, 'You make me sure of myself, whole' – complete as a man and as an artist. Lawrence freely admitted, 'It is hopeless for me to try to do anything, without I have a woman at the back of me. . . . A woman that I love sort of keeps me in direct communication with the unknown.' Lawrence's love for Frieda inspired his creative genius and led to one of the most productive periods of his life, for she believed in his genius, was intensely responsive to his work, helped him to imagine fictional scenes, provided certain seminal ideas, and was sympathetic yet critical about his books. He completed *Sons and Lovers* while living with Frieda in Gargnano in 1912–13, and she introduced him to Freud's ideas, which she had learned from Otto Gross and which were scarcely known in England at that time. These

concepts helped Lawrence to clarify the mother–son relationship in the novel and led to his residual sympathy for the
loutish yet attractive father. *Sons and Lovers* was published in
1913, a year before their marriage; and while writing his next
novel, *The Rainbow* (1915), Lawrence told Murry that 'he was
conscious of Frieda's participation in his work, to such an
extent that it depended upon her active goodwill.'

III

Though the Lawrences were basically content, they fought a
great deal; and the most striking aspect of their marriage was
the violent battles that astounded, repelled and fascinated all
their friends, but were a vital and necessary part of their relationship. Brigit Patmore recalls that Frieda 'offered herself to
his wrath with her gay gibes and wilfulness in the way a
tigress draws the play-fight of her cubs.' Douglas Goldring
observes that 'voluble, full-bosomed, Prussian Frieda was
built to weather storms. Like a sound ship, broad in the
beam, slow but seaworthy, she could stand any amount of
buffeting.' Cecily Lambert remarks that Lawrence 'appeared
to love an opportunity to humiliate her – whether from jealousy or extreme exasperation one could never tell. I was only
surprised that she listened to his abuse or obeyed his orders.'
And Frederick Leighton, the rather stiff American consul in
Mexico City, states:

> Never before or since have I heard a human being, in
> educated society, repeatedly release such a flow of obscene
> vile abuse on his wife (or on anyone) in the presence of
> comparative strangers as Lawrence did on Frieda; nor, I
> must admit, have I heard such apparently uninhibited
> response. Lawrence was far more eloquent, more varied in
> his vituperation, but Frieda hardly less emphatic.

Lawrence and Frieda's quarrels usually began with a trivial occurrence. Frieda might contradict one of his assertions or commands (L:'Not so much intensity, Frieda.' F:'If I want to be intense, I'll be intense, and you go to hell.') or he would attack her for smoking, cutting her hair, gluttony, ignorance or pretentiousness. Sometimes the mere mention of Frieda's children and her subsequent tears set off the explosive spark. Murry describes Lawrence's irrational behaviour when this happened at Chesham in October 1914:

> Lawrence, though passionately angry, had kept control; and it was the more frightening. He had had enough, he said: she must go, she was draining the life out of him. She must go, she must go now. She knew what money he had; he would give her her share – more than her share. He went upstairs, and came down again, and counted out on the table to me sixteen sovereigns. Frieda was standing by the door, crying, with her hat and coat on, ready to go – but where?

Katherine Mansfield, who wrote to their mutual friend Koteliansky, 'I don't know which disgusts me worse, when they are loving and playing with each other, or when they are roaring at each other and he is pulling out Frieda's hair and saying "I'll cut your bloody throat, you bitch,"' gives a lively and thorough scenario of one explosion that took place in Cornwall in May 1916:

> Frieda said Shelley's Ode to a Skylark was false. Lawrence said, 'you are showing off; you don't know anything about it.' Then she began. '*Now* I have had enough. Out of my house. You little God Almighty you. I've had enough of you. Are you going to keep your mouth shut or aren't you.' Said Lawrence: 'I'll give you a dab on the cheek to quiet you, you dirty hussy.' Etc. Etc. So I left the house. At dinner

time Frieda appeared. 'I have finally done with him. It is all over forever.' She then went out of the kitchen & began to walk round and round the house in the dark. Suddenly Lawrence appeared and made a kind of horrible blind rush at her and they began to scream and scuffle. He beat her, he beat her to death, her head and face and breast and pulled at her hair. All the while she screamed for Murry to help her. Finally they dashed into the kitchen and round and round the table. I shall never forget how L. looked. He was so white, almost green and he just hit, thumped the big soft woman. Then he fell into one chair and she into another. No one said a word. A silence fell except for Frieda's sobs and sniffs. In a way I felt almost glad that the tension between them was over for ever, and that they had made an end of their 'intimacy.' L. sat staring at the floor, biting his nails. Frieda sobbed. . . . And the next day, whipped himself, and far more thoroughly than he had ever beaten Frieda, he was running about taking up her breakfast to her bed and trimming her a hat.

Despite the passion and violence, their operatic playlet contains an element of slapstick and self-parody. Act One begins with Lawrence's destruction of Frieda's aesthetic evaluation, leads to her verbal abuse of his assumed omniscience, and ends with his colloquial threat of punishment and Katherine's exit. Act Two opens with Frieda's absolute judgment ('It's all over forever.') which is absolutely unconvincing, and leads to her exit and Lawrence's sudden reappearance as an avenging Fury. But the brutality of his attack is alleviated by the burlesque chase around the table and softened by the description of a green Lawrence thumping a pillow-like Frieda. The curtain falls on this act as both protagonists collapse with physical exhaustion, sobbing and biting nails, and as Katherine, acting as Chorus, makes another absolute pronouncement ('the tension was over for ever'). Act Three reveals a comic reversal of sexual roles, with the defeated male aggressor serving and wooing his lady love.

Though Katherine was horrified by what she called their degradation and humiliation, Mabel Luhan, who described a lively exchange in New Mexico in 1922, also saw the comical side of their combats: '"Take that dirty cigarette out of your mouth! And stop sticking out that fat belly of yours!" he yelled once, shaking his finger in her face. "You'd better stop that talk or I'll tell about *your* things," she taunted' – threatening to expose some horrible intimacies that only a wife could reveal. The Danish painter, Knud Merrild, recounts another fight in 1922 in which Lawrence swung at Frieda and missed, and then crushed and ground up her cigarettes in a hysterical rage. Dorothy Brett describes a quarrel in 1924 when Lawrence threatened to smash Frieda with a poker but destroyed a teapot instead. And Frieda's daughter Barbara recalls an argument in Italy in 1925 when Lawrence threw wine in Frieda's face. When Barbara attacked Lawrence and asked if he really cared for his wife, he incongruously replied: 'It's indecent to ask. Look what I've done for your mother! Haven't I just helped her with her rotten painting?' After a battle in Cornwall in 1916, Frieda retaliated by bringing a heavy plate down on his skull. Lawrence, who was so surprised that he forgot to strike back, exclaimed: 'That was like a woman! . . . No man could have done such a thing when the quarrel was over, and from behind too! . . . It was only lucky you didn't kill me.' Lawrence used this incident in the 'Breadalby' chapter of *Women in Love* when Hermione strikes Birkin from behind with a heavy piece of lapis lazuli.

Frieda, in a letter to Murry in December 1951, admitted Lawrence's manic violence (but not her own) and mentioned the brevity of his rage:

Sometimes he went over the edge of sanity. I was many times frightened but never the last bit of me. Once, I remember he had worked himself up and his hands were on my throat and he was pressing me against the wall and ground out: 'I am the master, I am the master.' I said: 'Is that all? You can be the master as much as you like, I don't care.' His hands dropped away, he looked at me in astonishment and was all right.

But in her autobiography Frieda explains and minimises the quarrels, and emphasises their blissful reconciliations:

What does it amount to that he hit out at me in a rage when I exasperated him, or mostly when the life around him drove him to the end of his patience? I didn't care very much. I hit back or waited till the storm in him subsided. We fought our battles outright to the bitter end. Then there was peace, such peace.

Frieda recognized that Lawrence periodically had to expel his violent hatred so that he could then express his love, and that their repulsion was a necessary element of their attraction. As he wrote in 'History' of the angel–demon play-fight in their marriage:

> Your life, and mine, my love
> Passing on and on, the hate
> Fusing closer and closer with love
> Till at last they mate.

Though Catherine Carswell believed that the rebellious Frieda 'submitted from the first to Lawrence's practical direction, as she did at the last (after a long fight) to his profounder guidance', Katherine Mansfield was more accurate when she stated that Lawrence was 'completely in her power.' The Lawrences' marriage represents the constant tension and struggle of conflicting sexual wills, with the ostensible, though not actual, submission of the subtly powerful woman. For just as Lawrence's outbursts were directly related to the constant pain of his tubercular disease, so Frieda's domination – and his dependence – were closely connected to her overwhelming physical strength. Intimates like Ottoline Morrell, Earl Brewster and Barbara Weekley all testified to Lawrence's intense need for Frieda and his unhappiness when separated from her. As he wrote to her mother when he was alone in Taormina in March 1921: 'The house very empty without F. Don't like it at all.'

IV

Lawrence's marriage suffered two major crises: one culminating in Cornwall in 1916 during the composition of *Women in Love*, the other in Mexico in 1923 when he was writing *The Plumed Serpent*. In the first crisis Lawrence turned away from Frieda toward Rananim in general and Murry in particular. The origin of Rananim (his plan for an ideal community) went back to Lawrence's youth, for Jessie Chambers recalls that 'when he was 17 or 18 he said to me how fine it would be if some day he could take a house, say one of the big houses in Nottingham Park, and he and all the people he liked could live together.'

In February 1916 Lawrence, who was then living with Frieda in Cornwall, intensified his campaign, begun in Lerici in 1913, to get the Murrys to live with them; and in March he pleaded: 'Really, you must have the other place. I keep looking at it. I call it already Katherine's house, Katherine's tower. There is something very attractive about it. It is very old, native to the earth.' Though Katherine was strongly opposed to Cornwall and distrusted the very idea of a community, the Murrys allowed themselves to be persuaded by Lawrence's desperate pleas, reluctantly left Bandol, and arrived in Tregerthen sitting on their possessions on top of a cart.

But Lawrence was immediately critical of the Murrys' marriage and prescribed a radically new foundation for their friendship. As Murry writes in his autobiography, *Between Two Worlds*:

> Lawrence believed, or tried to believe, that the relation between Katherine and me was false and deadly; and that the relation between Frieda and himself was real and life-giving: but that his relation with Frieda needed to be completed by a new relation between himself and me, which I evaded.... By virtue of this 'mystical' relation with Lawrence, I participate in this pre-mental reality, the 'dark sources' of my being come alive. From this changed personality, I, in turn, enter a new relation with Katherine.

The emotional yet abstract language does not explain precisely why Lawrence needs a completion that he could not get from Frieda nor how the Murrys recharge themselves on Lawrence's marital battery, but it is not difficult to see how these ideas offended Katherine, who quite naturally resented Lawrence's assaults on her marriage. She reacted against his powerful influence and his attempt to revitalise their existence through a passionate attachment to her husband.

Lawrence's violent fights with Frieda and his humiliating dependence on her revolted the rather reserved Katherine; and in a letter of May 1916 to her friend, Beatrice Campbell, she gave a precise and vivid description of Lawrence's rages, which embroiled her emotions, exhausted her and made it impossible to concentrate or to work:

> Once you start talking, I cannot describe the frenzy that comes over him. He simply *raves*, roars, beats the table,

abuses everybody. But that's not such a great matter. What makes these attacks insupportable is the feeling one has at the back of one's mind that he is completely out of control, swallowed up in an acute, *insane* irritation. After one of these attacks he's ill with fever, haggard and broken. It's impossible to be anything to him but a kind of playful acquaintance.

After Lawrence's frenzied behaviour, unsuccessful attempt to possess Murry and mad ravings when he screamed at his friend: 'I hate your love, I *hate it*. You're an obscene bug, sucking my life away,' the break between the couples was inevitable. The departure of the Murrys, with suitable excuses, at the end of May, symbolised the failure of Lawrence's most serious attempt to escape from his power-struggle with Frieda and to discover a kind of male love with Murry that could lead the way to a more meaningful form of marriage between man and woman.

After the Murrys left, the Lawrences' behaviour among the rural folk of coastal Cornwall, who were naturally suspicious during the war, was rather reckless. In October 1917, Lawrence and Frieda (whose cousin, Manfred von Richthofen, was the most famous German air ace of the war) were loudly singing German folk songs at the neighbouring house of the composer, Cecil Gray, when they were interrupted by the police. Gray reports that 'at the very time my light had been seen shining out to sea, a German submarine had been located in the vicinity. This, coupled with Frieda Lawrence's German nationality and Lawrence's reputation as an immoral and subversive writer, was more than enough to create a thoroughly unpleasant, not to say dangerous, situation for us all.'

The Lawrences were suspected of spying and forced to leave Cornwall within three days; and this persecution, combined with his humiliating medical examinations for military service, described in the 'Nightmare' section of *Kangaroo*; the suppression of *The Rainbow* for obscenity in 1915; his inability to publish *Women in Love*, which he completed in 1916; the break-up of his friendship with the Murrys as well as his constant poverty and ill-health, increased Lawrence's bitterness, intensified his temper and sent him around the world on his savage pilgrimage as soon as he could escape from his hateful country in 1919.

In September 1919, two months before leaving England, the Lawrences stayed at Cecily Lambert's farm (which he later used as the setting for 'The Fox'), and she provides some interesting insights into the marriage of the practical genius and his aristocratic wife:

> Frieda, I remember, started her visit to us by succumbing to bed for the first few days and expected to be waited on. Most of this fell to D. H. . . . To this day I can see D. H. in a raging temper, carrying a brimming chamber [pot] down to the front garden and emptying it over our flower beds which rather horrified us . . . . They occupied two bedrooms at Grimsbury Farm, and when I suggested to Frieda that it would ease things if they shared one, her reply was that she did not wish to be too much married. What that implied I have no idea. Maybe it was D. H. L.'s illness.

Though Lawrence felt that Frieda had taken advantage of his illness to bully and dominate him, and that he could 'really leave her now, without a pang,' Richard Aldington, like Lawrence's other friends, was sceptical about this and felt that 'no other woman meant anything to him, and those two were as certain to stay together as a river to run to the sea.'

V

In the summer of 1923, just after he completed the first draft of *The Plumed Serpent*, rootlessness, isolation, poverty, illness, sexual problems, Frieda's longing for her children and the revolutionary violence of Mexico intensified the Lawrences' eternal conflict and produced the second and most serious crisis of their marriage. Mabel Luhan reports, with some satisfaction, 'I had heard that he and Frieda had gone to New York to sail for England, but that they had quarrelled at the last moment and he had let her sail alone. . . . She told me, long afterwards, that she thought they had come to a final separation.' Catherine Carswell agrees that they had 'perhaps the very worst' quarrel of their lives, parted in anger and felt the separation would be final. Yet Lawrence longed for Frieda as soon as she had left, did not want to return to Mexico without her, was afraid she would not come back and could not bear to be alone. He rather desperately told the painter, Kai Götzsche: '"She will hate it before long" . . . biting his lower lip and nodding small, quick nods.'

Frieda, who does not mention this quarrel in her autobiography, was also unhappy without Lawrence and writes that in the autumn of 1923: 'I went to England alone and had a little flat in Hampstead to see something of my children. It was winter and I wasn't a bit happy alone there and Lawrence was always cross when I had this longing for the children upon me; but there it was, though now I know he was right: they didn't want me any more. They were living their own lives.' Frieda, rejected by Lawrence and ignored by her children, turned to Murry, who writes that she arrived in England completely out of love with her husband: Frieda had 'had enough of Lawrence in his Mexican "moods," and in fact she had left him. She felt – rightly enough – no more loyalty to him.' Katherine Mansfield had died of tuberculosis the previous January and Lawrence was in America, so Frieda and Murry decided to travel to Germany together.

'On the journey,' writes Murry:

> we declared our love to each other. She was sweet and lovely, altogether adorable, and she wanted us to stay together in Freiburg for a few days anyhow, and I wanted it terribly. The idea of our sleeping together, waking in each other's arms, seemed like heaven on earth. I was worn out with the long strain of Katherine's illness, and Frieda's love was the promise of renewal. And Lawrence had been horrible to her in Mexico – something really had snapped between them. So I felt free to take Frieda, or thought I did; but when it came to the point, I didn't. . . . 'No, my darling, I mustn't let Lorenzo down – I can't.'

The loyalty of Murry (who did not live with Katherine during the last six months of her life) seems insincere and unconvincing, for in his confusion of grief and love it is doubtful that the weak-willed man could have resisted the desires of the impulsive and dominant aristocrat. Murry probably slept with Frieda but did not take her away from Lawrence. E. W. Tedlock, who edited Frieda's *Memoirs and Correspondence* (1961) states that whether Frieda's relationship with Murry before her separation from Lawrence 'was intimate or not, is unclear; but that it became so now on her return to England is certain'; and Emile Delavenay, Lawrence's biographer, agrees with this judgment.

When Lawrence announced his return to England in December 1923, Frieda told Mark Gertler: 'Prepare yourself – Lorenzo's coming!' Lawrence instinctively knew what had happened, for Catherine Carswell reports that the sight of 'Murry and Frieda waiting for him so chummily together [at Waterloo Station] was enough to turn him greenish pale all over.' The Frieda–Murry liaison led to Murry's

Dostoyevskian confession during the embarrassing 'Last Supper' at the Café Royal that month, when Lawrence invited his close friends – Murry, Kot, Gertler, Brett, Mary Cannan and the Carswells – to dinner and then asked who would follow him back to New Mexico. According to Murry's biographer, F. A. Lea:

> Lawrence, drunk and despairing, appealed to Murry not to 'betray' him: and he, drunk too but 'clairvoyant,' spoke the celebrated words, 'I love you, Lorenzo, but I won't promise not to betray you.' They meant, as [Murry] explained later on, 'I am full of affection for you and pity for what you are suffering; but I won't promise to conceal my knowledge of why you are suffering.'

Lawrence's biographer, Harry Moore, explains that 'it is now known that Murry meant he would not betray Lawrence with Frieda, who had proposed that she and Murry become lovers.' But Tedlock is much closer to the truth when he writes, 'Murry confessed rather vaguely to a betrayer's role, and thereby increased Lawrence's scorn.' Catherine Carswell's version of the 'Last Supper' portrays Murry as Judas ('She felt – rightly enough – no more loyalty') and makes his confession quite explicit:

> Murry again embraced Lawrence, who sat perfectly still and unresponsive, with a dead-white face in which the eyes alone were alive. 'I *have* betrayed you, old chap, I confess it,' continued Murry. 'In the past I *have* betrayed you. But never again. I call you all to witness, never again.'
>
> It must have been almost immediately after the strange episode with Murry, that Lawrence, without uttering a sound, fell forward with his head on the table, was deadly sick, and became at once unconscious.

Catherine Carswell's convincing evidence was disputed by Murry in his *Reminiscences of D. H. Lawrence*; and Murry's fourth wife, Mary, attempted to perpetuate the myth of Murry's loyal friendship with Lawrence when she told Lea how Frieda told Murry that 'Lawrence had always looked on him as his greatest friend; how deeply he had loved him, and that he had held John's last letter to him in his hand when he was dying.' Lea dutifully records this improbably sentimental detail; and he also reports that after Lawrence's death in March 1930, Murry 'sped to the south of France to pay his last respects to Lawrence. There, however, he met Frieda: and this time, there was no holding back. "With her, and with her for the first time in my life, I knew what fulfilment in love really meant."' There is no trace of irony in Lea's account of Murry's 'last respects,' nor any comment on Murry's morbid compulsion to sleep with Frieda after his wife's and her husband's deaths. Murry was the most serious threat to the Lawrences' marriage – both in 1916 when Lawrence was attracted to him and in 1923 when Frieda was. But Aldous Huxley's perceptive analysis suggests why their marriage survived the latest crisis just as it had the earlier ones:

Frieda and Lawrence had, undoubtedly, a profound and passionate love-life. But this did not prevent Frieda from having, every now and then, affairs with Prussian cavalry officers and Italian peasants, whom she loved for a season without in any way detracting from her love for Lawrence or from her intense devotion to his genius. Lawrence, for his part, was aware of these erotic excursions, got angry about them sometimes, but never made the least effort to break away from her; for he realised his own organic dependence upon her.

VI

The only friend who agreed to follow Lawrence was the painter, Dorothy Brett, who had been at the Slade school with Gertler and had been a close friend of Katherine Mansfield. She came to New Mexico in the spring of 1924 as a kind of buffer between Frieda and Lawrence, who told Mabel: 'It's a little too hard, alone with [Frieda].' When they arrived in Taos Frieda had to contend with two rivals, for both Mabel and Brett were in love with Lawrence.

When Mabel told Frieda that she was not the right woman for Lawrence, Frieda defiantly challenged her: 'Try it yourself, living with a genius, see what it is like and how easy it is, take him if you can.' Though married to a monumental Indian (her fourth husband) Mabel did try to capture Lawrence – but was not very successful. When Lawrence began to write a novel based on Mabel's life, the vigilant Frieda objected to their *tête-à-têtes* and insisted they work in her house. But Mabel objected to this and cattily asked: 'How could I talk to Lawrence and tell him my feelings and experiences with *Frieda* in the room? To tell him was one thing – that was like talking to oneself – but one couldn't tell her *anything*. She wouldn't understand and she would make one terribly uncomfortable and self-conscious.' When Frieda triumphed, Mabel alluded to her as the Archangel Michael who banished Adam and Eve from Eden, and claimed that she had a secret but more profound sympathy with Lawrence than Frieda did: 'Though Frieda tried to stand with a flaming sword between him and all the others, he, subtle, exchanged with me more and more sympathy, but secretly.'

When in the spring of 1924 the Lawrences wanted to escape from Mabel's possessiveness and from the incestuous gossip of Taos, she generously offered to give Lawrence her Kiowa ranch, seventeen miles above the town. Though Lawrence, who hated presents and possessions, refused her gift, Frieda eagerly accepted the ranch when it was offered to her, and gave Mabel the manuscript of *Sons and Lovers* in exchange. (Mabel later used it to pay her psychiatrist's bills.)

Though freed from Mabel, Frieda still had to contend with Brett, who also became too involved in their lives and got on Frieda's nerves when they travelled together in Mexico in the winter of 1924. Brett relates, with admirable candour, that in Oaxaca in January 1925:

> [Frieda] accuses us, Lawrence and myself, of being like a curate and a spinster; she resents the fact that we do not make love to each other. She says that friendship between man and woman makes only half the curve. Well, maybe.
>
> 'But Frieda,' I say, 'How can I make love to Lawrence when I am your guest; would that not be rather indecent?' She stares at me suspiciously.
>
> 'Lawrence says he could not possibly be in love with a woman like you – an asparagus stick!'

Frieda's unconventional objection to Brett echoes her earlier objection to Ottoline Morrell in 1915: 'she wouldn't have minded L. and [Ottoline] having an ordinary affair – what she couldn't stand was all this "soul-mush."' When Frieda finally told Brett that she would have to leave them and return to New Mexico, and could not live with them on the ranch, Lawrence became angry and called Frieda a jealous fool, but in the end was relieved. And when Brett insisted on 'settling the problem' by renting a cabin on the neighbouring ranch and spying on the Lawrences with a telescope, Frieda strictly limited her visits to three times a week.

This trip to Mexico ended disastrously in February 1925 when Lawrence suffered a near fatal haemorrhage and was finally forced to submit to a medical examination. The doctor confirmed Frieda's greatest fears when he told her: 'Take him to the ranch; it's his only chance. He has T. B. in the third degree. A year or two at the most.' And Lawrence, who had always refused to face the gravity of his disease, also realised how close he had been to death and told Frieda: '"If I die, nothing has mattered but you, nothing at all." I was almost scared to hear him say it, that, with all his genius, I should have mattered so much. It seemed incredible.'

Lawrence made an amazing recovery at the ranch; they returned to Europe in the autumn of 1925 and rented a house at Spotorno on the Italian Riviera; and their conflict flared up again when Frieda had to contend with yet another rival. When Lawrence's younger sister, Ada, visited them, he complained to her about Frieda, who had to fight to free him from his past. One night Ada, who had told Frieda, 'I hate you from the bottom of my heart,' persuaded Lawrence to lock Frieda out of his room, which was the only time he really hurt her.

In February 1926 Lawrence and Ada left for Monte Carlo, and he travelled around Italy while Frieda's daughter visited her at Spotorno. Lawrence admired the way Barbara and Else stood up to and chastised their mother, perhaps because he could no longer do so himself, and in April 1926 he wrote to Kot: 'F's daughters are really very funny: they sit on their mother with ferocity, simply won't stand her cheek, and fly at her very much in her own style. It leaves her a bit flabbergasted, and is very good for her.' He told Brett that he planned to return to Frieda, who seemed quieter, and more friendly; and later sent Frieda a postcard of Jonah confronting the whale with the question: 'Who is going to swallow whom?' Lawrence and Frieda rented Villa Mirenda, outside Florence, in May; and while living there in July 1927 Lawrence had another grave haemorrhage: 'He called from his room in a strange, gurgling voice; I ran and found him lying on his bed; he looked at me with shocked eyes while a slow stream of blood came from his mouth.'

VII

Lawrence was an invalid throughout his life. When he lay
dying in Vence in 1930 he told Frieda, 'I have had bronchitis
since I was a fortnight old'; and as early as June 1913 David
Garnett noticed that after a fit of coughing Lawrence's handkerchief was 'spotted with bright arterial blood.' In January
1930, Dr Andrew Morland, the tuberculosis specialist who
came from London to Bandol to examine Lawrence, stated
he 'had obviously been suffering from pulmonary tuberculosis for a very long time – probably 10 or 15 years.' After
Lawrence's death Huxley said that for the last two years of
his life Lawrence had been like a flame that miraculously
burned on though it had no fuel to feed it.

Though Frieda was obviously worried about Lawrence's
health, she irritated Aldous and Maria Huxley by encouraging Lawrence's obstinate refusal to undergo medical treatment. As Huxley wrote to his brother Julian in July 1929:
'Frieda is worse than he is. We've told her that she's a fool and
a criminal; but it has no more effect than telling an elephant.
So it's hopeless. Short of handcuffing him and taking him to
a sanatorium by force, there's nothing to be done.' Frieda's
apparently irresponsible behaviour can be explained by her
own obstinacy (Huxley also called her 'the most maddening
woman I think I ever came across'), as well as by her loyalty
to Lawrence's wishes, her belief (shared by Lawrence and
Katherine Mansfield) that the depressing routine of a 'soul-
destroying clinic' would stifle his creative genius, and that her
own marvellous power could resurrect and cure – or at least
strengthen and revive – Lawrence. Huxley explains this
mysterious dependence on Frieda (he had to 'have a woman
at the back of him') in a fascinating letter of October 1932:

Lawrence was, in some strange way dependent on her
presence, physically dependent, as one is dependent on the

liver in one's belly, or one's spinal marrow. I have seen him on two occasions rise from what I thought was his death bed, when Frieda, who had been away, came back after a short absence. The mysteries of human relationships are impenetrably obscure.

At the end of his life, Lawrence feared that Frieda was 'a bit sick of my being so much in bed' and found 'the death in me repellent,' and in January 1930 he asked his sister to look after him so Frieda could have a rest. Lawrence asked Frieda to stay with him one night in February, and she described her inability to strengthen him during the final month of his life:

> One night he asked me: 'Sleep with me,' and I did . . . all night I was aware of his aching inflexible chest, and all night he must have been so sadly aware of my healthy body beside him . . . always before, when I slept by the side of him, I could comfort and ease him … now no more … He was falling away from life and me, and with all my strength I was helpless.

In the spring of 1930, Frieda wrote to Mabel Luhan about her admiration for Lawrence's courage in the face of death and the powerful love he had left behind for her:

> Yes, our Lorenzo is dead, but up to the end life never lost its glamour and its meaning. The courage, the courage with which he fought. I am so full of admiration that I can hardly feel much else. Dead, he looked so proud and so unconquered. I didn't know death could be so *splendid*. . . . His death has left me so full of love; it is very strange, no bitterness, no regret; I feel his love and protection, his 'ambiente,' more complete and whole than in his lifetime.

And she told Caresse Crosby, who had published Lawrence's story 'Sun': 'How I miss Lorenzo, in spite of his illness and all, miss his generosity and the life he gave me.' Frieda had relied completely on Lawrence, and felt lost until she could find another man to support her.

Ernest Weekley, who had kept in touch with Frieda through their children, made the surprising proposal that she become his wife again. But Frieda, after her brief affair with Murry, who 'paid his respects' to Lawrence in March 1930, returned to Captain Angelo Ravagli, who had been their landlord at the Villa Mirenda during 1926–29. Frieda, who never valued fidelity, later revealed that Lawrence had become sexually impotent toward the end of 1926 and that she had slept with Ravagli in October 1928, while Lawrence was in Port-Cros. In 1932 Frieda bought Ravagli out of the Italian army, he left his wife and three children, and they lived in Taos, near Mabel and Brett, from 1933 until her death in 1956.

VIII

Frieda was the greatest inspiration in Lawrence's life, and her character and ideas are found everywhere in his work. She helped him to clarify the filial relationship in *Sons and Lovers*, provoked the autobiographical *The Fight for Barbara* (1912) and *Look! We Have Come Through!* (1917), was portrayed as the 'queen-bee' in *Sea and Sardinia* (1921), was the model for Hannele in 'The Captain's Doll' (1923) and for the heroines of almost all the novels written after he met her: Ursula Brangwen in *The Rainbow* (1915) and *Women in Love* (1920), Tanny Lilly in *Aaron's Rod* (1922), Harriet Somers in *Kangaroo* (1923), Kate Leslie in *The Plumed Serpent* (1926) and Connie Chatterley in *Lady Chatterley's Lover* (1928). And in his stories 'The Fox,' 'The Princess,' 'The Virgin and the Gipsy' and 'St. Mawr' and novels *The White Peacock* and *The*

Lost Girl there is the recurrent Laurentian theme of a passionate man of the people who ravishes, against her conscious will but with her subconscious acquiescence, a beautiful, sensitive and frequently aristocratic woman.

There is an element of wish-fulfilment and imaginary triumph in Lawrence's novels, particularly at the end of *The Plumed Serpent*, when Kate learns, as none of the earlier heroines has learned, to submit to the powerful and dominant male will: 'Without Cipriano to touch me and limit me and submerge my will, I shall become a horrible, elderly female. I ought to *want* to be limited. I ought to be *glad* if a man will limit me with a strong will.' But Kate's submission is essentially unconvincing; and the real triumph and vindication of Lawrence's marriage is manifest in his last novel, which was written when Lawrence, weakened by tuberculosis, had abandoned his exhausting sexual combats with Frieda and achieved a final reconciliation. As Lawrence explained to Ottoline Morrell in December 1928: 'There is a brief time for sex, and a long time when sex is out of place. But when it is out of place as an activity there still should be the large and quiet space in the consciousness where it lives quiescent.' In *Lady Chatterley's Lover*, which portrays the vital affirmation of the self in opposition to the sterilising and destructive forces of the machine age, Lawrence expresses his aspirations in the virile and gentle woodsman, Mellors, and his fears in the impotent and decadent writer, Chatterley. This novel, which transcends the exercise of power and the subjection of women, describes Mellors' protective authority and Connie's passionate fulfilment, and expresses a 'new adjustment of consciousness,' a reciprocal tenderness and love.

Ernest Hemingway's Four Wives
THE WELL OF LONELINESS

'Anyone who marries three girls from St. Louis hasn't learned much.'

GERTRUDE STEIN on Hemingway

I

Fitzgerald and Hemingway represent two contrasting modes of marriage. Fitzgerald, who remained loyal to Zelda through alcoholism and insanity, and vulnerable to her predatory destructiveness, was willing to sacrifice his art in order to care for his wife. Hemingway exploited women, aggressively and brutally rejected their emotional needs, cast them off when they had served their purpose and indulged himself in a series of supportive marriages. He thought women should sacrifice themselves to his artistic success and personal welfare.

Like Tolstoy, who believed in emotional inspiration and told Turgenev, 'Before I am able to write anything, I must first of all experience the fever of love,' Hemingway felt 'the best writing is certainly when you are in love.' In the thirties, his friend Morley Callaghan developed the convincing 'theory that Ernest needs a new woman for each big book. There was one [Hadley Richardson] for the stories and *The Sun Also Rises*. Now there's Pauline [Pfeiffer]. *A Farewell to Arms* is a big book. If there's another big book I think we'll find Ernest has another wife.' Callaghan's prediction proved accurate, for during his marriages to Martha Gellhorn and Mary Welsh he wrote *For Whom the Bell Tolls* and *Across the River and Into the Trees*.

In his long and thorough biography of Hemingway Carlos Baker presents all the facts, but he resolutely refrains from interpreting Hemingway's life and analysing the relationship of his marriages to his art. Hemingway's attitude toward his parents and toward his first love strongly influenced his rigid and unrealistic ideas about women. His marriages failed partly because he refused to change or adapt his predetermined beliefs and kept trying to find an attractive, sophisticated and wealthy woman who would also become the passive victim of his overwhelming ego.

Hemingway was born in 1899 and grew up in Oak Park, a comfortable suburb of Chicago, under the contrasting influence of a weak father who enjoyed hunting and fishing, and a domineering and pretentious mother who had been an opera singer and forced her untalented son to practise the cello for six years. John Dos Passos exclaimed that 'Hem was the only man I ever knew who really hated his mother.' And Hemingway insisted that 'his hatred of his mother was non-Freudian, that she was an all-time, all-American bitch, and that the first big psychic wound in his life had come when he discovered that his father was a coward' and that his mother had driven his father to suicide in 1928. After the funeral, Hemingway's mother sent him the gun his father had used to kill himself.

Hemingway's 'non-Freudian' psychic wound, which made him dominate women and force them into the role of passive, devoted and inferior creatures, derives from the fear of his mother's power over his father. In his novels, this attitude toward women is implicit in the stoic virility of the (wounded) hero, and in the beauty and submissiveness of the romantic and tragic heroine who heightens his sense of manliness and well-being; and explicit in the attractive, aggressive and dangerous bitches who resist domination and threaten to destroy weak men. Just as the self-consciousness, philistinism and swaggering brutality of the sometime cello player represent a deliberate rejection of his mother's genteel values, so the sophistication and sexual freedom of his first novel, *The Sun Also Rises* (1926), which his mother called 'One of the filthiest books of the year,' was partly an answer to Gertrude Stein's deadly criticism of her provincial influence: 'Hemingway, after all, you are ninety percent Rotarian.'

Miss Stein, who knew precisely where Hemingway was most vulnerable, also remarked in the voice of Alice Toklas, 'Ernest is very fragile, whenever he does anything sporting something breaks, his arm, his leg, or his head.' Hemingway's desire to put a hook in every fish and a bullet in every beast, and his uncontrollable urge to punch all his adversaries in the nose, suggest a rather awkward attempt to defeat his mother and redeem his father by testing and proving his masculinity.

II

Apart from his mother, the most influential woman in Hemingway's life was Agnes von Kurowsky. Agnes, whose father was German, was trained at Bellevue as an American

Red Cross nurse and cared for him in the Milan hospital after he had been gravely wounded during the Austrian offensive at Fossalta in 1918. Little is known about Agnes except that she taught him, when he was defenceless and vulnerable, to accept the care and protection of a woman for the first time in his life, and that he fell madly in love with her. After their wartime separation, when she wrote to announce her engagement to an Italian lieutenant (whom she never married), Hemingway was devastated by her rejection.

He records this incident in 'A Very Short Story'; and Harry, the autobiographical hero of 'The Snows of Kilimanjaro,' alludes to Agnes when he thinks: 'He had written to her, the first one, the one who left him, a letter telling her how he had never been able to kill [the loneliness]. . . . How what she had done could never matter since he knew he could not cure himself of loving her.' The trauma of Agnes' betrayal, for that is how he interpreted it, forced him into instinctive self-protection. He guarded himself against betrayal and loneliness by conducting a liaison with a future wife during his current marriage; and when he had ensured his own emotional security, abandoned his wife before she could leave him.

Agnes was the model for the heroine of *A Farewell to Arms* (1929), Catherine Barkley, who like Maria in *For Whom the Bell Tolls* (1940), is revealed and reflected in the man she loves. Hemingway idealises Catherine, emphasises her fine background and flawless physical attributes as well as her rather military virtues of loyalty and self-sacrifice, and makes her a suitable object for the attention and pleasure of the wounded hero, Frederic Henry. She 'came from very good people,' wore a nurse's uniform with 'a dark blue cape and a soft felt hat . . . was blonde and had a tawny skin and grey eyes.' She also 'had wonderfully beautiful hair ... a lovely face and body and lovely smooth skin too.'

She calls herself, while unmarried, 'a very old-fashioned wife' and when they spend the night in a Milan hotel, demurely exclaims, 'I never felt like a whore before.... It isn't nice to feel like one.' But their relationship, however charming, is one-dimensional and *donnée*, and they communicate in rhetorical banalities and platitudes:

> 'Oh, darling, I love you so.'
> 'Don't we have a fine time? . . .'

> 'Don't I make you a good wife?'
> 'You're a lovely wife.'

But the essence of Catherine's tragedy is her unwanted baby, and for this aspect of the novel Hemingway transposes on to Agnes his resentment against the accidental pregnancy of his first wife, Hadley, whom he married in September 1921.

Hemingway met Hadley, who had red hair and a trust fund income of about $3000 a year, in Chicago in 1920. Max Eastman described her as 'a likeable though not alluring girl, rather on the square side, vigorously muscular and independent; I think of her as a natural born "hiker."' Hemingway impressed her with his boyish charm, extraordinary good looks (Clark Gable with biceps) and swirling Italian cape, his skill in boxing, fishing and writing, and his courageous war record. Like Othello, he could claim: 'She loved me for the dangers I had passed, / And I loved her that she did pity them.' Though eight years older than Hemingway, Hadley wondered if she would not prefer him as her papa.

Hemingway missed his friends and newspaper cronies when they moved to Paris right after their marriage and lived a poverty-stricken existence in dingy flats. But in the nostalgic *A Moveable Feast* (1964) – which he wrote when he was cushioned by wealth and fame – he portrayed as idyllic their life near a dance hall and above a saw mill in the poor quarters of Paris. The ever helpful Gertrude Stein, not content with teaching Hemingway how to write, 'advised him on how he might acquire paintings by limiting the purchase of clothing, particularly his wife's clothing. Hadley Hemingway, glancing at Gertrude's "steerage" outfit, listened with dismay.' Harold Loeb reports that when Hemingway followed her advice and bought Miró's painting, *The Farm*, a friend said 'it was not his taste that she disapproved of, but his lack of consideration. "Hadley's a perfect fool to take it. Her clothes are falling off. She can't even show herself on the street. And it's her money."' Yet in early stories like 'Cat in the Rain,' which record the dissolution of their marriage, he portrays Hadley as selfish, materialistic and demanding: 'And I want to eat at a table with my own silver and I want candles. And I want it to be spring and I want to brush my hair out in front of a mirror and I want a kitty and I want some new clothes.'

The Hemingways quarrelled bitterly when he left to cover the Greco-Turkish war in September 1922. Two months later, Hadley lost in the Gare de Lyon a suitcase containing the originals and the carbons of all his unpublished type-scripts, and this literary castration had a disastrous effect on their marriage. A third crisis developed when Hadley became pregnant early in 1923, and Hemingway (like Conrad) revealed his selfishness and immaturity by blaming her and refusing to take responsibility for the mishap. Gertrude Stein writes that he came to her house in the morning and 'stayed until about ten o'clock at night and then all of a sudden he announced that his wife was enceinte and then with great bitterness, said, I am too young to be a father.' And Robert McAlmon reports that after the birth of his first son, 'Hemingway was most unhappy because he feared he was again to become a father. He told Hadley it would be no fun at all any more if they had too many children at his age. She wouldn't be a good playmate any more either. He was tragic about it, and Hadley, too, became upset.'

In 'Cross Country Snow' the wife's untimely pregnancy interrupts the hero's fun and good skiing; and in *A Farewell to Arms* Catherine expresses the guilt that Hemingway imposed upon Hadley (who at the age of thirty may have felt she was *not* 'too young' to have children) and the insecurity of a woman who is purely a sexual object and does not want to 'make trouble':

'You aren't angry are you, darling?'
'No.'
'And you don't feel trapped?'
'Maybe a little. But not by you ...'

'She won't come between us, will she? The little brat. . . .
I was afraid because I'm big now that maybe I was a bore
to you. . . . I know I'm no fun for you, darling. I'm like a
big flour barrel.'

The magnanimous Hemingway ('Maybe a little. But not by you.') also transforms his private accident, and his lack of responsibility and loyalty, into a kind of malign retribution for romantic love: 'That was the price you [i.e., *he*] paid for sleeping together. That was the end of the trap. That was what people got for loving each other.' (Kafka's version of this human dilemma, which reveals the superficiality of Hemingway's, is much more terrible, for he believes 'Coitus is punishment for the happiness of being together.') In the novel, Hemingway continues the hunting metaphor of the trap and compares the newborn baby to a freshly skinned rabbit in order to dissociate himself from the realities of paternity. Frederic Henry (who like Hemingway had a son instead of the expected daughter) confesses, 'I had no feeling for him. He did not seem to have anything to do with me.

I had no feeling of fatherhood.' And Catherine has a series of uncontrollable haemorrhages that lead to her death. Though Catherine 'leaves' Frederic, her death represents Hemingway's rejection and desertion of Hadley and his first son, John.

In the later and less idyllic part of *A Moveable Feast*, with thirty years and three marriages between himself and Hadley, Hemingway portrayed the break-up of his first marriage in the form of a parable in which Hadley was the innocent victim, Hemingway the passive prize and Pauline Pfeiffer the treacherous friend in their Eden: 'an unmarried young woman becomes the temporary best friend of another young woman who is married, goes to live with the husband and wife, and then unknowingly, innocently and *unrelentingly* sets out to marry the husband.' The disparity between the first two and the italicised adverb casts considerable doubt on Hemingway's version of this incident, which transfers all his own guilt to the (now divorced) Pauline. The situation becomes even more false – and more heartrending – when he describes his inability to leave Pauline in Paris and return to Hadley and John who awaited him in the Austrian mountains:

> I should have caught the first train from the Gare de l'Est. But the girl I was in love with was in Paris then . . . and where we went and what we did, and the unbelieveable wrenching, killing happiness, selfishness, and treachery of everything we did gave me such a terrible remorse that I did not take the second or the third. . . . When I saw my wife again standing by the tracks . . . I wished I had died before I ever loved anyone but her.

In another discussion of his first marriage, Hemingway tended to praise Hadley and blame himself: 'Hadley, of course, had been good. The fault was his own in every way . . . . She had supported him with her patrimony while he wrote all his early books, and he could never have done them without her loyal, self-sacrificing, stimulating, loving and "actual cash support."' Despite her exemplary qualities, they got divorced, he admitted in a moment of truth, 'because I am a son of a bitch' – which was both literally and figuratively true. Yet in the final and most convincing version of the story, he once again blamed Pauline for his infidelity just as he had blamed Hadley for getting pregnant. Though Hemingway had criticised Hadley for a Zelda-like desire to buy things, he now revealed his own materialistic motives and frankly said that 'Pauline had stolen him away from her good friend Hadley. Pauline had the wealth that Hadley lacked and that he needed at the time.'

Hemingway was always rather sentimental about his former wives, and was pleased when the odd and even ones got on well together. When he was making the transition from Pauline to Martha in 1939, he wrote to Hadley for moral support and gave her a dubious compliment: 'The more he saw of women, the more he admired her. If heaven was something that people enjoyed on earth, then he and she had known a good slice of theirs in the Black Forest and at Cortina and Pamplona in 1922–23.' It is significant that Hemingway felt the best years were before the birth of their son and that in *The Sun Also Rises* he excluded Hadley from the experiences he had shared with her in Paris and Pamplona. There was no place for a passive, pregnant woman among the glamorous expatriates of France and Spain.

III

Like her close friend Hadley, Pauline Pfeiffer had gone to school in St Louis, and was older and much richer than Hemingway. She was an ardent Catholic who converted Hemingway to her religion for the duration of their marriage (1927–40); a graduate of the University of Missouri school of journalism who had worked for *Vogue* in Paris; and one of the sophisticated and gilded Americans of the Paris twenties, who were exemplified by Gerald and Sara Murphy and portrayed in Fitzgerald's *Tender is the Night*. McAlmon describes her as 'small-boned and lively as a partridge ... with dark bangs on her forehead and long, emerald-jewelled earrings hanging from the neat lobes of her ears.' And Baker, who says she was 'chic, well-dressed and highly articulate about the current fashions, [and] glanced sympathetically at Hadley's worn and simple clothes,' does not record *her* response to the Miró painting.

The predatory Pauline appropriately features in Hemingway's hunting tales: *The Green Hills of Africa* (1935) and 'The Snows of Kilimanjaro' (1936). She gets a good press in the book where she is praised for her bravery, beauty and devotion, and portrayed as an impressive possession, like a gun or a trophy. 'Her courage was so automatic and so much a simple state of being that she never thought of danger. . . . She was always lovely to look at asleep, sleeping quietly, close curled like an animal.' When Tarzan returns from the hunt, Jane says: 'I've spent all my time praying for you.'

The personal theme of corruption by money, which emerges in *The Green Hills*, is developed at some length in 'Kilimanjaro.' He knowingly discourses on what harms a writer and rather wittily lists: 'Politics, women, drink, money, ambition. And the lack of politics, women, drink, money and ambition.' Hemingway, who by this time was fairly well off and could afford luxurious safaris, elaborates this theme by stating: 'We destroy them in many ways. First, economically. They make money. . . . Our writers when they have made some money increase their standard of living and they are caught. They have to write to keep up their establishments, their wives, and so on, and they write slop.' Though Hemingway speaks generally of writers in the plural, he had his own establishments and wives and slop.

In 1936 Hemingway met Martha Gellhorn in Key West and wrote 'The Snows of Kilimanjaro.' In that story, which marks a turning-point in his marriage to Pauline, he gratuitously attacks Fitzgerald and obliquely accuses Pauline of corrupting his talent and wrecking his first marriage.

'Your bloody money,' he said.
'That's not fair,' she said. 'It was always yours as much as mine. I left everything and I went wherever you wanted to go and I've done what you wanted to do. But I wish we'd never come here....'

Each day of not writing, of comfort, of being that which he despised, dulled his ability and softened his will to work so that, finally, he did no work at all....

He had never quarrelled much with this woman, while with the women that he loved he had quarrelled so much they had finally, always, with the corrosion of the quarrelling, killed what they had together.

Though her denials are just, Harry's wife, like Pauline, cannot escape the guilt *he* feels about marrying her for money. Though Pauline had learned from Hadley's experience, as Mary Welsh would learn from Martha's, not to oppose Hemingway's wishes, her non-combatant role reduced their quarrels but did not solve their problems. Though Harry represents a degree of corruption and sterility that Hemingway had not yet reached, his troubles cut close to Hemingway's bone and accurately foreshadow his own artistic degeneration.

Though Pauline and Hemingway had two sons (Patrick was born in 1928, the year Hemingway's father committed suicide, and Gregory in 1931), Hemingway, many years after 'Kilimanjaro,' blamed the failure of his second marriage on sexual maladjustment. Though he was then a Catholic, he complained that 'he had been obliged to practice coitus interruptus with Pauline after two Caesarean births because further children would endanger her life, and birth control was barred by *her* religion.' He also hoped to have a daughter with Martha Gellhorn, who naively confessed to Pauline that she spent so much time in their Key West House, she nearly became a fixture there. Martha eventually displaced Pauline, who had also lived with the Hemingways, just as Pauline had ousted Hadley.

IV

Martha Gellhorn, a tall, handsome, blonde writer, was born in 1908. She had been to Bryn Mawr, had married a French marquis and had published two novels before she met Hemingway. Just as Hadley is associated with expatriate Paris and Pauline with Key West and hunting in Africa, so Martha (who found Finca Vigia) belongs to Cuba and the war years in Spain and France. She and Hemingway were correspondents during the Civil War, visited the front together and were discovered as lovers when a shell burst the hot-water tank in their Madrid hotel.

Martha was a friend of Eleanor Roosevelt and arranged for a showing at the White House of *The Spanish Earth,* the Loyalist film that Hemingway had helped to make. Just as Hadley had tried to prevent Hemingway from reporting the Turkish war, so Pauline attempted to keep him from returning to the Spanish war, but he ignored her objections and returned for a second six-month tour with Martha. Baker writes that:

While he and Martha celebrated a quiet Catalonian Christmas [in 1937], Pauline reached Paris alone and unannounced in a last-ditch attempt to save her marriage.

She had even let her hair grow in a long bob like Martha's
. . . . They were quarrelling bitterly over Martha, and
Pauline had threatened to jump off the balcony of their
hotel room.

Pauline's extreme behaviour did not fail to arouse
Hemingway's all-too-human emotions, for he felt she had
been 'a hell of a fine girl' before she turned sour. And Baker
reports, with some pride, that 'His rejection of Pauline in
favor of Martha stirred up the remorse that had remained
quiescent ever since his rejection of Hadley.' Hemingway
regretted that he had lost one of his best critics and said that
'Pauline now hated him so much that she refused to look at
the book. This was a damned shame because she had the best
literary judgment of any of them.'

Dorothy Bridges, the heroine of Hemingway's play about
the Spanish Civil War, *The Fifth Column* (1938), was based on
the physical and personal characteristics of Martha. The love-
stricken hero of the play insists: 'I want to make an absolutely
colossal mistake' with Dorothy; and in September 1940 Scott
told Zelda, with a bittersweet mixture of satisfaction and
envy, Hemingway and Pauline 'are getting divorced after ten
years and he is marrying a girl named Martha Gellhorn.'

The dedication of Hemingway's novel about Spain, *For
Whom the Bell Tolls* (which Pauline refused to read), boldly
asserted: 'This book is for Martha Gellhorn'; and the heroine,
Maria, is a portrait of Martha as Hemingway would have
liked her to be. Though beautiful, Maria is subservient and
submissive, docile and devoted; and like a domestic pet, she
is grateful for the attention of Robert Jordan: 'Jordan reached
his hand out and patted her head. She stroked under his hand
like a kitten. Then he thought that she was going to cry. But
her lips drew up again and she looked at him and smiled.'

Maria has been traumatised by the political execution of
her father and her rape by the fascists, and is ready to be

rescued and revived by Jordan. Despite her violation, which makes her more sexually exciting, she has retained her essential innocence without losing her sexual desire. She instantly responds to Jordan's touch, which embarrasses even Pilar, takes the initiative and asks where he is sleeping so she can come to him in the night.

> He ran his hand over the top of her head. He had been wanting to do that all day and now he did it, he could feel his throat swelling. She moved her head under his hand and smiled up at him and he felt the thick but silky roughness of the cropped head rippling between his fingers. Then his hand was on her neck and then he dropped it. 'Do it again,' she said.'I wanted you to do it all day.' 'Later,' Robert Jordan said and his voice was thick

– with the pride of seduction, the pleasure of restraint and the prospect of satisfaction. Though Maria, who remains static throughout the novel, is an extremely limited character, her 'silky roughness' makes her as good a comrade in arms as in bed.

Unlike Maria, Hadley, Pauline and Mary Welsh, Martha did not meekly submit to her hero's wishes, and she refused to relinquish her successful career as a foreign correspondent for *Collier's* magazine. When she reported the war in Finland in 1939, Hemingway referred dramatically to 'the dark depths of his loneliness without her.' And just after their marriage in 1940, when she left to cover the war in China, the abandoned husband sardonically remarked that her idea of fun 'was to celebrate the rest of their honeymoon on the Burma road.' At home, Hemingway was extremely domineering and egoistic, and during the war his abortive submarine-hunting expeditions were usually followed by compensatory drinking sprees and terrible fights at the Finca Vigia. On one occasion (which recalled the Fitzgeralds' grimmer moments), when Martha insisted on driving because he was drunk, he slapped her and she drove his beloved Lincoln across the ditch and into the trees.

Martha longed to return to journalism and used her career to threaten Hemingway. Her refusal to submit to his will puzzled and hurt him, and he was unable to understand her unwillingness 'to tag along and like it' as Hadley and Pauline had done. When they began to lead separate lives, he once again recalled the sentimental memories of his first marriage, and complained to Hadley about the absence of Martha – the only woman, apart from his mother, who had ever opposed and defied him. He accepted the blame for the break-up of all his marriages, except the one to Martha; and when they got divorced in 1945 after five years together, he was already deeply involved with Mary Welsh.

V

Hemingway and Martha were rival war correspondents in London in 1944. When Martha ignored him after he was seriously injured in a car accident, he was nursed by Mary Welsh, a small, attractive, thirty-six-year-old blonde from Minnesota, who worked as a feature writer for the *Daily Express* and was married to an Australian reporter. Though consoled by Mary, Hemingway got even with Martha by inviting her to dinner, undressing and pretending to attack her when she came to his room.

Though Martha, not Hemingway, landed in Normandy on D-Day, he exaggerated his military exploits with the Fourth Infantry Division in order to impress Mary (as he had once impressed Hadley) and was reunited with her after he 'liberated' the Ritz Hotel from the Germans. Mary, whom Hemingway married in March 1946, failed to achieve literary immortality in his works, but she was the subject of two embarrassingly bad love poems that emphasise her role as an anodyne for loneliness. In 'To Mary in London,' written during the war and published posthumously by her, he describes her:

> Coming small-voiced and lovely
> To the hand and eye
> To bring your heart back that was gone
> To cure all loneliness.

Though Hemingway had deserted his three sons, he still wanted a daughter. When Mary suffered a grave miscarriage in August 1946, he helped to save her life, sent her to Key West to recover from her illness and was surprised to see how much his second and fourth wives liked each other. Though the heroine of the first novel written during their marriage, Renata in *Across the River and Into the Trees,* was inspired by a young Venetian beauty, Adriana Ivancich, it was dutifully dedicated 'To Mary with Love.'

When Mary recovered, Hemingway noted with pleasure that she fished and swam well and liked the Cuban climate, cats and the sea; and he told his comrade, Colonel Lanham, that 'she was brave, kind, unselfish, adaptable and "beautifully tanned"' – that is, as Lillian Ross reveals in her profile of Hemingway, decorative and amenable to his whims. Robert Manning, who visited the Hemingways in Cuba, rather fulsomely confirms that 'Hemingway's fourth wife cared for him well, anticipated his moods and his desires, played bountiful hostess to his friends, and diplomatically turned aside some of the most taxing demands on his time and generosity.'

Mary was Hemingway's wife during the years of his greatest fame and most radical deterioration, the years of the Hollywood films and the Nobel Prize as well as of the 'Papa' persona and the egotistical articles for the slick magazines.

Though Mary believed, in contrast to Martha, in *laissez-faire*: 'He didn't marry a policeman. It's better if I let him alone,' he could still be cruel to her. When she broke her elbow, he complained that it ruined his plans for a hunting trip, just as he had condemned Hadley's pregnancy for spoiling his skiing. Though Mary served as his secretary and 'retyped as usual, correcting spelling and punctuation and consulting him about phrases which I thought needed reorganization', he aroused her jealousy in 1959, as he had done with Adriana Ivancich ten years earlier, by adopting Valerie Danby-Smith as his second-string secretary in the belief – shared by Ben Jonson's *Volpone* – that 'a miraculous renewal of youth could be achieved by association with a nineteen-year-old girl.'

Mary supported Hemingway during his bouts of morbid depression and electric shock treatments, and loyally if ineffectively tried to conceal his suicide. After his death she found the typescript of *A Moveable Feast* in the basement of the Ritz and 'went over the book and gave it the same hard-headed editing I would have done if I had been copying from Ernest's original typing and handscript as I used to do in Cuba.'

VI

Hemingway's four marriages were significantly reflected in his work, and there is a close correspondence between his personal and imaginative defects, between his treatment of women and the decline of his art. As Hemingway became more famous, he wanted more beautiful, wealthy, successful and worldly wives. He therefore discarded the sweet but provincial Hadley, a good sport whom he had admired during their courtship for attending a college football game with a sprained ankle. She had suited the first phase of his career and outlived her usefulness. Though he admired Pauline, Martha and Mary, who were professional writers and could help him with his work, he was unable to accept women as equals and unwilling to allow them to have an independent existence.

In his best novel, *The Sun Also Rises,* his most successful heroine, Brett Ashley (inspired by Lady Duff Twysden who aroused Hemingway's violent jealousy when she ran off with Harold Loeb), dominates and controls the men in the novel. But in his later works, Hemingway does not permit his fictional women, like his actual wives, to live a life of their own and makes them all subservient to the heroes of his books. Hemingway wanted women to be ciphers, portrayed them as such and controlled in his novels what he could not always control in his life.

Hemingway's aesthetic as well as emotional need for the love and inspiration of women was complemented by the legacy of his mother: a fundamental hostility to women; a profound resentment of his dependence upon them; and a desire to escape to the less complicated world of fish, game, bulls, and men without women. As Edmund Wilson observed of Hemingway's antagonism to women, 'This instinct to get the woman down presents itself frankly as a fear that the woman will get the man down.'

In 'The Short Happy Life of Francis Macomber,' for example, the beautiful and bitchy Mrs Macomber, who punishes her husband for his cowardice by sleeping with Wilson, the white hunter, exemplifies the kind of women who are 'the hardest in the world; the hardest, the cruelest, the most predatory and the most attractive and their men have softened or gone to pieces nervously as they have hardened.' At the climax of the story, Mrs Macomber shoots her husband because he has recovered his courage and Wilson's respect, and has become strong enough to leave her.

In his last book, *The Old Man and the Sea* (a poor man's *Moby Dick*), Hemingway eliminated women entirely and replaced sexual conflict with a sentimentalised relationship of

a man and a fish. The world of war and sport was attractive
to Hemingway because it removed his greatest source of
anxiety – women – and provided an excellent opportunity
to test his courage and assert his masculinity. His compulsive
glorification of the manly virtues of bravery and endurance,
and his emphasis on *cojones*, *machismo* and grace under pressure, betrays the legacy of his father: the basic insecurity
about his own virility, which forced him to dominate,
oppress and abandon the women he married, and to assuage
his loneliness by continuously confirming his capacity to
conquer and to love.

Scott and Zelda Fitzgerald
THE ARTIST AND THE MODEL

"'I used to think until you're eighteen nothing matters."
"That's right. And afterwards it's the same way."'
FITZGERALD, Tender is the Night

I

Fitzgerald wrote about himself and lived his books; and this confusion of his life and his art, which like the phoenix was nourished and consumed by the same source, led inevitably to the tragic conclusion of his brilliant career. He was convinced he had talent and that his talent would make him *great*, but he had imaginative limitations and lacked the confidence to invent. His only material was his private life, so he meticulously observed and carefully recorded his family and friends, and created his fiction out of immediate, personal experience.

Fitzgerald was absorbed in adolescent image-making and role-playing. Writing about what had happened to him seemed to certify reality and help to define – or recover – his idea of himself, which remained elusive behind a romantic façade. As he ingenuously observed, 'I don't know whether I'm real or whether I'm a character in one of my own novels.' After he had created the public *personae* which he and Zelda felt obliged to imitate and embody, and which revealed the disparity between their projected and actual lives, he admitted 'we scarcely knew any more who we were and we hadn't a notion what we were.' And when this rift fissured into a crack-up in the 1930s he lost his created identity and confessed, 'there was not an "I" any more. . . . It was strange to have no self.'

Fitzgerald met Zelda Sayre at a country club dance in Montgomery, Alabama in July 1918 when she performed as a southern belle and he paraded as an infantry officer. Their attraction was immediate, intense and narcissistic, for she was as beautiful as he was handsome and they looked sufficiently alike to be taken for brother and sister. Zelda told him, 'I don't want to be famous and fêted – all I want is to be very young always and very irresponsible,' and he 'fell in love with her courage, her sincerity and her flaming self respect.' To the young man who grew up in Buffalo and went to school in Hackensack (like Orwell, Fitzgerald had been a poor boy in a rich boy's school), Zelda represented the essence of the girls he desired and the glamorous life he hoped to live.

But Fitzgerald had to overcome the romantic rivalry of the golfer Bobby Jones as well as his own Irish Catholic background. He drank too much, had dropped out of Princeton and was a failure just after the war: mediocre in the advertising world and unable to get started as a writer.

Zelda, who was scarcely enchanted by the prospect of life in a small Bronx apartment and very cagey about throwing in her lot with a penniless suitor, broke with him in 1919. Like Gatsby, who lost Daisy because he was poor, Fitzgerald had already experienced with the wealthy socialite, Ginevra King, what he called 'one of those tragic loves doomed for lack of money.' Though he could lament with Marvell:

> My love is of a birth as rare
> As 'tis, for object, strange and high;
> It was begotten by Despair
> Upon Impossibility,

he was determined to win Zelda from her southern half-backs and golfing beaux.

Zelda's esteem, from the very beginning, was inextricably linked with his success as a writer, and he was inspired by her challenge to his latent creative genius. He portrayed her as Rosalind in 'The Debutante' section of his first novel, *This Side of Paradise*, they became engaged when the book was accepted; and were married in April 1920, a week after publication, as the novel went into its second printing. It sold 33,000 copies in the first eight months and launched them into a vertiginous fame.

Though Scott's literary image was daring, nonconformist and unconventional, he had a provincial, puritanical streak and an element of sensitive boorishness. He was excited by Zelda's *Je m'en fiche* attitude and attracted to the aristocratic manners of the girl who lashed the elevator door with her belt so that it would be ready when she was. Like the auto-biographical heroine of her novel, *Save Me the Waltz*, Zelda lived without premeditation: 'You took what you wanted from life, if you could get it, and you did without the rest.' Arthur Mizener describes their extravagance and practical jokes, and how they circled around a revolving door for half an hour, 'rode down Fifth Avenue on the tops of taxis because it was too hot or dove into the fountain in Union Square or tried to undress at the *Scandals,* or, in sheer delight at the splendor of New York jumped, dead sober, into the Pulitzer fountain in front of the Plaza.' As late as 1927, during a party in Hollywood, they boiled all the ladies' purses in a large pot of tomato sauce, but failed to amuse the guests.

This familiar catalogue of infantile pleasures is often admired ('in sheer delight') by the chroniclers of the Fitzgerald legend who accept it as an expression of their youthful vitality. But it also suggests a tiresome self-absorption, self-importance and striving for complete irresponsibility as well as a rather desperate hedonism that threatened to burn itself out and lapse into boring repetition (five minutes in the revolving door would have been sufficient). For lack of anything better to do they jumped into *two* fountains (they could not have *dived* into the shallow water) and merely 'tried' to undress at the theatre instead of actually doing so.

It is important to distinguish, however, between the motives of Scott and of Zelda. Though they both felt the need to act up to their reputation and sometimes resembled a vaudeville team in their public performances, it was Zelda who always exploited the dramatic possibilities of a scene, gave what she called 'a damned good show,' self-consciously fulfilled her madcap role and created Scott's fictional material. During a farewell dinner on the Riviera she drawled, 'Nobody has offered our departing heroes any gifts to take with them. I'll start off.' And she charitably stepped out of her black lace panties and threw them at the stunned and delighted guests. During a tennis match in 1931, which was passively umpired by Fitzgerald, she gradually stripped off all her clothes until her male opponent was 'playing with a stark naked woman . . . and having a terrible time returning her shots.' In *Tender is the Night* Nicole insists, 'I think we should do something spectacular. I feel that all our lives have been too restrained,' and Fitzgerald observes: 'There is something awe-inspiring in one who has lost all inhibitions, who will do anything.'

Though Scott's drunkenness frequently precipitated his adolescent pranks, he deliberately encouraged Zelda to be childish and wild so that he could later write about the bizarre things she had done. He was attracted to the qualities that were at first essential to his work and that would later destroy him; and it is possible to see, in the borderland between their awareness and abandon, the origins of his alcoholism and her insanity. Fitzgerald later realised this when he unconsciously echoed Wordsworth's description of the manic-depressive:

> But, as it sometimes chanceth, from the might
> Of joy in minds that can no farther go,
> As high as we have mounted in delight
> In our dejection do we sink as low,

and wrote of his early success in 'The Crack-Up': 'Riding in a taxi one afternoon between very tall buildings under a mauve and rosy sky, I began to bawl because I had everything I wanted and knew I would never be so happy again.'

II

The Fitzgeralds were rivals and combatants as well as partners and lovers, and both ambitiously sought attention, publicity and fame. At first Zelda was the proud and shy helpmate who told Scott, 'It's nice to know you *can* really do things – *anything* – and I love to feel that maybe I can help just a little.' Encouraged by her willingness and passivity, Fitzgerald artistically exploited their personal relationship and appropriated Zelda as his raw material. During their courtship he felt a conflict between his personal and artistic desires, and records, 'My enchantment with certain things that she felt and said was already paced by an anxiety to set them down in a story.' Scott fell in love with Zelda as well as with his imaginative transformation of her, spun her wit and wildness into his fiction, and later admitted to his Princeton friend, Edmund Wilson: 'The most enormous influence on me in the four and a half years since I met her has been the complete, fine and full-hearted selfishness and chill-minded-ness of Zelda.' But he failed to realise that he had betrayed her confidence and exposed her feelings, and that her para-doxical coolness and selfishness would not always remain full-hearted.

The expropriation and direct transcription of Zelda's diaries, letters and creative ideas, as well as her personality and behaviour, are evident in stories like 'Jelly Bean' and 'Ice Palace' and in his second novel, *The Beautiful and the Damned* (1922). This book, which included Zelda's famous *mot*, 'I want to marry Anthony, because husbands are so often "husbands" and I must marry a lover,' portrayed some of the more negative aspects of their life. In a coy review of the novel in the *New York Tribune* Zelda disguised her consider-able resentment, like a cat's claws, beneath a velvety exterior: 'It seems to me that on one page I recognize a portion of an old diary of mine, which mysteriously disappeared shortly after my marriage, and also scraps of letters which, though considerably edited, sound to me vaguely familiar.'

In order to get higher fees, Scott published all Zelda's stories under his own name; and when George Jean Nathan wanted to publish her diaries in *Vanity Fair,* Fitzgerald insisted that they were vital to his own work. While Zelda rightly felt that Scott was stifling her creative impulse, he resented his dependence on her inspiration and her criticism: 'Referring everything to Zelda – a terrible habit,' he wrote to his editor, Maxwell Perkins, 'nothing ought to be referred to anybody until it's finished.' By recklessly confusing Zelda with his fictional heroines and demanding exclusive literary rights to her life and works, Scott set up an explosive clash of egos that eventually destroyed them.

Their extravagance, quarrels, jealousy and destructive drunkenness were apparent from the very beginning of their public marriage, for they refused to suppress the ugliness that lay beneath the glamour. During their earliest revels in New York, Fitzgerald's college friend, Alexander McKaig, noted in his diary of 1920:

Terrible party. Fitz & Zelda fighting like mad – say themselves marriage can't succeed.

They continued their fight while here. . . . Fitz should let Zelda go & not run after her. Like all husbands he is afraid of what she might do in a moment of caprice.

[Flat] looks like a pigsty. If she's there Fitz can't work – she bothers him – if she's not there he can't work – worried of what she might do.

Zelda was even more extravagant than Scott, and Max Perkins reports that 'money went through her fingers like water; she wanted everything, she kept him writing for the magazines.' They were soon deeply in debt and Fitzgerald claimed that in 1923 he wrote stories twelve hours a day for five weeks 'to rise from abject poverty back into the middle class.' But he was never able to repeat this heroic feat.

Alabama Beggs, the autobiographical heroine of *Save Me the Waltz*, blames her husband's absorption in his painting for the monotony of their lives. And in *A Moveable Feast* Hemingway confirms that 'Zelda was jealous of Scott's work and as we got to know them, this fell into a regular pattern . . . . He would start to work and as soon as he was working well Zelda would begin complaining about how bored she was, and get him off on another drunken party.'

Despite the grave problems observed by McKaig, Perkins and Hemingway, Fitzgerald kept up a brave front and wrote to his college friend, John Peale Bishop: 'Zelda and I sometimes indulge in terrible four-day rows that always start with a drinking party but we're still enormously in love and about the only truly happily married people I know.' Emotional chaos had become an essential part of their existence and seemed to sustain them in a cataclysmic sort of way.

The Fitzgeralds may have been enormously in love but they were not truly happy. Though Scott's ideal was to protect his youth, his success and his passion for Zelda from the passage of time and the demands of reality, their marriage reached its first serious crisis during the summer of 1924 when Zelda had a brief affair with the handsome French aviator, Edouard Josanne. Fitzgerald was proud of Zelda's beauty and her ability to attract men, but he may have been too egotistically sure of her fidelity. After the birth of their daughter Scottie in October 1921 and Zelda's abortion a few months later in March 1922, she must have feared a physical decline. She was bored, she resented Scott's success, she wanted to make him jealous and, as her novel makes clear (Fitzgerald considered it proof of her adultery) she was overwhelmed by the romantic Frenchman who made daredevil flights over their luxurious villa.

When Scott realised what was happening, he delivered an ultimatum and forced Zelda to banish Josanne from her life. She reacted by taking an overdose of sleeping pills, the first of her three suicide attempts. Zelda's crack-up was also foreshadowed by other ominous events. In the summer of 1925 in Vence she rose from the table and suddenly threw herself down a long dark flight of steps; and in October 1929 she suddenly said, 'I think I'll turn off here,' and tried to drive off the high cliffs of the Grande Corniche.

Fitzgerald never recovered from Zelda's affair, which permanently scarred their marriage. He retaliated three years later in Hollywood when he had his affair with Lois Moran, 'fresh, blonde, blue-eyed, just seventeen and unspoiled by her success as an actress.' Scott not only slept with Lois but also praised her at Zelda's expense and claimed that she 'did something with herself, something that required not only talent but effort.' After a fight about Lois, Zelda threw her platinum and diamond watch out of a train window; and a few months later he smashed her favourite blue vase, she called his father an Irish policeman, and he slapped her so hard that her nose bled. This violence was a manifestation of their artistic rivalry and struggle for personal survival as well as their jealousy and sexual problems. They were unable to have a second child, Zelda complained of his inability to satisfy her and accused him of a homosexual attachment to Hemingway. Fitzgerald remembered his early traumas with Zelda when in 1938 he wrote to a dejected writer who had sought his advice: 'I think a great deal of your problem will depend on whether you have a sympathetic wife who will realise calmly and coolly, rather than emotionally, that a talent like yours is worth saving.'

III

When Zelda interfered with his work, undermined his self-confidence and drove him to drink, Fitzgerald tried to strengthen himself with college connections and male friendships. He spent many weekends at his Princeton club after his marriage, wrote collegiate musicals, loyally followed the football team to the end of his life and died with the *Princeton Alumni Weekly* in his hands. He was the son of a weak and unsuccessful father, and sought moral authority from Zelda's father, intellectual authority from Edmund Wilson, and aesthetic authority from Ernest Hemingway. Before going to Hollywood in 1927 Fitzgerald knelt before Judge Sayre and pleaded, 'Tell me you believe in me.' 'Scott,' the Judge grudgingly replied, 'I think you will always pay your bills.'

Fitzgerald's relationship with Hemingway was far more complicated. Though Fitzgerald had gone to college, and was an older and far more successful writer (he introduced Hemingway to Scribner's and helped him toward recognition), he always stood in awe of his artistic rival and heroic ideal. Morley Callaghan relates, 'It seemed to give [Fitzgerald] pleasure to be able to tell stories about a man whose life was so utterly unlike his own. He gave Ernest's life that touch of glamour that he alone could give.'

In 'The Crack-Up' Fitzgerald writes of his 'two juvenile regrets at not being big enough (or good enough) to play football in college, and at not getting overseas during the war,' and he regrets 'the shoulder-pads worn for one day on the Princeton freshman football field and the overseas cap never worn overseas.' Though these seem to be superficial symbols of puerile regrets, they can be traced back to 1920 when Edmund Wilson and John Bishop compiled an ironic exhibit of Fitzgeraldiana which included an 'Overseas cap never worn overseas' and a 'Photograph of the Newman [prep school] football team with Fitzgerald as half-back.' The symbols specifically represent the athletic prowess and combat experience (in Italy as well as in Spain) that Hemingway had and Fitzgerald, with his 'non-combatant's shell shock,' sadly lacked.

The hero of Fitzgerald's last, absurd project, *Philippe, Count of Darkness*, was modelled on Hemingway as he might have existed in the middle ages. He recorded in his Notebooks that 'he had always longed to absorb into himself some of the qualities that made Ernest attractive, and to lean on him like a sturdy crutch in times of psychological distress.' But Hemingway, who was unusually vindictive toward his benefactors, despised Fitzgerald's weakness, drunkenness and self-pity, and tended to bully him. He told Perkins that 'Fitzgerald had gone from youth to senility without manhood in between,' and when Scott was particularly vulnerable he cruelly attacked him in the original version of 'The Snows of Kilimanjaro' (Scott's name was later changed to Julian): 'He remembered poor Scott Fitzgerald and his romantic awe of [the rich]. . . . He thought they were a special glamorous race and when he found out they weren't it wrecked him just as much as any other thing wrecked him.' Fitzgerald was so disturbed by the story that he attempted suicide, but vomited from the overdose of morphine.

Hemingway, who was ruthless with anyone who interfered with his work or his wishes, selfishly discarded a sequential series of sometimes rich and always devoted wives, while Fitzgerald remained loyal to Zelda in her madness. Hemingway agreed with H. L. Mencken that 'Scott would never amount to anything until he got rid of his wife,' and bluntly told Fitzgerald: 'Of all people on earth you needed discipline in your work and instead you marry someone who is jealous of your work, wants to compete with you and ruins you. It's not as simple as that and I thought Zelda was crazy the first time I met her and you complicated it even more by being in love with her and, of course, you're a rummy.' In a notorious passage in *A Moveable Feast*, Hemingway describes Fitzgerald's complaint about Zelda's attempt at psychological castration : 'You know I have never slept with anyone but Zelda. . . . Zelda said the way I was built I could never make any woman happy and that was what upset her.' After a personal inspection in the toilet, the patronising man-of-the-world paternally reassures Scott about his physical equipment and says, with some justice, 'Zelda just wants to destroy you.'

Fitzgerald's convincing statement in 'The Crack-Up' that he had slept with prostitutes as an undergraduate in 1917 ('that night was the first time that I hunted down the specter of womanhood that, for a little while, makes everything else seem unimportant') casts doubt on Hemingway's version of the incident. Though he exaggerated Fitzgerald's innocence and naivety and tried to make him look ridiculous, there is no doubt that Zelda attacked Scott's sexual capacity.

Though Fitzgerald was always embarrassed by the contrast between Hemingway's success and his own failure, his analysis of his former friend was extremely perceptive. He said that Hemingway was just as 'nervously broken down' as he was, but that the manifestations took different forms: 'His inclination is toward megalomania, and mine toward melancholy.'

IV

In the late 1930s Scott wrote of Zelda; 'Never in her whole life did she have a sense of guilt, even when she put other lives in danger – it was always people and circumstances that oppressed her.' Fitzgerald had once admired and encouraged Zelda's egoistic hedonism; but in his attempt to discover what went wrong in their lives, he blamed her for lacking the sense of guilt that had overwhelmed him during the last decade of his life. His profound regrets about his estrangement from Zelda and Scottie are portrayed in his most moving story, 'Babylon Revisited.' He also realised that his artistic manipulation and suppression of Zelda and their unstable and itinerant life provided the personal and circumstantial factors that made her feel oppressed and led to her mental breakdown in the spring of 1930.

Zelda's intense need to express her various talents and achieve artistic recognition was partly inspired by Scott's success and by his invidious comparison of Zelda with professionals, like Lois Moran, who *did* something. In mid-1927 she started taking ballet lessons in Philadelphia, but failed to see that she was too old to begin a professional career in dance and that her manic efforts were doomed from the start. Zelda's novel reveals her unrealistic, dangerous and compensatory commitment to the discipline of ballet, for she writes that Alabama wanted to change 'the certain disillusions of the past into uncertain expectancies of the future. . . . It seemed to Alabama that, reaching her goal, she would drive the devils that had driven her.'

Dance dominated Zelda's life in the late twenties for she had great ambitions and pushed herself mercilessly. She hoped to join the Diaghilev troupe, her teacher Egorova said she had ability and could take secondary roles in the Massine Ballet in New York, and she was actually asked to join the San Carlo Opera Ballet in Naples. Though Zelda never went to Naples, Alabama did go – and came to disaster.

Mizener shrewdly observes of Zelda's dancing that Scott 'appeared unable to endure Zelda's successful – if neurotic – display of will when he felt that self-indulgence and dissipation were ruining him.' And when his career and his wife collapsed at about the same time he wrote to Edmund Wilson about her balletomania, neglect of Scottie, artistic rivalry and emotional isolation: 'I'm relieved that the ballet was over anyhow as our domestic life was cracking under the strain and I hadn't touched a novel for a year. She was drunk with music that seemed a crazy opiate to her and her whole cerebral tradition was something locked in such an absolutely impregnable safe inside her that it was months after the break before doctors could reach her at all.' But if Zelda was drunk with music, Scott was drunk with alcohol, and it was more his own fault than Zelda's that he was not writing. He began using drink as a stimulant to work in 1928, and by mid-1930 he had become an alcoholic and had to hire a registered nurse to restrain him during his binges.

Zelda had become schizophrenic, enclosed in a horrible mask of nervous eczema. 'For two months she had lain under it,' Scott wrote in his novel, 'as if imprisoned in the Iron Maiden. She was coherent, even brilliant, within the limits of her special hallucinations.' At a time when Fitzgerald was earning less than ever before, Zelda began fifteen months of expensive treatment with Dr Forel and consultations with Dr Bleuler at Prangins in Switzerland, a country where, Scott felt, 'few things begin but many things end.'

From that hospital Zelda sent a stream of despairing and accusing letters, shot through with lucid insight, that emphasised Scott's responsibility, exacerbated his guilt and undermined his dwindling capacity to work: 'Every day it seems to me that things are more barren and sterile and hopeless. . . . At any rate one thing has been achieved: I am thoroughly and completely humiliated and broken if that was what you wanted. . . . I wish I could see you: I have forgotten what it's like to be alive with a functioning intelligence. . . . *Please* help me. Every day more of me dies with this bitter and incessant beating I'm taking. . . . I wonder why we have never been very happy and why all this has happened.'

As they sank, like two drowning victims, into their interlocking agonies of madness and drink, Scott attempted, with a new clarity and perception, to analyse their lives and discover the source of their tragedy. He had to defend himself yet accept responsibility, and explain things to Zelda without accusing her. 'I had to get drunk before I could leave you so sick and not care,' he wrote to her. 'Things were always the same. The apartments that were rotten, the maids that stank – the ballet before my eyes, spoiling a story to take the Troubetskoys [her teacher] to dinner, poisoning a trip to [North] Africa. You were going crazy and calling it genius – I was going to ruin and calling it anything that came to hand . . . your almost megalomaniacal selfishness and my insane indulgence in drink.' Though he concluded, 'We have ruined ourselves – I have never honestly thought that we ruined each other,' it was clear that they fell into chaos as blindly as they had fallen in love.

Scott also told Zelda's doctor about the origins of their

mutually destructive relationship: 'Perhaps 50 per cent of our friends and relatives would tell you in all honest conviction that my drinking drove Zelda insane – the other half would assure you that her insanity drove me to drink. . . . Liquor on my mouth is sweet to her; I cherish her most extravagant hallucinations.' This neatly balanced statement suggested their parasitic masochism but was not entirely accurate. For Fitzgerald, who had been a heavy drinker in college, wrote to Perkins in September 1930: 'I must not drink anything, not even wine, for a year, because drinking in the past was one of those things that haunted her in delirium.'

Scott began to decline as Zelda slowly improved, and he had to be treated at her clinic for alcoholism. Andrew Turnbull relates that Scott 'had a collection of photographs put out by some temperance society, showing the ill effects of alcohol on the kidneys and other organs, and he would mull over them and joke about them in a lugubrious way.' He told one friend that he drank because he felt he could never be a first-rate writer and would always be 'at the top of the second class.' Yet in his more euphoric moods he blamed Zelda for sharing this belief: 'A strange thing was I could never convince her I was a first-rate writer. She knew I wrote well but she didn't recognize how well. When I was making myself from a popular writer into a serious writer, a big-shot, she didn't understand or try to help me.' Though Fitzgerald saw himself as a 'big-shot,' his self-esteem and success still depended on Zelda's approval and support.

After Zelda's breakdown, when he had to nurse her as well as protect Scottie, keep the household together and try to finish *Tender is the Night,* he could not manage. For Scott was no Leonard Woolf and could not assume the sacrificial and supportive role. 'Zelda is sick as hell,' he told Perkins, 'and the psychiatrist who is devoting almost his entire time to her is an expensive proposition. I was so upset in June when hopes for her recovery were so black that I could do practically no work.'

Zelda, sensing Scott's weakness, began to take the offensive: 'Your leisure is eaten up by habits of leisure, your money
by habitual extravagance, your hope by cynicism and mine
by frustration, your ambition by too much compromise.' She
began a new spurt of therapeutic creativity, first in fiction
and then in painting. Scott sent his agent, Harold Ober, 'three
stories which Zelda wrote in the dark middle of her nervous
breakdown' and praised their originality and style: 'I think
you'll see that apart from the beauty and richness of the
writing they have a strange haunting and evocative quality
that is absolutely new.' In April 1934 Zelda held at Cary
Ross' studio in New York an exhibition of her paintings and
drawings that exposed her deepest fears and included 'many
crucifixions with faces hauntingly like her own and ballet
dancers with enormous, swollen limbs.'

While Zelda and her 'fellow maniacs' surrealistically
survived 'in vaporous places peopled with one-dimensional
figures and tremulous buildings,' Scott, in Turnbull's phrase,
'lived in the phases of Zelda's illness.' His emotional and
artistic life were inextricably connected to Zelda by bonds of
love and guilt, and he wrote that 'Our love was one in a
century. Life ended for me when Zelda and I crashed. If she
would get well, I would be happy again and my soul would
be released. Otherwise never. . . . I left my capacity for hoping
on the roads that led to Zelda's sanatorium.' But he could
never learn to cope with the disturbing moods of her
schizoid behaviour. Shortly after her father's death in 1931,
'She went into the other personality and was awful to me at
lunch. After lunch she returned to the affectionate tender
mood, utterly normal, so that with pressure I could have
maneuvered her into intercourse, but the eczema was almost
visibly increasing so I left early. Toward the very end she was
back in the schizophrenia.'

In July 1935 he confessed to Harold Ober, 'the awful
strangling heartrending quality of this tragedy has gone on

now for more than six years, with two brief intervals of hope' during Zelda's periods of temporary sanity. She remained in Prangins from June 1930 until September 1931, and lost her good looks and self-assurance. 'Isn't it terrible,' she asked Scott while confined, for the second time, in Phipps Clinic, Baltimore, from February to June 1932, 'when you have one little corner of your brain that needs fixing?' Zelda's brother committed suicide in 1933; and while in the Pratt Hospital outside Baltimore from May 1934 to April 1936, she tried to throw herself under a train.

Fitzgerald could never free himself from the syndrome of guilt and drink that prevented him from writing and led to increasing debts, insomnia and a profound sense of sterility and waste. He was finally forced to admit, 'I was trading my health for her sanity, and I was through.' In June 1935 he wrote to Mrs Bayard Turnbull: 'When I do face the whole tragedy of Zelda it is simply a day lost. I think I feel it more now than at any time since its inception. She seems so help-less and pitiful. Liquor used to help put it out of mind.' He conscientiously tried to control his drinking throughout 1935 and 1936, but did not succeed until the end of 1937.

In the spring of 1936 he published the revealing and ther-apeutic 'Crack-Up' articles which, he said, 'helped me personally but rather hurt me professionally.' Everyone assumed, despite the power of his confession, that he was finished as a writer. In a cruel and devastating front-page interview of September 1936, Michael Mok emphasised Fitzgerald's 'restless pacing, his trembling hands, his twitching face with its pitiful expression of a cruelly beaten child. . . . He spent the day as he spends all his days – trying to come back from the other side of Paradise, the hell of despondency in which he has writhed for the last couple of years.' In 1935 Ober was having difficulty selling Scott's stories at any price. He made a financial and emotional recovery during his third trip to Hollywood in 1937 when he earned $1000 a week at MGM and had his famous love affair with Sheilah Graham. But his total royalties in 1939, when he had nine books in print but no sales, was only $33.

Zelda was a patient in Highland Hospital in Asheville, North Carolina from April 1936 to April 1940, again from August 1943 to February 1944, and finally from early 1946 until March 1948 when she died in the fire that swept through the institution. In April 1938, after a brief but disastrous trip to Virginia Beach, when Zelda ran shrieking through the hotel corridors accusing Scott of insanity, he wrote to her doctor that he had 'no desire ever again to personally undertake her supervision. That period has gone, and each time that I see her something happens to me that makes me the worst person for her rather than the best, but a part of me will always pity her with a sort of deep ache that is never absent from my mind for more than a few hours: an ache for the beautiful child that I loved and with whom I was happy as I shall never be happy again.'

Scott now felt Zelda was a nostalgic yet painful memory, and stopped sleeping with her. But they had been capable of achieving moments of profound communion. As Scott wrote tenderly in 1935, 'she was fine, almost herself, has only one nurse now and has no more intention of doing away with herself. It was wonderful to sit with her head on my shoulder for hours and feel as I always have even now, closer to her than to any other human being.' In one of his last letters to Scottie he stressed Zelda's remoteness and amorality, and told her, 'The insane are always mere guests on the earth, eternal strangers carrying around broken decalogues that they cannot read.' But Fitzgerald, despite debts, disease and depression, tried to uphold what he considered the moral law – as well as his own self-esteem – and wrote to Perkins: 'Such stray ideas as sending my daughter to a public school, putting my wife in a public insane asylum, have been proposed to me by intimate friends, but it would break something in me.'

V

Save Me the Waltz (1932) and *Tender is the Night* (1934) are intimate revelations, refracted through personal and distorted visions, of the fight for survival in the Fitzgeralds' disastrous marriage. Though Zelda's novel is more transparently auto-biographical and less artistically successful than Scott's, both novels provide some fascinating insights about their creators. Scott violently objected to the publication of Zelda's novel, which she had secretly sent to Perkins. She had read the first 50,000 words of his unfinished book, and he felt she had imitated his plot, dialogue and style, and attacked him personally. As the future author of the confessional 'Crack-Up' told Zelda's doctor: 'Turning up in a novel signed by my wife as a somewhat anaemic portrait painter with a few ideas lifted from Clive Bell, Leger, etc. puts me in an absurd & Zelda in a ridiculous position. The mixture of fact & fiction is calculated to ruin us both, or what is left of us.' And in a medical interview of May 1933, after her book – but not his – had been published, he brutally glorified himself at Zelda's expense and revealed his own weakness and insecurity: 'You are a third rate writer and a third rate ballet dancer. . . . I am a professional writer, with a huge following. I am the highest paid short story writer in the world. . . . I am the professional writer, and I am supporting you. That is all my material. None of it is your material. . . . I want you to stop writing fiction.'

Zelda had heard and ignored this argument before and recorded it in her novel when David tells Alabama: 'I hope you realise that the biggest difference in the world is between the amateur and the professional in the arts.' Fitzgerald reit-erated this point in his novel when Dick says of Nicole: 'The frontiers that artists must explore were not for her, ever. She was finespun, inbred – eventually she might find rest in some quiet mysticism.' And in a letter to Harold Ober in February 1936 he tried to censor Zelda's book and relate it to her personal as well as artistic defects: 'Please don't have anybody read Zelda's book because it is a bad book! But by glancing over it yourself you will see that it contains all the material a tragedy should have, though she was incapable as a writer of realizing where tragedy lay as she was incapable of facing it as a person.' Though this was probably true, it was Zelda's personal tragedy that gave Scott the inspiration for his finest novel.

Save Me the Waltz, which was aptly abbreviated to *Save Me*, faithfully relates the story of Zelda's childhood, marriage, her husband's youthful success, the birth of her daughter, travels in Europe, brief affair with a French aviator and husband's retalitory affair, her passion for dancing and invitation to the San Carlo Theatre in Naples where (in the novel) she gets blood poisoning from an infected foot and is forced to give up her career. She returns to her home in the south and after the death of her father must begin her life again.

Alabama's physical illness obviously represents Zelda's insanity, and estranges her from both her husband and other people. For David 'felt of a different world to Alabama; his tempo was different from the sterile, attenuated rhythms of the hospital.' The novel is certainly not a personal attack on Fitzgerald, but a tragedy of stagnation and frustration. Its most remarkable feature is perhaps Zelda's ingenuous portrayal of her own extravagance, domestic incompetence, recklessness, jealousy, infidelity, ambition and responsibility for the dissolution of their marriage. *Save Me the Waltz*, which suffered from over-writing and under-editing (Perkins' weakest point) had mixed reviews, did not sell well and earned Zelda $120 in royalties.

Fitzgerald wrote that his intention in *Tender is the Night* was to 'show a man who is a natural idealist, a spoiled priest, giving in for various causes to the ideas of the haute bourgeoisie, and in his rise to the top of the social world losing his idealism, his talent, and turning to drink and dissipation. Background one in which the leisure class is at their truly most brilliant and glamorous.' The characters that surround Dick Diver subtly and effectively portray his temptations and weaknesses: Baby Warren, money; Abe North, liquor; Tommy Barban, anarchy; Albert McKisco, self-betrayal; Rosemary Hoyt, infidelity. The immorality of the class that leads Dick from idealism to corruption is symbolised by sexual disorders: Campion and Dumphrey are homosexuals, Mary North and Lady Caroline pose as lesbians, Baby is onanistic, Dick is mistaken for a rapist and Devereux Warren has committed incest with his daughter, Nicole.

Tender is the Night was published when Zelda was insane, when Scottie was thirteen years old and showing the first signs of womanhood, and when Fitzgerald began to transfer his love for his wife to his daughter. Zelda's relationship with Scottie was always rather remote, and after she had lost emotional control in 1926 they seemed more like two children playing together than like mother and daughter. Zelda admitted that during her dancing mania 'I lived in a quiet, ghostly, hypersensitized world of my own,' and Scott maintained that his namesake 'was not, and had probably never been, dependent upon her mother for either direction or emotional sustenance' – though this deficiency should have caused concern rather than satisfaction. He spoke to Scottie about the 'sense of partnership with you that sprang out of your mother's illness'; and in a letter to Gerald and Sara Murphy contrasted his indulgence of Zelda and discipline of Scottie: 'In an odd way, perhaps incredible to you, [Zelda] was always my child (it was not reciprocal as it often is in marriage), my child in a sense that Scottie isn't, because I've brought Scottie up as hard as nails.'

Fitzgerald constantly emphasises Scottie's distance from Zelda and closeness to himself, and their sense of almost marital partnership that developed when Zelda left the family. If Zelda seemed more like a child than Scottie, Scottie must have seemed, at times, more like a wife than Zelda; and it is quite possible that the incest theme that accounts for Nicole's insanity in the novel is a fictional transformation of Scott's unconscious desire for his daughter. The incest theme is also related to Dick's affair with the actress, Rosemary Hoyt, for they had assumed a father–daughter role before they became lovers. Her famous film, *Daddy's Girl*, ends with a 'lovely shot of Rosemary and her parent united at last in a father complex so apparent that Dick winced for all psychologists at the *vicious* sentimentality.'

Tender is the Night reflects the Fitzgeralds' lives in a number of other significant ways. Dick wants 'to be the greatest psychologist that ever lived' just as Scott had told Edmund Wilson that he wanted 'to be one of the greatest writers that ever lived.' Dick makes an unsuccessful attempt to perform aquatic feats for Rosemary just as Scott, who liked to show off, once dislocated a shoulder while trying an impressive high dive for a girl. Both Fitzgerald and his hero were involved in drunken brawls with the police. Scott describes Zelda's extravagance and absorption in spending when 'Nicole bought from a great list that ran two pages, and bought the things in the windows besides.' Although Zelda had slept with Josanne *before* Scott met Lois Moran, Fitzgerald becomes the betrayer – not the cuckold – in the novel. Dick first has the affair with Rosemary, and Nicole later retaliates with Tommy Barban.

Fitzgerald wrote seven versions of the novel between 1925, when he published *The Great Gatsby,* and 1934 (the first draft concerned matricide), but started the final version from a new plan after Zelda's breakdown. Nicole's mental illness forms the emotional core of the novel just as Dick's responsibility for his wife is the moral centre: its dominant theme is the recovery of the sick at the expense of the healthy. Nancy Milford justly observes that Scott used Zelda's letters from Prangins 'with very little regard for Zelda's reaction or for the precarious balance of her sanity. . . . That she might object to it, be wounded by it, did not seem to have disturbed him. He saw it only from a writer's point of view.' Though Scott was emotionally committed to Zelda, he was still capable of exploiting her intimate feelings in order to create a novel that would represent and explain their private life. Though he could not prevent their destruction, he was able to observe and record it.

While treating Nicole in a mental clinic Dick is warned by an older colleague not to marry her and 'devote half your life to being doctor and nurse and all – never!' But Dick ignores this sound advice; and when his work becomes confused with Nicole's problems, he learns to 'harden himself about her, making a cleavage between Nicole sick and Nicole well.' Dick's defensive response, like Scott's, is expressed in a painful yet necessary coldness, indifference and neglect. It was 'difficult now to distinguish between his self-protective professional detachment and some new coldness in his heart. As an indifference cherished, or left to atrophy, becomes an emptiness, to this extent he had learned to become empty of Nicole, serving her against his will with negations and emotional neglect.' At the end of the novel Dick is forced to confess, like Scott, 'I can't do anything for you any more, I'm trying to save myself.'

The hopeful phases of Nicole's illness are made more poignantly bitter by the certain knowledge that they cannot last: 'She had come out of her first illness alive with new hopes, expecting so much, yet deprived of any subsistence except Dick, bringing up children she could only pretend gently to love, guided orphans.' But the brilliance and versatility of her madness, which Fitzgerald compares to water seeping through a dyke, forces itself to the surface. In one of the great scenes of the novel Nicole, like Zelda, attempts to drive the car off a high, steep road:

> He had turned up a hill that made a short cut to the clinic and now, as he stepped on the accelerator for a short, straightaway run parallel to the hillside, the car swerved violently left, swerved right, tipped on two wheels and, as Dick, with Nicole's voice screaming in his ear, crushed down the mad hand clutching the steering wheel, righted itself, swerved once more and shot off the road; it tore through low underbrush, tipped again, and settled slowly at an angle of ninety degrees against a tree.
>
> The children were screaming and Nicole was screaming and cursing and trying to tear at Dick's face.

This incident is described as Dick experiences it, in all the confusion of violence and screams, and without the later comprehension of Nicole's desire to terrify or kill him, even if it involves 'putting other lives in danger.'

Dick is forced to participate in her disintegration, and though he barely manages to save himself it is clear that Nicole's recovery is based on his own decline. He accuses her of cherishing her illness as an instrument of power and tries to blame his failure on Nicole. But when she no longer has to play a planet to Dick's sun she gains a new psychological insight from her freedom and thinks: 'I'm almost complete. I'm practically standing alone, without him.' When she tries to help Dick, to do something for *him*, he rejects her and she declares: 'You used to want to create things – now you seem to want to smash them up.' Zelda provided Scott with the true material of tragedy, and his intense involvement in her illness gave him the requisite courage, vision, maturity and detachment to transform it into art. Though Zelda helped to destroy Scott, she also inspired him.

The Fitzgeralds' marriage never evolved from a youthful love affair into a stabilising and supportive alliance, for they shared the same virtues and defects. Their emotional parabola swung too widely, and if they loved more passionately than others, they also hated more bitterly. In October 1939 Scott, who suffered from recurrent attacks of tuberculosis, begged Zelda: 'I ask only this of you – leave me in peace with my haemorrhages and my hopes.' A few months later she described herself as 'middle-aged, untrained, graduate of half-a-dozen mental Institutes.' Yet Scott recognised her intuitive lucidity, thought 'Possibly she would have been a genius if we had never met,' and generously admitted to Scottie just before his death in 1940: 'She was a great original in her way, with perhaps a more intense flame at its highest than I ever had.' And after his death Zelda wrote nostalgically from Highland that Scott was 'as spiritually generous a soul as ever was. . . . In retrospect it seems as if he was always planning happiness for Scottie and me . . . Books to read – places to go. Life seemed so promising always when he was around.'

Select Bibliography

Tolstoy, Leo. *Journal of Leo Tolstoy, 1895–1899.* trans. Rose Strunsky. New York, 1917.

Tolstoy, Leo. *Last Diaries, 1910.* trans. Lydia Weston-Kesich. New York, 1960.

Tolstoy, Sofya. *The Diary of Tolstoy's Wife, 1860–1891.* trans. Alexander Werth. London 1928.

Tolstoy, Sofya. *Countess Tolstoy's Later Diary, 1891–1897.* trans. Alexander Werth. London, 1929.

Tolstoy, Sofya. *The Final Struggle – Countess Tolstoy's Diary for 1910.* trans. Aylmer Maude. London, 1936.

Polner, Tikhon. *Tolstoy and His Wife.* trans. Nicholas Wreden. New York, 1945.

Simmons, Ernest. *Leo Tolstoy.* 2 vols. New York, 1946.

Tolstoy, Alexandra. *Tolstoy: A Life of My Father.* trans. Elizabeth Hapgood. New York, 1953.

Troyat, Henri. *Tolstoy.* trans. Nancy Amphoux. New York, 1965.

Shaw, George Bernard. *Collected Letters, 1874–1897.* ed. Dan Laurence. London, 1965.

Shaw, George Bernard. *Collected Letters, 1898–1910.* ed. Dan Laurence. London, 1972.

Bernard Shaw and Mrs. Patrick Campbell: Their Correspondence. ed. Alan Dent. London, 1952.

Shaw, George Bernard. *Sixteen Self-Sketches.* New York, 1949.

Dunbar, Janet. *Mrs. G.B.S.: A Portrait.* New York, 1963.

Ervine, St. John. *Bernard Shaw: His Life, Work and Friends.* London, 1959.

Pearson, Hesketh. *George Bernard Shaw: His Life and Personality.* New York, 1950.

Webb, Beatrice. *Diaries, 1912–1924.* ed. Margaret Cole. London, 1952.

Webb, Beatrice. *My Apprenticeship.* London, 1926.

Conrad, Joseph. *Conrad to a Friend: 150 Selected Letters from Joseph Conrad to Richard Curle.* ed. Richard Curle. London, 1928.

Conrad, Joseph. *Letters from Joseph Conrad, 1895–1924.* ed. Edward Garnett. Indianapolis, 1928.

Conrad, Jessie. *Joseph Conrad as I Knew Him.* London, 1926.

Conrad, Jessie. *Joseph Conrad and His Circle.* London, 1935.

Aubry, Georges Jean. *Joseph Conrad: Life and Letters.* 2 vols. New York, 1927.

Baines, Jocelyn. *Joseph Conrad: A Critical Biography.* London, 1960.

Curle, Richard. *The Last Twelve Years of Joseph Conrad.* London, 1928.

Ford, Ford Madox. *Joseph Conrad: A Personal Remembrance.* London, 1924.

Meyer, Bernard. *Joseph Conrad: A Psychoanalytic Biography.* Princeton, 1967.

Joyce, James. *Letters.* ed. Stuart Gilbert and Richard Ellmann. 3 vols. New York, 1966.

Joyce, James. *Selected Letters.* ed. Richard Ellmann. New York, 1975.

Colum, Mary and Padraic. *Our Friend James Joyce.* London, 1959.

Ellmann, Richard. *James Joyce.* New York, 1959.

Joyce, Stanislaus. *My Brother's Keeper.* London, 1958.

Lidderdale, Jane and Mary Nicholson. *Dear Miss Weaver.* London, 1970.

McAlmon, Robert. *Being Geniuses Together.* London, 1938.

Reynolds, Mary 'Joyce and Nora: The Indispensable Countersign.' *Sewanee Review*, 72 (1964), 29–64.

Trilling, Lionel. 'James Joyce in His Letters.' *Commentary*, 45 (February 1968), 53–64.

Woolf, Virginia. *Letters, 1888–1912*. vol. 1. ed. Nigel Nicolson and Joanne Trautmann. London, 1975.

Woolf, Virginia and Lytton Strachey. *Letters*. ed. Leonard Woolf and James Strachey. London, 1956.

Woolf, Virginia. *A Writer's Diary*. ed. Leonard Woolf. New York, 1954.

Woolf, Leonard. *Beginning Again*. London, 1964.

Woolf, Leonard. *Downhill All the Way*. London, 1967.

Woolf, Leonard. *The Journey Not the Arrival Matters*. London, 1970.

Bell, Quentin. *Virginia Woolf*. 2 vols. London, 1972.

Holroyd, Michael. *Lytton Strachey*. 2 vols. London, 1968.

Noble, Joan, ed. *Recollections of Virginia Woolf*. New York, 1972.

Mansfield, Katherine. *Journal*. ed. J. M. Murry. New York, 1954.

Mansfield, Katherine. *Letters*. ed. J. M. Murry. 2 vols. London, 1928.

Mansfield, Katherine. *Letters to John Middleton Murry, 1913–1922*. ed. J. M. Murry. London, 1951.

Mansfield, Katherine. *Scrapbook*. ed. J. M. Murry. London, 1939.

Alpers, Anthony. *Katherine Mansfield*. London, 1954.

Berkman, Sylvia. *Katherine Mansfield: A Critical Study*. New Haven, 1951.

Carco, Francis. *Memoires d'une autre vie*. Genève, 1942.

Moore, Lesley. *Katherine Mansfield: The Memories of Lesley Moore*. London, 1971.

Murry, John Middleton. *Between Two Worlds: An Autobiography*. London, 1936.

Lawrence, D. H. *Letters.* ed. Aldous Huxley. London, 1932.

Lawrence, D. H. *Collected Letters.* ed. Harry Moore. 2 vols. New York, 1956.

Lawrence, Frieda. *Not I, But the Wind.* London, 1934.

Lawrence, Frieda. *Memoirs and Correspondence.* ed. E. W. Tedlock. London, 1951.

Carswell, Catherine. *The Savage Pilgrimage.* London, 1932.

Lucas, Robert. *Frieda Lawrence.* London, 1973.

Nehls, Edward, ed. *D. H. Lawrence: A Composite Biography.* 3 vols. Madison, 1958.

Moore, Harry. *The Priest of Love.* London, 1973.

Murry, John Middleton. *Reminiscences of D. H. Lawrence.* London, 1933.

Hemingway, Ernest. *A Moveable Feast.* London, 1964.

Hemingway, Mary. 'The Making of Books: A Chronicle and a Memoir.' *New York Times Book Review,* 10 May 1964, pp. 26–27.

Baker, Carlos. *Ernest Hemingway: A Life Story.* New York, 1969.

Cowley, Malcolm. 'A Portrait of Mr. Papa.' *Life,* 25 (10 January 1949), 86–101.

Hemingway, Leicester. *My Brother, Ernest Hemingway.* New York, 1962.

Hotchner, A. E. *Papa Hemingway: A Personal Memoir.* London, 1966.

Ross, Lillian. *Portrait of Hemingway.* New York, 1961.

Stein, Gertrude. *The Autobiography of Alice B. Toklas.* New York, 1933.

Young, Philip. *Ernest Hemingway: A Reconsideration.* University Park, Penna., 1966.

Fitzgerald, F. Scott. *Letters.* ed. Andrew Turnbull. New York, 1963.

Fitzgerald, Zelda. *Save Me the Waltz.* New York, 1932.

Callaghan, Morley. *That Summer in Paris.* New York, 1963.

Graham, Sheilah and Gerald Frank. *Beloved Infidel.* London, 1959.

Latham, John. *Crazy Sundays: F. Scott Fitzgerald in Hollywood.* London, 1972.

Milford, Nancy. *Zelda.* New York, 1970.

Mizener, Arthur. *The Far Side of Paradise.* New York, 1951.

Tomkins, Calvin. *Living Well is the Best Revenge.* New York, 1971.

Turnbull, Andrew. *Scott Fitzgerald.* New York, 1962.